Anonymous

Regents manual of the laws and orders governing the university

Anonymous

Regents manual of the laws and orders governing the university

ISBN/EAN: 9783337233792

Printed in Europe, USA, Canada, Australia, Japan

Cover: Foto ©Suzi / pixelio.de

More available books at **www.hansebooks.com**

Regents' Manual

The Laws, Orders, Etc., Governing the University.

BERKELEY.
1884.

THE BOARD OF REGENTS.

ARTICLE 1.

EX OFFICIO REGENTS.

His Excellency GEORGE STONEMAN, Sacramento,
Governor, ex officio President of the Board.

His Honor JOHN DAGGETT, Oakland,
Lieutenant-Governor.

Hon. H. M. LaRUE, Sacramento,
Speaker of the Assembly.

Hon. Professor W. T. WELCKER, Sacramento,
Superintendent of Public Instruction.

Hon. P. A. FINIGAN, San Francisco,
President of the State Agricultural Society.

P. B. CORNWALL, Esq., San Francisco,
President of the Mechanics' Institute.

W. T. REID, A.M., Berkeley,
President of the University.

ARTICLE 2.

APPOINTED REGENTS.

(In order of appointment.)

Rev. Horatio Stebbins, San Francisco ....Term expires March 1, 1894
Hon. John S. Hager, San Francisco ....Term expires March 1, 1896
Hon. John F. Swift, San Francisco................Term expires March 1, 1888
A. S. Hallidie, Esq., San Francisco................Term expires March 1, 1892
Hon. Joseph W. Winans, San Francisco ....Term expires March 1, 1890
Hon. William T. Wallace, San Francisco................Term expires March 1, 1886
John L. Beard, Esq., Centerville, Alameda County ....Term expires March 1, 1892
Hon. A. L. Rhodes, San José................Term expires March 1, 1888
Prof. William Ashburner, San Francisco ....Term expires March 1, 1896
Hon. J. West Martin, Oakland ....Term expires March 1, 1898
Hon. T. G. Phelps, Belmont................Term expires March 1, 1896
Isaias W. Heilman, Esq., Los Angeles ....Term expires March 1, 1886
George T. Marye, Esq., San Francisco ....Term expires March 1, 1898
Arthur Rodgers, Esq., San Francisco ....Term expires March 1, 1890
George J. Ainsworth, Esq., Temescal, Alameda County.Term expires March 1, 1900

J. H. C. BONTÉ, Secretary of the Board of Regents, of the Academic Senate, and Superintendent of Grounds.

J. HAM HARRIS, Land Agent and Assistant Secretary.

TERMS OF REGENTS.

When Appointed or Elected.	Names.	Remarks.	Years—Term.	Term Expires.
I.				
June 12, 1868	Friedlander, I.	Honorary, elected	Two years	March 1, 1870
August 31, 1869	Sachs, Louis	Vice Friedlander, resigned	Unexpired term	March 1, 1870
July 29, 1870	Sachs, Louis	Elected	Sixteen years	March 1, 1886
October 19, 1875	Wallace, William T.	Vice Sachs, resigned	Unexpired term	March 1, 1886
II.				
June 12, 1868	Tompkins, Edward	Honorary, elected	Four years	March 1, 1872
April 8, 1872	Tompkins, Edward	Elected	Sixteen years	March 1, 1888
December 13, 1872	Haight, Henry H.	Vice Tompkins, deceased	Unexpired term	March 1, 1888
April 20, 1876	Casserley, Eugene	Vice Haight, resigned	Unexpired term	March 1, 1888
January 19, 1880	Rhodes, A. L.	Vice Casserley, resigned	Unexpired term	March 1, 1888
III.				
June 12, 1868	Moss, J. Mora	Honorary, elected	Six years	March 1, 1874
March 5, 1874	Moss, J. Mora	Vice self, appointed	Sixteen years	March 1, 1890
December 6, 1880	Curtis, N. Greene	Vice Moss, deceased	Unexpired term	March 1, 1890
March —, 1883	Rodgers, Arthur	Vice Curtis, resigned	Unexpired term	March 1, 1890
IV.				
June 12, 1868	Butterworth, S. F.	Honorary, elected	Eight years	March 1, 1876
December 24, 1873	Hallidie, A. S.	Vice Butterworth, resigned	Unexpired term	March 1, 1876
April 22, 1874	Hamilton, J. M.	Vice Hallidie, resigned	Unexpired term	March 1, 1876
January 18, 1876	Beard, J. L.	Vice Hamilton, term expired	Sixteen years	March 1, 1892
V.				
June 12, 1868	Moulder, A. J.	Honorary, elected	Ten years	March 1, 1878
November 27, 1868	Hager, John S.	Vice Moulder, resigned	Unexpired term	March 1, 1878
April 4, 1878	Hager, John S.	Vice Hager, term expired	Sixteen years	March 1, 1894
VI.				
June 12, 1868	Bowie, A. J.	Honorary, elected	Twelve years	March 1, 1880

Date	Name	Vice / Action	Term	Term expired
March 3, 1880	Ashburner, William	Vice Bowie, term expired	Sixteen years	March 1, 1896
VII.				
June 12, 1868	Low, Frederick F.	Honorary, elected	Fourteen years	March 1, 1882
November 27, 1868	Ralston, William C.	Vice Low, resigned	Unexpired term	March 1, 1882
September 3, 1875	Pixley, Frank M.	Vice Ralston, deceased	Unexpired term	March 1, 1882
March 3, 1880	Redding, B. B.	Vice Pixley, resigned	Unexpired term	March 1, 1882
	Redding, B. B.	Vice Redding, term expired	Sixteen years	March 1, 1898
	Stanford, Leland	Vice Redding, deceased	Unexpired term	March 1, 1898
March 30, 1883	Marye, George T.	Vice Stanford, resigned	Unexpired term	March 1, 1898
VIII.				
June 12, 1868	Felton, John B.	Honorary, elected	Sixteen years	March 1, 1884
May 14, 1877	Davidson, George	Vice Felton, deceased	Unexpired term	March 1, 1884
		Vice Davidson, term expired	Sixteen years	March 1, 1900
IX.				
May 21, 1868	Merritt, Samuel	Appointed	Two years	March 1, 1870
May 28, 1870	Merritt, Samuel	Appointed	Sixteen years	March 1, 1886
June 23, 1874	Mills, D. O.	Vice Merritt, resigned	Unexpired term	March 1, 1886
July 1, 1881	Hellman, I. W.	Vice Mills, resigned	Unexpired term	March 1, 1886
March 30, 1883	Hellman, I. W.	Vice Hellman, resigned	Unexpired term	March 1, 1886
X.				
May 21, 1868	Doyle, John T.	Appointed	Four years	**March 1, 1872**
March 19, 1872	Swift, John F.	Vice Doyle, term expired	Sixteen years	**March 1, 1888**
XI.				
May 21, 1868	Hammond, R. P.	Appointed	Six years	March 1, 1874
December 24, 1873	Winans, J. W.	Vice Hammond, resigned	Unexpired term	March 1, 1874
March 5, 1874	Winans, J. W.	Vice Winans, term expired	Sixteen years	March 1, 1890
XII.				
May 21, 1868	Dwinelle, John W.	Appointed	Eight years	March 1, 1876
October 12, 1874	Meek, William	Vice Dwinelle, resigned	Unexpired term	March 1, 1876
March —, 1876	Hallidie, A. S.	Vice Meek, term expired	Sixteen years	March 1, 1892

Terms of Regents—Continued.

When Appointed or Elected.	Names.	Remarks.	Years—Term.	Term Expires.
	XIII.			
May 21, 1868	Stebbins, Horatio	Appointed	Ten years	March 1, 1878
April 4, 1878	Stebbins, Horatio	Vice Stebbins, term expired	Sixteen years	March 1, 1894
	XIV.			
May 21, 1868	Archer, Lawrence	Appointed	Twelve years	March 1, 1880
March 3, 1880	Bidwell, John	Vice Archer, term expired	Sixteen years	March 1, 1896
December 6, 1880	Pholps, T. G.	Vice Bidwell, resigned	Unexpired term	March 1, 1896
	XV.			
May 21, 1868	Watt, William	Appointed	Fourteen years	March 1, 1882
November 29, 1871	Martin, J. West	Vice Watt, resigned	Unexpired term	March 1, 1882
	Martin, J. West	Vice Martin, term expired	Sixteen years	March 1, 1898
	XVI.			
May 21, 1868	McKee, Samuel B.	Appointed	Sixteen years	March 1, 1884
May 9, 1883	Ainsworth, George J.	Vice McKee, resigned	Unexpired term	March 1, 1884
	Ainsworth, George J.	Vice Ainsworth, term expired	Sixteen years	March 1, 1900

TITLE ONE.

FEDERAL LEGISLATION.

TITLE ONE—FEDERAL LEGISLATION.

CHAPTER I.

An Act to provide for the survey of the public lands in California, the granting of preëmption rights therein, and for other purposes.

[Approved March 3, 1853. U. S. Stats. at Large, Vol. 10, p. 244.]

ARTICLE 3.

SECTION 12. *And be it further enacted,* That the quantity of two entire townships, or seventy-two sections, shall be and the same is hereby granted to the State of California for the use of a seminary of learning, said lands to be selected by the Governor of the State, or any person he may designate for that purpose, in legal subdivision of not less than a quarter section, of any of the unsold, unoccupied, and unappropriated public lands therein, subject to the approval of the Secretary of the Interior, and to be disposed of as the Legislature shall direct; *provided, however,* that mineral land, or lands reserved for any public purpose whatever, or lands to which any settler may be entitled under the provisions of this Act, shall not be subject to such selection.

ARTICLE 4.

SECTION 13. *And be it further enacted,* That there shall be and is hereby granted to the State of California the quantity of ten entire sections of land, for the purpose of erecting the public buildings of that State, said lands to be selected by the Governor, or any persons he may designate, in legal subdivisions of not less than a quarter section of any of the unsold, unoccupied, and unappropriated public lands in that State, and subject to the approval of the Secretary of the Interior; *provided, however,* that none of said selections shall be made of mineral lands, or lands reserved for any public purpose whatever, or lands to which any settler may be entitled under the provisions of this Act.

NOTE.—The "Seminary Fund," and the "Public Building Fund," were derived from the sale of land donated by this Act.

CHAPTER II.

[Act of Congress approved July 2, 1862, donating 150,000 acres. 12 U. S. Stats. at Large, 503.]

*An Act donating public lands to the several States and **Territories** which may provide colleges **for** the benefit of **agriculture and** the mechanic arts.*

ARTICLE 5.

SECTION 1. *Be it enacted **by** the Senate and House of Representatives of the United States of America in Congress assembled,* That there **be** granted to the several States, for the purposes hereinafter mentioned, an amount of public land, to be apportioned to each State, a quantity equal to thirty thousand **acres** for each Senator and Representative in Con**gress** to **which** the States are respectively entitled by the apportionment under the census of eighteen hundred and sixty; *provided,* that no mineral lands shall be selected or purchased under the provisions **of** this Act.

ARTICLE 6.

SECTION 2. *And be it further enacted,* That the land aforesaid, after being surveyed, shall be apportioned to the several States in sections, or subdivisions of sections not less than one quarter of a section; and whenever there are public lands in a State subject to sale at private entry at one dollar and twenty-five cents per acre, the quantity to which said State shall be entitled shall be selected from such lands within the limits of such State, and the Secretary of the Interior **is** hereby directed to issue to each of the States in which there is **not the** quantity of public lands subject to sale at private **entry at** one dollar and twenty-five cents **per** acre, to which said State may be entitled under **the** provisions of this Act, land scrip to the amount in acres for the deficiency of its distributive share; said scrip to be sold by said States and the proceeds thereof applied to the uses and purposes prescribed in this Act, and for no other **use** or purpose whatsoever; *provided,* that in no case shall any State to which land scrip may thus be issued be allowed to locate the same within the limits of any other State, **or** of any Territory of the United States, but their assignees may thus locate said land scrip upon any of the unappropriated lands of the United States subject to sale at private entry at one dollar and twenty-five cents, or less, per acre; *and, provided further,* that not more than one million acres shall be located by such assignees in any one of the States; *and, provided further,* that no such location shall be made before one year from the passage of this Act.

ARTICLE 7.

SECTION 3. *And be it further enacted,* That all the expenses of management, superintendence, and taxes from the date of selection of said lands, previous to their sales, and all expenses incurred in the management and disbursement of the money which may be received therefrom, **shall** be paid by the States to which they may belong, **out of the treasury** of said States, **so** that the entire proceeds **of the sale of said** lands shall be applied, without any **diminution whatever,** to the purposes hereinafter mentioned.

ARTICLE 8.

SECTION 4. ***And be*** *it further enacted,* That all moneys derived from the sale of the lands aforesaid by the States to which the lands are apportioned, and from the sale of land scrip hereinbefore provided for, shall be invested in stock of the United States, or of the States, or some other safe stocks, yielding not less than five per centum upon the par value of said stocks; and that the moneys so invested shall constitute a perpetual fund, the capital of which shall remain forever undiminished (except so far as may be provided in section fifth of this Act), and the interest of which shall be inviolably appropriated, by each State which may take and claim the benefit of this Act, to the endowment, support, and mainte-nance of at least one college where the leading object shall be, without excluding other scientific and classical studies, and including military tactics, to teach such branches of learning as are related to agriculture and the mechanic arts, in such manner as the Legislatures of the States may respect-ively prescribe, in order to promote the liberal and practical education of the industrial classes in the several pursuits and professions in life.

ARTICLE 9.

SECTION 5. ***And be*** *it further enacted,* That the grant of land and land scrip hereby authorized shall be made on the following conditions, **to** which, as **well** as the provisions here-inbefore contained, the previous assent of the several States shall be signified by legislative Acts:

First—If **any** portion of the fund invested, **as** provided **by** the foregoing **section,** or any portion of the interest thereon, shall, by any action or contingency, be diminished or lost, it shall be replaced by the State to which it belongs, so that the capital of the fund shall remain forever undiminished; and the annual interest shall be regularly applied without dimin-**ution to** the purposes mentioned **in the** fourth section of this Act, except that a sum, not exceeding ten per centum upon the amount received by any State under the provisions of **this Act,** may be expended for **the** purchase of lands for sites or experimental farms, whenever authorized by the respective Legislatures of said States.

Second—No portion of said fund, nor the interest thereon, shall be applied, directly or indirectly, under any pretense whatever, to the purchase, erection, preservation, or repair of any building or buildings.

Third—Any State which may take and claim the benefit of the provisions of this Act, shall provide, within five years, at least not less than one college, as described in the fourth section of this Act, or the grant to such State shall cease; and said State shall be bound to pay the United States the amount received of any lands previously sold, and that the title to purchasers under the State shall be valid.

Fourth—An annual report shall be made regarding the progress of each College, recording any improvements and experiments made, with their costs and results, and such other matters, including State industrial and economical statistics, as may be supposed useful, one copy of which shall be transmitted by mail, free, by each to all the other Colleges which may be endowed under the provisions of this Act, and also one copy to the Secretary of the Interior.

Fifth—When lands shall be selected from those which have been raised to double the minimum in price, in consequence of railroad grants, they shall be computed to the State at the maximum price, and the number of acres proportionately diminished.

Sixth—No State, while in a condition of rebellion or insurrection against the Government of the United States, shall be entitled to the benefit of this Act.

Seventh—No State shall be entitled to the benefits of this Act unless it shall express its acceptance thereof, by its Legislature, within two years from the date of its approval by the President.

ARTICLE 10.

SECTION 6.   *And be it further enacted,* That land scrip issued under the provisions of this Act shall not be subject to location until after the first day of January, one thousand eight hundred and sixty-three.

ARTICLE 11.

SECTION 7.   *And be it further enacted,* That the land officers shall receive the same fees for locating land scrip issued under the provisions of this Act, as is now allowed for the location of military bounty land warrants under existing laws; *provided,* their maximum compensation shall not be thereby increased.

ARTICLE 12.

SECTION 8. *And be it further enacted,* That the Governors of the several States to which scrip shall be issued under this Act, shall be required to report annually to Congress all sales made of such scrip, until the whole shall be disposed of, the amount received for the same, and **what** appropriation **has** been made of the proceeds.

CHAPTER III.

[Act of Congress, approved July 23, 1866.   Vol. 14, U. S., p. 208.]

ARTICLE 13.

NOTE.—This Act merely amends Section 5 of Act of July, 1862, extending the time within which the provisions of said Act may be accepted, and such colleges established, to three years thereafter in which to express such acceptance, and five years within which to provide such colleges.

CHAPTER IV.

Relating to the selection of lands.

[Approved June 8, 1868.   Vol. 15, p. 68 of U.S. Stats. at Large, Fortieth Congress.]

ARTICLE 14.

SECTION 4. *And be it further enacted,* That the lands granted to the State of California for the establishment of an Agricultural College by the Act of July second, eighteen hundred and sixty-two, and Acts amendatory thereto, may be selected by said State from any lands within said State subject to preemption and sale; *provided,* that this privilege shall not extend to lands upon which there may be rightful claims under the preëmption and homestead laws, nor to mineral lands; *and provided further,* that if lands be selected as aforesaid, the minimum price of which is two dollars and fifty cents **per** acre, each acre so selected shall be **taken** by **the** State in satisfaction **of two** acres, the minimum **price of** which **is** one dollar and **twenty-**five cents **per acre;** *and provided further,* that such selections shall be **made in** every other respect subject to the condition, restrictions, **and** limitations contained in the Acts hereby modified.

CHAPTER V.

Act of March 3, 1871.

[Approved March 3, 1871.   Vol. 16, p. 581 of U. S. Stats. at **Large**.]

ARTICLE 15.

Be it enacted by the Senate and House of Representatives of the United States of America in Congress assembled, That section four of an Act entitled "An Act to further provide for giving effect to the various grants of public lands to the State of Nevada," be, and the same is hereby, amended so as to read as follows: And it is further enacted that the lands granted to the State of California for the establishment of an Agricultural College, by the Act of July second, eighteen hundred and sixty-two, and Acts amendatory thereto, may be selected by said State from any lands within said State, subject to preëmption, settlement, entry, sale, or location, under any laws of the United States. Such selection may be made in any legal subdivisions, adjoining by sides, so as to constitute bodies of not less than one hundred and sixty acres; or they may be made in separate subdivisions of forty, eighty, or one hundred and twenty acres, respectively; *provided,* that this privilege shall not extend to lands upon which there may be rightful claims under the preëmption and homestead laws, nor to mineral lands; *and provided further,* that if lands be selected as aforesaid, the minimum price of which is two dollars and fifty cents per acre, they shall be taken, acre for acre, in part satisfaction of the grant, and the State of California shall pay to the United States the sum of one dollar and twenty-five cents per acre for each acre so selected, when the same shall be patented to the State by the United States; *provided further,* that where lands, sought to be selected for the Agricultural College, are unsurveyed, the proper authorities of the State shall file a statement to that effect with the Register of the United States Land Office, describing the land by township and range, and shall make application to the United States Surveyor-General for a survey of the same, the expenses of the survey for field-work to be paid by the State, provided there be no appropriation by Congress for that purpose. The United States Surveyor-General, as soon as practicable, shall have the said lands surveyed, and the township plats returned to the United States Land Office, and lands so surveyed and returned shall, for thirty days after the filing of the plats in the United States Land Office, be held exclusively for location for the Agricultural College; and within said thirty days the proper authorities of the State shall make application to the United States Land Office for the lands sought to be located by sections and parts of sections; *provided*, that any rights, under the preëmption or homestead laws, acquired prior to the filing of the required statement with the United States Register, shall not be impaired or affected by this Act; *and provided further*, that such selections shall be made in every other respect subject to the conditions, restrictions, and limitations contained in the Acts hereby modified.

CHAPTER VI.

An Act to amend an Act donating public lands to the several States and Territories which may provide Colleges for the benefit of agriculture and the mechanic arts.

[Act of Congress approved March 3, 1883.   Vol. 22, U. S., 484.]

ARTICLE 16.

Be it enacted by the Senate and House of Representatives of the United States of America in Congress assembled, That the fourth section of the Act donating public lands to the several States and Territories which may provide Colleges for the benefit of agriculture and the mechanic arts, approved July second, eighteen hundred and sixty-two, be and the same is hereby amended so as to read as follows:

"SECTION 4. That all moneys derived from the sale of lands aforesaid by the States to which the lands are apportioned, and from the sales of land scrip hereinbefore provided for, shall be invested in stocks of the United States, or of the States, or some other safe stocks; or the same may be invested by the States having no State stocks in any other manner, after the Legislatures of such States shall have assented thereto and engaged that such funds shall yield not less than five per centum upon the amount so invested, and that the principal thereof shall forever remain unimpaired; *provided*, that the moneys so invested or loaned shall constitute a perpetual fund, the capital of which shall remain forever undiminished (except so far as may be provided in section five of this Act), and the interest of which shall be inviolably appropriated by each State which may take and claim the benefit of this Act, to the endowment, support, and maintenance of at least one College, where the leading object shall be, without excluding other scientific and classical studies, and including military tactics, to teach such branches of learning as are related to agriculture and the mechanic arts, in such manner as the Legislatures of the States may respectively prescribe, in order to promote the liberal and practical education of the industrial classes in the several pursuits and professions in life."

2

CHAPTER VII.

G. O. 74, H. Q. A., July 19, 1884.

ARTICLE 17.

[Extract from the Revised Statutes of the United States, as amended by the Act of Congress approved July 5, 1884.]

"Section 1225. The President may, upon the application of any established college or university within the United States, having capacity to educate, at the same time, not less than one hundred and fifty male students, detail an officer of the army to act as President, Superintendent, or professor thereof; but the number of officers so detailed shall not exceed * * * [forty] at any time, and they shall be apportioned throughout the United States, as nearly as may be practicable, according to population. Officers so detailed shall be governed by general rules prescribed from time to time by the President. The Secretary of War is authorized to issue at his discretion and under proper regulations to be prescribed by him, out of any small arms or pieces of field artillery belonging to the Government and which can be spared for that purpose, such number of the same as may appear to be required for military instruction and practice by the students of any college or university under the provisions of this section; and the Secretary shall require a bond in each case, in double the value of the property, for the care and safe keeping thereof, and for the return of the same when required."

ARTICLE 18.

REGULATIONS.

The following regulations, in regard to the detail of officers of the army at established colleges and universities within the United States, are prescribed by the President, under the above law:

1. Details "shall be apportioned throughout the United States as nearly as may be practicable according to population;" such States as do not contain sufficient population to entitle them to one officer will be grouped with one or more contiguous States or Territories, so that the combined population of the group will allow the detail of one or more officers, to the extent of forty officers in all.

2. As a rule, Captains of companies, regimental staff officers, or officers who have served less than three years with their regiments or corps, or who have recently completed a tour of detached duty, will not be eligible. No details will be made that will leave a battery, troop, or company without

two officers for duty with it. The period of detail will not be longer than three years.

3. No officer will be detailed at any institution except upon an application from its proper representatives.

4. Applications for details of officers should be addressed to the Secretary of War, and should be accompanied by a certificate as to the number of male students the college or university has the capacity to educate, and also by the last printed catalogue.

5. Officers of the army desiring a detail at colleges or universities may make application therefor to the Adjutant-General through the usual military channels, and their names will, if the officers are available, be furnished to such institutions as may desire such details.

The following are the regulations prescribed by the Secretary of War for the issue of arms, etc., required for military instruction and practice at colleges and universities, under Section 1225, Revised Statutes:

1. The number of pieces of field artillery, with necessary implements, and of small arms and accouterments, which may be issued for the purpose of military instruction to each selected college and university having an officer of the army stationed thereat, is limited to the following, viz.: 2 3-inch rifled guns, wrought iron, model 1861, at $450, $900; 2 carriages and limbers, 3-inch gun, at $325, $650; 2 gunner's haversacks, at $3 35, $6 70; 2 handspikes, trail, at $1, $2; 4 lanyards, at 10 cents, 40 cents; 2 priming wires, at 10 cents, 20 cents; 4 sponges and rammers, 3-inch, at $1, $4; 4 sponge covers, 3-inch, at 30 cents, $1 20; 2 tube pouches, at $1 50, $3; 4 thumbstalls, at 20 cents, 80 cents; 2 tompions, 3-inch, at 30 cents, 60 cents; 2 vent covers, at 40 cents, 80 cents; 1 pendulum hausse, 3-inch, $2 50; 1 pendulum hausse seat, 60 cents; 1 pendulum hausse pouch, 75 cents; 2 paulins, 12 by 15 feet, at $11 75, $23 50; 150 Springfield "cadet" rifles, caliber .45, with appendages, etc., at $18, $2,700; 150 bayonet scabbards, steel, cadet, at 91 cents, $136 50; 150 waist belts and plates, at 50 cents, $75; 150 cartridge boxes, caliber 45, at $1 25, $187 50.

2. Issue of the above stores will be made by the Chief of Ordnance to any selected institution upon its filing a bond in the penal sum of double the value of the property, conditioned that it will take good care of and safely keep and account for the same, and will, when required by the Secretary of War, duly return the same, within thirty days, in good order, to the Chief of Ordnance or such officer or person as the Secretary of War may designate to receive it.

3. To conform to the requirements of the law, the terms "college" and "university" herein used are held to relate to "State institutions, incorporated or public," and not to "mere schools, private or municipal."

4. (Prescribes the form of bond.)

5. For practice-firing, the following allowances of ammuni-

tion will be made annually to each of the various institutions, viz.: 1,000 carbine metallic ball cartridges, cal. .45; 1,000 metallic blank cartridges, cal. .45; 100 rounds blank cartridges for 3-inch gun; 300 friction primers.

This ammunition will be issued upon requisitions to be forwarded to the Chief of Ordnance by the Presidents or Superintendents of the institutions; and as annual allowances date in all cases from July first of each year, requisitions should be forwarded before or as soon after that date as practicable for the prospective year's supply. Undrawn allowances of one year cannot be drawn in the succeeding year.

6. Regular property returns will be rendered quarterly to the Chief of Ordnance by each President or Superintendent of an institution supplied with arms, etc., accounting for all ordnance and ordnance stores issued to the institution under his charge. These returns will be made on the blank forms to be supplied by the Chief of Ordnance.

7. Whenever any institution shall fail to return the public property in its charge within thirty days after demand made by the Secretary of War, the delinquency will be promptly referred to the Attorney-General, that the bond of the institution may forthwith be put in suit.

8. All expense of repairs of stores are to be borne by the institution using the same, the Ordnance Department supplying spare parts for repairs at cost price.

The Act of Congress approved May 4, 1880, relating to the detail of retired officers at colleges provides:

That upon the application of any college, university, or institution of learning, incorporated under the laws of any State within the United States, having capacity at the same time to educate not less than one hundred and fifty male students, the President may detail an officer of the army on the retired list to act as President, Superintendent, or professor thereof; and such officer may receive from the institution to which he may be detailed the difference between his retired and full pay, and shall not receive any additional pay or allowance from the United States.

The details authorized by this Act will be in addition to the forty allowed by Section 1225, Revised Statutes, as amended by the Act of Congress approved July 5, 1884, and may be made to institutions of learning of the requisite grade in any State, without reference to population or to the number of officers already serving therein.

By command of Lieutenant-General Sheridan.

CHAUNCEY McKEEVER,
Acting Adjutant-General.

TITLE TWO.

STATE LEGISLATION.

DIVISION ONE—CONSTITUTIONAL PROVISIONS.

CHAPTER I.

Constitution of California 1849 and 1862—Article IX.

ARTICLE 19.

SECTION 4. The Legislature shall take measures for the protection, improvement, or other disposition of such lands as have been or may hereafter be reserved or granted by the United States, or any person or persons, to this State, for the use of a University; and the funds accruing from the rents or sale of such lands, or from any other source, for the purpose aforesaid, shall be and remain a permanent fund, the interest of which shall be applied to the support of said University, with such branches as the public convenience may demand, for the promotion of literature, the arts and sciences, as may be authorized by the terms of such grant. And it shall be the duty of the Legislature, as soon as may be, to provide effectual means for the improvement and permanent security of the funds of said University.

CHAPTER II.

Constitution of California 1879—Article IX, Section 9.

ARTICLE 20.

SECTION 9. The University of California shall constitute a public trust, and its organization and government shall be perpetually continued in the form and character prescribed by the organic Act creating the same, passed March twenty-third, eighteen hundred and sixty-eight (and the several Acts amendatory thereof), subject only to such legislative control as may be necessary to insure compliance with the terms of its endowments and the proper investment and security of its funds. It shall be entirely independent of all political or sectarian influence, and kept free therefrom in the appointment of its Regents, and in the administration of its affairs; *provided*, that all the moneys derived from the sale of public lands donated to this State by Act of Congress, approved July second, eighteen hundred and sixty-two, and the several Acts amendatory thereof, shall be invested as provided by said Acts of Congress, and the interest of said moneys shall be inviolably appropriated to the endowment, support, and maintenance of at least one College of Agriculture, where the leading objects shall be (without excluding other scientific and classical studies, and including military tactics) to teach such branches of learning as are related to scientific and practical agriculture and the mechanic arts, in accordance with the requirements and conditions of said Acts of Congress; and the Legislature shall provide that if, through neglect, misappropriation, or any other contingency, any portion of the funds so set apart shall be diminished or lost, the State shall replace such portion so lost or misappropriated, so that the principal thereof shall remain forever undiminished. No person shall be debarred admission to any of the collegiate departments of the University on account of sex.

DIVISION TWO—JOINT RESOLUTIONS.

CHAPTER 1.

[Adopted April 22, 1863. Stats. of Cal., 1863, p. 793.]

ARTICLE 21.

Appointing a Commission to report on the feasibility of establishing a University.

CHAPTER II.

[Resolution adopted December 12, 1863. Stats. of Cal., 1863–4, p. 541.]

ARTICLE 22.

Appointing a Commission to ascertain action necessary to secure United States land grant.

CHAPTER III.

Accepting benefits of Act of Congress of July 2, 1862, donating land for colleges.

[Resolution adopted March 31, 1864.   Stats. of Cal., 1863–4, p. 559.]

ARTICLE 23.

Resolved by the Senate, the Assembly concurring, That the State of California doth hereby accept the benefits of the Act entitled "An Act donating public lands to the several States and Territories which may provide colleges for the benefit of agriculture and mechanic arts," passed July second, A. D. eighteen hundred and sixty-two.

CHAPTER IV.

[Adopted February 26, 1868.   Stats. of Cal., 1867–8, p. 732.]

ARTICLE 24.

Requesting that Congress authorize selection of lands within railroad reservation.

CHAPTER V.

[Approved March 30, 1868.   Stats. of Cal., 1867–8, p. 742.]

ARTICLE 25.

Requesting that Congress shall permit investment of the proceeds of 150,000 acre donation in unincumbered productive real estate.

CHAPTER VI.

Senate Joint Resolution No. 1, asking Congressional action on behalf of the University of California.

[Approved February 1, 1883.   Stats. of Cal., 1883, p. 386.]

ARTICLE 26.

WHEREAS, The Act of Congress, approved July second, eighteen hundred and sixty-two, donating one hundred and fifty thousand acres of public land to the State of California for an Agricultural and Mechanic Arts College (which donation was by **said State** conferred upon **said** University of California), **required** the investment of the funds obtained from the **sale of** said lands, in safe stocks, yielding not less than five per centum upon the **par** value **of** said **stocks;** and whereas, **in the present** situation of financial affairs in this State it is **impossible to comply** with **said conditions;** be it

Resolved by the Senate and Assembly of the State of California, That our Senators be instructed and our Representatives be requested to use their best endeavors to have a law passed allowing the Regents of the University of California to invest said funds in the safest and best possible manner; and be it further

Resolved, That his Excellency the Governor be requested to transmit a copy of these resolutions to each of the Senators and Representatives in Congress from the State of California.

CHAPTER VII.

Assembly Concurrent Resolution No. 10, relative to the establishment of Experimental Stations in connection with Agricultural Colleges.

[Adopted April 16, 1884.]

ARTICLE 27.

WHEREAS, There is now pending before Congress a bill to establish National Experimental Stations in connection with the Agricultural Colleges of the various States; therefore, be it

Resolved by the Assembly, the Senate concurring, That our Senators and Representatives in Congress be requested to use their utmost endeavor to secure the passage of said bill.

Resolved, That the Governor of the State of California be requested to transmit a copy of this resolution to each of our Senators and Representatives.

DIVISION THREE — ACTS OF THE LEGISLATURE — STATUTES.

CHAPTER I.

[Approved April 27, 1863. Stats. of Cal., 1863, p. 592.]

ARTICLE 28.

An Act to provide for the sale of certain lands belonging to the State.

CHAPTER II.

[Approved March 31, 1866. Stats. of Cal., 1865-6, p. 504.]

ARTICLE 29.

An Act to establish an Agricultural, Mining, and Mechanical Arts College.

CHAPTER III.

[Approved April 2, 1866. Stats. of Cal., 1865-6, p. 674.]

ARTICLE 30.

An Act to provide for selection of lands and endowment of Colleges of Agriculture and Mechanic Arts.

NOTE.—Repealed by Act approved March 28, 1868. See Art. 23.

CHAPTER IV.

[Approved April 2, 1866. Stats. Cal., 1865-6, p. 784.]

ARTICLE 31.

An Act requiring biennial reports.

CHAPTER V.

Act authorizing incorporation of institutions of learning, under which the Board of Regents incorporated.

[Approved March 21, 1868. Stats. of Cal., 1867-8, p. 204.]

ARTICLE 32.

SECTION 1. Whenever the Legislature shall provide by enactment for the creation of any State university, college, academy, or other State institution of learning, science, or art, and shall, in and by such enactment, direct and provide for the creation of a corporation for such purpose, any three of the persons named or indicated in and by such enactment as Trustees or Directors of such corporation may unite in a certificate to the effect that they have associated themselves together for the purposes mentioned in and by such enactment, and to form a corporation for such purposes by the name and style designated in and by such enactment. The execution of such certificate shall be acknowledged before, and certified by, the Secretary of State, or any Notary Public, and said certificate thereupon filed in the office of the Secretary of State; and thereupon the persons named therein, their associates and successors, shall become a corporation under the name and style designated in and by such enactment.

ARTICLE 33.

SEC. 2. Every such corporation, as such, shall have power:

First—To have succession by its corporate name for the period limited; and where no period is limited, perpetually

Second—To sue and be sued in any Court.

Third—To make and use a common seal, and alter the same at pleasure.

Fourth—To hold, purchase, and convey such real and personal estate as the purposes of the corporation shall require, not exceeding the amount limited by law.

Fifth—To make by-laws, not inconsistent with any existing law, for the management of its property and the regulation of its affairs.

ARTICLE 34.

SEC. 3. In addition to the powers enumerated in the preceding section, no such corporation shall possess or exercise any corporate powers except such as shall be necessary to the exercise of the powers so enumerated and given, and such further powers as may be enumerated and given in and by the enactment providing for the creation of the institution so incorporated; and any and all provisions of such enactment specially limiting the powers of such corporation shall be binding upon the same.

Sec. 4. This Act shall take effect from and after its passage.

———

CHAPTER VI.

Act to create and organize the **University** *of California.—The* " *Organic Act.* "

[Approved March 23, 1868. Stats. of Cal., 1867-8, p. 248.]

ARTICLE 35.

SECTION 1. A State University is hereby created, pursuant to the requirements of section four, article nine, of the Constitution of the State of California; and, in order to devote to the largest purpose of education the benefaction made to the State of California under and by the provisions of an Act of Congress passed July second, eighteen hundred and sixty-two, entitled an Act donating land to the several States and Territories which may provide colleges for the benefit of agriculture and the mechanic arts. The said University shall be called the University of California, and shall be located upon the grounds heretofore donated to the State of California by the President and Board of Trustees of the College of California. The said University shall be under the charge and control of a Board of Directors, to be known and styled "The Regents of the University of California." The University shall have for its design to provide instruction and complete education in all the departments of science, literature, art, industrial and professional pursuits, and general education, and also special courses of instruction for the professions of agriculture, the mechanic arts, mining, military science, civil engineering, law, medicine, and commerce, and shall consist of various colleges, namely.

First—Colleges of Arts;

Second—A College of Letters;

Third—Such professional and other colleges as may be added thereto or connected therewith.

ARTICLE 36.

SEC. 2. Each full course of instruction shall consist of its appropriate studies, and shall continue for at least four years, and the faculty, instructors, and body of students, in each course, shall constitute a college, to be designated by its appropriate name. For this purpose there shall be organized as soon as the means appropriated therefor shall permit:

First—The following Colleges of Arts: a State College of

Agriculture; a State College of Mechanic Arts; a State College of Mines; a State College of Civil Engineering; and such other Colleges of Arts as the Board of Regents may be able and find it expedient to establish.

Second—A State College of Letters.

Third—Colleges of Medicine, Law, and other like professional colleges.

ARTICLE 37.

SEC. 3. A proper degree of each college shall be conferred at the end of the course upon such students as, having completed the same, shall, at the annual examination, be found proficient therein; but each college shall also have a partial course for those who may not desire to pursue a full course therein; and any resident of California, of the age of fourteen years or upwards, of approved moral character, shall have the right to enter himself in the University as a student at large, and receive tuition in any branch or branches of instruction at the time when the same are given in their regular course, on such terms as the Board of Regents may prescribe. The said Board of Regents shall endeavor so to arrange the several courses of instruction that the students of the different colleges and the students at large may be largely brought into social contact and intercourse with each other by attending the same lectures and branches of instruction.

ARTICLE 38.

SEC. 4. The College of Agriculture shall be first established; but in selecting the professors and instructors for the said College of Agriculture the Regents shall, so far as in their power, select persons possessing such acquirements in their several vocations as will enable them to discharge the duties of professors in the several Colleges of Mechanic Arts, of Mines, and of Civil Engineering, and in such other colleges as may be hereafter established. As soon as practicable a system of moderate manual labor should be established in connection with the Agricultural College, and upon its agricultural and ornamental grounds, having for its object practical education in agriculture, landscape gardening, the health of the students, and to afford them an opportunity, by their earnings, of defraying a portion of the expenses of their education. These advantages shall be open in the first instance to students in the College of Agriculture, who shall be entitled to a preference in that behalf.

ARTICLE 39.

SEC. 5. The College of Mechanic Arts shall be next established; and in organizing this or any other college, the same regard hereinbefore indicated shall be had for the general acquirements of each professor and instructor, so that he may be able to give general and special instruction in as many classes and courses of instruction as possible; and inasmuch as the original donation, out of which the plan of a State University has had its rise, was made to the State by virtue of the aforesaid Act of Congress, entitled an Act donating land to the several States and Territories which may provide colleges for the benefit of agriculture and the mechanic arts, approved July second, eighteen hundred and sixty-two, the said Board of Regents shall always bear in mind that the College of Agriculture and the College of Mechanic Arts are an especial object of their care and superintendence, and that they shall be considered and treated as entitled primarily to the use of the funds donated for their establishment and maintenance by the said Act of Congress.

ARTICLE 40.

SEC. 6. The College of Mines and the College of Civil Engineering shall be next established, and such other colleges of arts as the Board of Regents may be able to establish with the means in their possession or under their control; and in order to fulfill the requirements of the said Act of Congress all able-bodied male students of the University, whether pursuing full or partial courses in any colleges, or as students at large, shall receive instruction and discipline in military tactics, in such manner and to such extent as the Regents shall prescribe, the requisite arms for which shall be furnished by the State.

ARTICLE 41.

SEC. 7. The Board of Regents, having in regard the said donation already made to the State by the President and Board of Trustees of the College of California, and their proposition to surrender all their property to the State, for the benefit of the State University, and to become disincorporate and go out of existence as soon as the State shall organize the University by adding a Classical College to the College of Arts, shall, as soon as they deem it practicable, establish a College of Letters. The College of Letters shall be coexistent with the aforesaid Colleges of Arts, and shall embrace a liberal course of instruction in languages, literature, and philosophy, together with such courses or parts of courses in the aforesaid Colleges of Arts as the authorities or the University shall prescribe. The degree of Bachelor of Arts, upon due examination, and afterward the degree of Master of Arts, in usual course, shall be conferred upon graduates of this college. But the provisions herein and hereinbefore contained, regarding the order in which the said colleges shall be organized, shall not be construed as directing or per-

mitting the organization of any of the specified colleges to be
unnecessarily delayed, but only as indicating the order in
which said colleges shall be organized, beginning with the College of Agriculture, and adding in succession to the body of
instructors in that and the other colleges such other instructors as may be necessary to organize the other colleges succes-
sively in the order above indicated. Only the first year's course
of instruction shall be provided for in each college at first, the
other successive years' courses being added in each year as
the students advance to the same until the full course in each
college is established; *provided, however,* that the Board of
Regents may organize at once the full course of the College of
Letters, if in their judgment it is expedient so to do, in order
to allow the College of California to immediately convey the
residue of its property to the State for the benefit of the
University, and to become disincorporate and go out of existence pursuant to its proposition to that effect.

ARTICLE 42.

SEC. 8. The Board of Regents may affiliate with the University and make an integral part of the same, and incorporate therewith any incorporated College of Medicine or
of Law, or other special course of instruction now existing,
or which may hereafter be created, upon such terms as to
the respective corporations may be deemed expedient. And
such college or colleges so affiliated shall retain the control
of their own property, with their own Boards of Trustees
and their own Faculties and Presidents of the same, respectively; and the students of those colleges, recommended by
the respective Faculties thereof, shall receive from the University the degrees of those colleges; *provided, however,* that
the President of the University shall be, ex officio, a member
of the Faculty of each and every college of the University,
and President of such Faculty.

ARTICLE 43.

SEC. 9. The examinations for degrees shall be annual,
and the Board of Regents shall take measures to make such
examinations thorough and complete. Students who shall
have passed not less than a full year as resident students
in any college, academy, or school in this State, and after
examination by the respective Faculty of such college,
academy, or school, are recommended by such Faculty as
proficient candidates for any degree in any regular course of
the University, shall be entitled to be examined therefor at
the annual examination; and, on passing such examination,
shall receive such degree for that course and the diploma of
the University therefor, and shall rank and be considered, in
all respects, as graduates of the University All students of

the University who have been resident students thereof for not less than one year, and all graduates of the University, in any course, may present themselves for examination in any other course or courses at the annual examinations, and, on passing such examination, shall receive the degree and diploma of that course. Upon such examinations each professor and instructor of that course shall cast one vote upon each application for recommendation to the Board of Regents for a degree, and the votes shall be by ballot. In case the College of California shall surrender its property to the University, and said donation shall be accepted by the Board of Regents, and said College of California shall thereafter become disincorporate in pursuance of its proposition heretofore made, to that effect, the graduates and those who shall have received the degrees of that college shall receive the degrees from the University, and be considered, in all respects, graduates of the same; and the last above expressed provision shall apply to the previous graduates of any incorporated college of medicine, law, or other professional college which shall become affiliated with the University, as herein otherwise provided. The Board of Regents shall also confer certificates of proficiency in any branch of study upon such students of the University as, upon examination, shall be found entitled to the same. The style of diplomas and degrees shall be: "University of California, College of Agriculture," or with the name of the other respective college; but honorary degrees for the higher degrees, not lower than that of Master of Arts, may be conferred, with the designation of the University alone, upon persons distinguished in literature, science, and art.

ARTICLE 44.

SEC. 10. Scholarships may be established in the University by the State, associations, or individuals, for the purpose of affording tuition in any course of the University, free from the ordinary charges, to any scholar in the public schools of the State who shall distinguish himself in study, according to the recommendation of his teachers, and shall pass the previous examination required for the grade at which he wishes to enter the University, or for the purpose of private benefaction; *provided,* that the said scholarships shall be approved and accepted by the Board of Regents.

ARTICLE 45.

SEC. 11. The general government and superintendence of the University shall vest in a Board of Regents, to be denominated the "Regents of the University of California," who shall become incorporated under the general laws of the State of California by that corporate name and style.

The said Board shall consist of **twenty-two members, all of whom shall be** citizens and **permanent residents of the State of California, as** follows:

Firstly—Of **the** following ex officio members, namely: His Excellency **the** Governor; the Lieutenant-Governor, or the person acting as such, the Speaker, for the time being, of the Assembly; the State Superintendent of Public Instruction; the President, for the time being, of the State Agricultural Society, and the President **of** the Mechanics' Institute **of the** City and County of San Francisco.

Secondly—Of eight **other** appointed members, to be nominated by the Governor, by and with the advice and consent of **the Senate,** who shall hold their office for the term of sixteen years; *provided*, that such members first so appointed shall be classified by **lot** at the first meeting **of** the Board of Regents, so that one of the numbers so appointed shall go out of office at the end of **every** successive two **years;** and after that the full term to be sixteen years, and the record of such classification shall be transmitted by said Board of **Regents to the** Secretary of State and filed in his office.

Thirdly—Of eight additional honorary members, to be chosen from the body of the State by the official and appointed members, who shall hold their office for the term **of** sixteen years; *provided*, that such honorary members first so chosen shall be classified by lot when so appointed, by the Board of Regents so appointing them, so that one of the members so chosen shall go out of office at the end of each successive two years, and after that the full term to be sixteen years, and the record of such classification shall be transmitted by said Board of Regents to the Secretary of State, to be filed in his office. Each member of the said Board, whether official, appointed, or honorary, shall, if present, **be** entitled to one vote at all the meetings of said Board. The first official year from which the terms of office shall **be** computed **to** run, shall be the first day of March, in the year eighteen hundred and sixty-eight. Vacancies in the office of appointed members of the Board, occurring in the recess of the Legislature, shall **be** filled for the rest of the term by appointment of the Governor. Vacancies **in** the office of honorary members, occurring from any cause other than the expiration of the term by limitation, shall be filled for the rest of the term by appointment of **the** Board of Regents. **In case** the Senate shall adjourn before the Governor shall have nominated the first appointed members of the Board **of** Regents, under this Act, or before it shall have confirmed **his** nomination in their behalf, the Governor shall appoint **the** same by his sole act. No member of the Board of Regents, or of the University, shall be deemed **a** public officer by virtue of such membership, or required **to** take any **oath** of office, but his employment as such shall be held and deemed **to be** exclusively **a private trust;** and **no** person who **at the**

time holds any executive office, or appointment under the
State, shall be a member of said Board, except the executive
officers above mentioned. The Governor shall be President
of the Board of Regents, and in his absence the Board shall
appoint a President pro tempore.

ARTICLE 46.

SEC. 12. The said Board of Regents, when so incorporated,
shall have the custody of the books, records, buildings, and
all other property of the University. The lands and other
property heretofore donated to the State by the President
and Trustees of the College of California, and which are
situated in the Township of Oakland, in the County of Alameda, for the purpose of erecting thereon an Agricultural
College, and for other purposes mentioned in the deed of
conveyance by which the same were so conveyed, shall be
and forever remain vested in the State of California; as shall
also be vested in the said State all property which shall be
purchased by the funds of the State, or from the proceeds of
donations made to the State for the purpose of the University, or of any of the colleges or professorships thereof; and
the said Board of Regents shall have no power to alienate or
incumber, by mortgage, hypothecation, lien, or otherwise, any
portion of said property except on terms such as the Legislature shall have previously approved; any act of the said
Regents, or of any other person, which shall purport to have
that effect, shall be wholly null and void. All lands, moneys,
bonds, securities, or other property, which shall be donated,
conveyed, or transferred to the said Board of Regents by
gift, devise, or otherwise, including such property as may
hereafter be donated and conveyed by the President and
Board of Trustees of the College of California, in trust or
otherwise, for the use of said University, or any college
thereof, or of any professorship, chair, or scholarship therein,
or for the library, observatory, or any other purpose appropriate thereto, shall be taken, received, held, managed,
invested, reinvested, sold, transferred, and in all respects
managed, and the proceeds thereof used, bestowed, invested,
and reinvested by the said Board of Regents in their corporate name and capacity, for the purposes and under the
terms, provisions, and conditions respectively prescribed by
the act of gift, devise, or other act in the respective case. In
case any incorporated College of Law, Medicine, or the like,
shall be brought into the said University by affiliation, as
herein otherwise provided, such college so affiliated may
retain its own property then possessed by it or thereafter to
be acquired, to be vested in and held and managed by its own
corporation, and the said Board of Regents shall have no
right of property in or power or control over the same, nor
shall be liable for any acts or contracts of such affiliated
corporation.

ARTICLE 47.

SEC. 13. The Regents and their successors in office, when so incorporated, shall have power, and it shall be their duty, to enact laws for the government of the University; to elect a President of the University, and the requisite number of professors, instructors, officers, and employés, and to fix their salaries; also the term of office of each; and to determine the moral and educational qualifications of applicants for admission to the various courses of instruction. They shall also consider and determine whether the interests of the University and of the students, as well as those of the State, and of the great body of scientific men in the State, whose purpose is to devote themselves to public instruction, will not be greatly promoted by committing those courses of instruction which are brief and special to professors employed for short terms, and for only a portion of each year in their special departments, and to be termed non-resident professors; and their decision in that regard may be reconsidered by them as often as they deem it expedient. And it is expressly provided that no sectarian, political, or partisan test shall ever be allowed or exercised in the appointment of Regents, or in the election of professors, teachers, or other officers of the University, or in the admission of students thereto, or for any purpose whatsoever. Nor at any time shall the majority of the Board of Regents be of any one religious sect, or of no religious sect; and persons of every religious denomination, or of no religious denomination, shall be equally eligible to all offices, appointments, and scholarships.

ARTICLE 48.

SEC. 14. For the time being an admission fee and rates of tuition, such as the Board of Regents shall deem expedient, may be required of each pupil, except as herein otherwise provided; and as soon as the income of the University shall permit, admission and tuition shall be free to all residents of the State; and it shall be the duty of the Regents, according to population, to so apportion the representation of students, when necessary, that all portions of the State shall enjoy equal privileges therein.

ARTICLE 49.

SEC. 15. The President of the University shall be President of the several Faculties, and the executive head of the institution in all its departments, except as herein otherwise provided. He shall have authority, subject to the Board of Regents, to give general direction to the practical affairs of the several colleges, and, in the recess of the Board of Regents, to remove any employé or subordinate officer, not a member of any Faculty; and to supply, for the time being, any vacancy thus created; and, so long as the institution require it, he shall be charged with the duties of one of the professorships. A competent person, who is a practical agriculturist by profession, competent to superintend the working of the agricultural farm, and of sufficient scientific acquirements to discharge the duties of Secretary of the Board of Regents, as prescribed in this Act, shall be chosen by said Board as their Secretary, and, in addition to his special duties as such, as prescribed in this Act, he shall perform such other duties as they shall impose. He shall receive for his services such reasonable salary as the Board of Regents shall prescribe. The Board of Regents may also appoint a Treasurer of the University and prescribe the form and sureties of his bond as such, which shall be executed, approved by them, and filed with the Secretary, before any such Treasurer shall go into office. The Secretary and Treasurer shall be subject to summary removal by the Board of Regents.

ARTICLE 50.

SEC. 16. The Secretary of the Board of Regents shall reside and keep his office at the seat of the University. It shall be his duty to keep a record of the transactions of the Board of Regents, which shall be open at all times to the inspection of any citizen of this State. He shall also have the custody of all books, papers, documents, and other property which may be deposited in his office; also, keep on file all reports and communications which may be made to the University from time to time by county, State, and district agricultural societies; horticultural, vinicultural, mechanical, and mining societies; and of all correspondence from other persons and societies appertaining to the business of education, science, art, husbandry, mechanics, and mining; address circulars to societies, and to the best practical farmers, mechanics, and miners in this State and elsewhere, with the view of eliciting information upon the latest and best modes of culture of the products, vegetables, trees, etc., adapted to the soil and climate of the State, and also on all subjects connected with field culture, horticulture, stock raising, and the dairy. He shall also correspond with established schools of mining and metallurgy in Europe, and obtain such information respecting the improvements of mining machinery adapted to California, and publish from time to time such information as will be of practical benefit to the mining interests and the working of all ores and metals; receive and distribute such rare and valuable seeds, plants, shrubbery, and trees as may be in his power to procure from the General Government and other sources, as may be adapted to our climate and soil, or to purposes of experiment therein. To effect these objects he shall correspond with the Patent

Office at Washington, and with the representatives of our National Government abroad, and, if possible, procure valuable contributions to agriculture from these sources. He shall aid, as far as possible, in obtaining contributions to the museum and the library of the said college, and thus aid in the promotion of agriculture, science, and literature. He shall keep a correct account of all the executive acts of the President of the University, and an accurate account of all moneys received into the treasury, as well as those paid out.

ARTICLE 51.

SEC. 17. The seeds, plants, trees, and shrubbery received by the Secretary and not needed by the University, shall be, so far as possible, distributed without charge equally throughout the State, and placed in the hands of those farmers and others who will agree to cultivate them properly and return to the Secretary's office a reasonable proportion of the products thereof, with a full statement of the mode of cultivation, and such other information as may be necessary to ascertain their value for general cultivation in the State. Information in regard to agriculture, the mechanic arts, mining, and metallurgy may be published by him from time to time, in the newspapers of the State, as matters of public importance, provided it does not involve any expense to the State.

ARTICLE 52.

SEC. 18. The immediate government and discipline of the several colleges shall be intrusted to their respective Faculties, to consist of the President and the resident Professors of the same, each of which shall have its own organization, regulate the affairs of its own college, recommending the course of study and the text-books to be used for the approval of the Board of Regents, and in connection with the President as its executive officer, have the government of its students. All the Faculties and instructors of the University shall be combined into a body which shall be known as the Academic Senate, which shall have stated meetings at regular intervals, and be presided over by the President, or a President pro tempore, and which is created for the purpose of conducting the general administration of the University and memorializing the Board of Regents; regulating in the first instance, the general and special courses of instruction, and to receive and determine all appeals couched in respectful terms, from acts of discipline enforced by the Faculty of any college. Its proceedings shall be conducted according to rules of order, and every person engaged in instruction in the University, whether resident Professors, non-resident Professors, lecturers, or instructors, shall have permission to participate in its discussions; but the right of voting shall be confined to the President and the resident and non-resident Professors. But the Regents shall have power to supervise the general course of instruction, and on the recommendation of the several Faculties, prescribe the authorities and text-books to be used in the several courses and colleges, and also to confer such degrees and grant such diplomas as are usual in Universities, or as they shall deem appropriate; *provided*, that no honorary degree of any college or course shall be granted by the Regents, nor shall any degree, certificate, or diploma for any course or branch of instruction, be granted by the Regents unless upon examination therefor as prescribed in this Act, except the substituted degrees and diplomas provisionally provided for those having received degrees from the College of California, in case the said college becomes extinct and disincorporates, and for the graduates of affiliated professional colleges as herein otherwise provided.

ARTICLE 53.

SEC. 19. At the close of each fiscal year the Regents, through their President, shall make a report in detail to the Governor, exhibiting the progress, condition, and wants of each of the colleges embraced in the University, the course of study in each, the number of professors and students, the amount of receipts and disbursements, together with the nature, cost, and results of all important investigations and experiments, and such other information as they may deem important; one printed copy of which shall be transmitted, free, by their Secretary, to all colleges endowed under the provisions of the Congressional Act of July second, eighteen hundred and sixty-two, hereinbefore referred to; also one printed copy to the Secretary of the Interior, as provided in said Act.

ARTICLE 54.

SEC. 20. For the endowment and support of the University, and its buildings and improvements, there are hereby appropriated:

Firstly—The capital, income, proceeds, securities, avails, and interest that have accrued, or may hereafter accrue, from the sale of the seventy-two sections of land granted to the State for a seminary of learning by an Act of Congress entitled "An Act to provide for the survey of the public lands in California, the granting of preemption rights therein, and for other purposes," approved March third, eighteen hundred and fifty-three, and from the sale of the ten sections of land granted to the State for public buildings by said Act of Congress, which shall be forthwith, so far as the same have been received, and hereafter as fast as the same shall be received by any **of** the officers of the State, shall be paid over to the said Board of Regents upon their order therefor.

Secondly—The income, revenue, and avails which shall be **derived** or received from the investment of the proceeds of **the sale** of the lands, or of the script therefor, or of any part **thereof,** granted to this State by an Act of Congress entitled an **Act** donating public lands to the several States and Territories of the United States, for the benefit of agriculture and the mechanic arts, approved July second, eighteen hundred and sixty-two, which are hereby appropriated to, and from time to time, as the same shall be received, shall be paid into the State Treasury, carried to the credit of said Board of Regents, and paid over to the Treasurer of the University, for the use and behoof of the said University, and expended by said Board as elsewhere prescribed in this Act; and said lands shall be located and sold under the direction of the Board of Regents, and for such price, and on such terms only **as** they shall prescribe.

. *Thirdly*—All such contributions to the endowment or other funds, **as** may be derived from appropriations by the State, from the United States, or from public or private bounty. The entire income of said funds shall be placed at the disposition of the Board of Regents, for the support of the University, and of the several colleges and schools thereof, as herein otherwise provided, with the exception of such affiliated incorporated colleges as shall preserve their own property and the income thereof, as herein otherwise provided; *and, provided moreover*, that all means derivable from either public or private bounty shall be exclusively devoted to the specific objects for which they shall have been designed by the grantor. The Board of Regents may appoint competent persons to solicit and collect private contributions for the endowment of the University, and pay them for their services **in** that behalf, out of the funds so obtained by them, such **reasonable** compensation as the said Board may prescribe.

Fourthly—All such appropriations as may be made for that purpose by the Legislature.

SEC. 21. For the current expenditures of the University, specific sums of **money** shall be set aside out of the funds at their disposal, by **the** Board of Regents, which shall be liable to disbursement for that purpose, and shall be subject to the warrants of the President **of** the Board drawn upon the Treasurer of the University, **in** pursuance of the orders of . the Board **of** Regents. All moneys received from labor and incidental sources shall be paid into the treasury and expended in the same manner as other moneys. All moneys which may at any time be in the State Treasury, and subject to the use of said Board of Regents, may be drawn therefrom by the President of the Board, upon the order of said Board, in favor of **the** Treasurer of the University.

Sec. 22. Meetings of the Board of Regents may be called in such a manner as the Regents shall determine, seven of whom shall constitute a quorum for the transaction of business; but a less number may adjourn from time to time. No member of the Board shall receive any compensation for his services as such member, nor be entitled to reimbursement for his traveling or other expenses while employed on the business of the Board.

Sec. 23. The Regents shall, when they shall be in possession of funds for that purpose, organize and put into operation the first year's course of instruction in as many of the said colleges as possible. If the buildings of the University are not sufficiently completed at that time to be occupied for that purpose, the Regents are authorized to make temporary arrangements for sufficient buildings, the use of apparatus, and for other needful purposes, in the City of Oakland, if the same shall be practicable.

Sec. 24. The collection by the State Geological Survey shall belong to the University; and the Regents shall, in their plans, have in view the early and secure arrangement of the same for the use of the students of the University, and of giving access to the same, to the public at large, and to visitors from abroad; and shall in every respect, by acts of courtesy and accommodation, encourage the visits of persons of scientific tastes and acquirements from other portions of the United States, and of other countries, to California.

The said collections shall be arranged by the resident professors of the University in a separate building, which shall be denominated the "Museum of the University." To this museum shall also be added, as fast as the means of the University shall permit, collections of agricultural implements, and objects illustrative of the mechanic arts, science, architecture, and the fine arts.

The collection of a library shall be commenced at once, and increased and expanded as fast as the Board of Regents are placed in possession of funds for that purpose. But the Board of Regents may allow duplicates to be taken from said collections of the State Geological Survey, and made a part of some other museum under the care of an incorporated academy of science, which shall become responsible for the custody and return of the same.

Sec. 25. The Regents shall devise, and with the funds appropriated for that purpose, cause to be constructed, such buildings as shall be needed for the immediate use of the University.

The dormitory system shall not be adopted. Such a plan shall be adopted as shall set aside separate buildings for separate uses, and yet group all such buildings upon a general plan, so that a larger and central building hereafter erected may bring the whole into harmony as parts of one design. The construction and equipment of said buildings shall be let out, in every instance, to the lowest responsible bidder, who shall previously give adequate security, upon sealed proposals, upon specifications, after advertisement for not less than ten days in at least two daily newspapers published in the City of San Francisco; but they may reject any bid, and advertise anew.

They shall also take immediate measures for the permanent improvement and planting of the grounds of the University, and may make such contracts therefor, or for any part of that work, as they may deem advisable.

SEC. 26. An Act entitled an Act to establish an Agricultural, Mining, and Mechanical Arts College, approved March thirty-first, eighteen hundred and sixty-six, and all Acts or parts of Acts inconsistent with this Act, are hereby repealed, so far as they conflict with the provisions of this Act. But the Board of Directors of the Agricultural, Mining, and Mechanic Arts College of this State are authorized and directed to transfer and convey all its property, real and personal, and all its effects, rights, and interests of property, to the Regents of the University of California; and said Regents may accept and take possession of said property, and may, if they approve the same, ratify and confirm any contracts executed or unexecuted, made by said Directors; and for the purpose of carrying out the purposes of this section, said Directors are continued in office until the powers herein conferred shall be fully executed.

SEC. 27. This Act shall take effect immediately from and after its passage.

CHAPTER VII.

[Approved March 26, 1868.   Stats. of Cal. 1867-8, p. 357.]

ARTICLE 55.

An Act relating to transfer of funds.

CHAPTER VIII.

[Approved March 28, 1868.   Stats. of Cal. 1867-8, pp. 507-530.]

ARTICLE 56.

An Act providing for the management and sale of lands belonging to the State.

CHAPTER IX.

[Approved March 30, 1868.   Stats. of Cal. 1867-8, pp. 583-588.]

ARTICLE 57.

Acts providing for sale of marsh and tide lands and appropriating $200,000 of proceeds for the University.

CHAPTER X.

[Approved January 6, 1870.   Stats. of Cal. 1869-70, p. 4.]

ARTICLE 58.

An Act authorizing Regents to establish a Preparatory Department.

CHAPTER XI.

An Act organizing University Cadets.

[Approved March 4, 1870.   Stats. of Cal. 1869-70, p. 119.]

ARTICLE 59.

SECTION 1.   The students of the State University of California shall, as soon as practicable, be organized into a body, to be known as the "University Cadets," for the purpose of physical training and military drill and instruction.

ARTICLE 60.

SEC. 2.   The officers of said Cadets, above and including the rank of Second Lieutenant, and below and including the rank of Colonel, shall be appointed by the Faculty, on a competitive examination, involving both scholarship and capacity for command, and they shall be commissioned by the Governor of the State.

ARTICLE 61.

SEC. 3.   The Adjutant-General of the State shall issue such arms, munitions, and equipments to carry out the objects of this bill as the Board of Regents may require.

ARTICLE 62.

SEC. 4. Upon graduating or retiring from the University, such officers may resign their commissions, or hold the same as retired officers of the University Cadets, liable to be called into service by the Governor in case of war, invasion, insurrection, or rebellion. The Military Instructor shall make quarterly reports to the Adjutant-General of the State, showing the number, discipline, and equipments of the Cadets.

ARTICLE 63.

SEC. 5. The Board of Regents shall make such further regulations in carrying out the objects of this law as they shall deem proper and consistent with the Constitution and laws of this State.

ARTICLE 64.

SEC. 6. It is not the intent of this law to lessen, encroach upon, or retard the academic and scientific courses provided for in said University, but to secure a system of physical training, with habits of order and dicipline, in aid of mental and moral advancement.

CHAPTER XII.

Act requiring biennial (and upon request special) reports of Regents.

[Approved March 18, 1870.   Stats. of Cal. 1869-70, p. 333.]

ARTICLE 65.

SECTION 1. The Controller, State Treasurer, Secretary of State, Attorney-General, Surveyor-General, Adjutant-General, Superintendent of Public Instruction, State Librarian, Directors, Visiting Physicians, and Resident Physicians of the Insane Asylum, Directors of the State Prison, State Capitol Commissioners, Trustees of the State Reform School, Trustees of the Institution for the education and care of the Deaf, Dumb, and Blind, Board of State Harbor Commissioners, Tide Land Commissioners, Regents of the University of the State of California, and all other officers and Boards of officers who now are, or who may hereafter be required by law, to make reports to the Governor or to the Legislature, shall send such reports to the Governor on or before the first day of August, eighteen hundred and seventy-one, and every two years thereafter; and *provided*, that such biennial reports shall be made in the form and manner now prescribed by law.

ARTICLE 66.

SEC. 2. It shall be lawful for the Governor to require of any officer or Board of officers who now are, or may hereafter be required by law to make biennial reports, such special reports as he may deem necessary concerning the business of their respective offices; and it is hereby made the duty of such officers or Boards of officers to make such special reports to the Governor, when required by him to do so.

CHAPTER XIII.

An Act to provide for competitive scholarships for the benefit of meritorious young men desirous of entering the State University.

[Approved April 1, 1870.   Stats of Cal. 1869–70, p. 546.]

ARTICLE 67.

SECTION 1. The Regents of the University of the State of California are hereby authorized and empowered to establish and maintain five competitive scholarships, embracing the full four years course in the University.

ARTICLE 68.

SEC. 2. The competitive examination for scholarships shall be made by the Faculty. The applicants for such examination shall be bona fide residents of California, and shall have been chiefly educated in any of the schools of this State, and shall, at the time of application, satisfy the Regents in respect to character and to the inability of the applicant to provide his own maintenance at the University.

ARTICLE 69.

SEC. 3. Each scholarship shall be entitled to three hundred dollars, to be appropriated out of the funds belonging to the University, and shall be applied, under the direction of proper officers of the Faculty, to the superintendence and support of the scholar during his University course; *provided,* the Regents may, upon the recommendation of the Faculty, revoke any scholarship for improper conduct or violating of established rules, and shall have power to fill all vacancies which may occur in scholarship under competitive examination.

CHAPTER XIV.

Act for the Endowment of the University of California.

[Approved April 2, 1870.   Stats. of Cal. 1869–70, p. 668.]

ARTICLE 70.

SECTION 1. The Treasurer of State shall place to the credit of the University Fund so much of any moneys that may be received by him from the net proceeds of sale of any salt marsh and tide lands lying in and around the Bay of San Francisco, belonging to the State of California, as, being invested in the bonds of said State, or of the United States, shall yield an annual income of fifty thousand dollars ($50,000)

ARTICLE 71.

SEC. 2. Said moneys shall be a fund, the capital of which shall remain undiminished, and the interest of which shall be inviolably applied to the support of the University of California; *provided*, that if at any time the income accruing to the University from the fund created by this Act, and the net income derived from all other sources, shall together exceed an average for the preceding years, reckoning from the date of the passage of this Act, of fifty thousand dollars per annum, then the excess above said average of fifty thousand dollars per annum shall be paid into the Common School Fund of the State.

ARTICLE 72.

SEC. 3. Whenever the sum paid into the University Fund from the proceeds of the sale of salt marsh and tide lands, as directed in section one, shall amount to fifty thousand dollars, net proceeds, it shall be the duty of the Treasurer to advertise in two daily newspapers published in English, in each of the Cities of San Francisco and Sacramento, for sealed proposals for the surrender of any of the civil bonds of the State of California, or of any gold-bearing bonds of the United States.   He shall state in such advertisement the amount of money on hand applicable to the purchase of bonds, and he shall accept such proposals as will yield the greatest amount of annual interest in gold coin of the United States.

ARTICLE 73.

SEC. 4. All bonds thus purchased shall be indorsed "University Fund," and shall be held by the Treasurer of State, who shall collect the interest thereon, which interest, when collected, shall be paid into the University Fund to the extent provided for in section two of this Act, and paid out therefrom semi-annually, to the Regents of the University, upon their order, to be by them expended for University purposes; *provided*, no portion of said interest so received shall be used for the erection or purchase of buildings nor for the purchase of lands.

ARTICLE 74.

SEC. 5. Whenever the principal of any of the bonds indorsed "University Fund," in the hands of the Treasurer, shall be paid, the amount so paid shall be reinvested in like manner as is provided for in section three.

CHAPTER XV.

[Approved February 1, 1872. Stats. of Cal. 1871-2, p. 48.]

ARTICLE 75.

Act relating to Brayton property in Oakland.

CHAPTER XVI.

[Approved February 2, 1872. Stats. of Cal. 1871-2, p. 55.]

ARTICLE 76.

Act authorizing delivery of report of State Geological Survey to the University.

CHAPTER XVII.

[Approved March 7, 1872. Stats. of Cal. 1871-2, p. 275.]

ARTICLE 77.

Act amending Act of April first, eighteen hundred and seventy, establishing scholarship. (See chapter thirteen, article twenty-eight.)

CHAPTER XVIII.

[Approved March 26, 1872.   Stats. of Cal. 1871-2, p. 554.]

ARTICLE 78.

An Act to provide for the support of the University (temporary).

———

CHAPTER XIX.

An Act to amend an Act entitled "An Act to create and organize the University of California," approved March twenty-third, eighteen hundred and sixty-eight.

[Approved March 28, 1872.   Stats. of Cal. 1871-2, p. 655.]

ARTICLE 79.

SECTION 1. Section twenty-five of said Act is hereby amended so as to read as follows:

Section 25. The Regents shall devise, and with the funds appropriated for that purpose, cause to be constructed such buildings as shall be needed for the immediate use of the University. Such a plan shall be adopted that separate buildings may be constructed and set aside for separate uses, yet such buildings shall be grouped upon a general plan so that a large and central building thereafter erected may harmonize therewith, and each building be a part of one design. The construction and equipment of the buildings shall in every instance be let out upon specifications and advertisement of not less than ten days in at least two daily newspapers of the City and County of San Francisco, to the lowest responsible bidder, upon sealed proposals. The Regents may require adequate security from all bidders, and shall have power to reject any and all bids and advertise anew. They shall also take measures for the immediate and permanent improvement of the grounds of the University, and may make such contracts therefor, or any part thereof, as they may deem advisable. The provisions of Chapter DXIX of the laws of eighteen hundred and sixty-nine–seventy shall not apply to buildings erected for the University

SEC. 2. This Act shall take effect immediately.

CHAPTER XX.

[Approved April 1, 1872. Stats. of Cal. 1871-2, p. 747.]

ARTICLE 80.

An Act appropriating $300,000 to Regents for building purposes.

CHAPTER XXI.

[Approved December 22, 1873. Stats. of Cal. 1873-4, p. 6.]

ARTICLE 81.

An Act providing for conversion of $65,000 United States 5-20 Bonds into State Bonds of Funded Debt of 1873.

CHAPTER XXII.

An Act to prohibit the sale of intoxicating liquors within two miles of the University of California.

[Approved December 23, 1873. Stats. of Cal. 1873-4, p. 12.]

ARTICLE 82.

SECTION 1. It shall not be lawful for any person or persons to keep or expose for sale, or sell, or give, or permit others to take, for a consideration, directly or indirectly, any malt, spirituous, or other alcoholic liquors, upon or within two miles of the grounds belonging and adjacent to the University of California in Alameda County.

ARTICLE 83.

SEC. 2. Any violation of section first of this Act shall be deemed a misdemeanor, punishable by fine or imprisonment in the county jail of Alameda County, or both. The fine to be not less than fifty dollars nor more than one hundred dollars; and the imprisonment to be not less than thirty nor more than ninety days, for each offense.

SEC. 3. This Act shall take effect from and after the first day of February, one thousand eight hundred and seventy-four.

4

CHAP. XXIII.

An Act concerning the selection and sale of University Lands.

[Approved March 13, 1874. Stats. of Cal. 1873–4, p. 356.]

ARTICLE 84.

SECTION 1. In all cases when a contest shall arise between two or more persons concerning the right of such persons to purchase any portion of the one hundred and fifty thousand acres of land granted to the State for the use of an Agricultural College, if either party shall demand a trial in the Courts of the State, the Land Agent of the University, as the agent of the State, shall make an order referring said contest to the District Court of the county in which the land involved is situated, and shall enter said order in the proper record book of his office; *provided*, that the party making such demand shall prosecute his contest to judgment within six months from the date of such demand, unless for cause satisfactory to the Court. Either party may bring an action in the District Court of the county in which the land in question is situated, to determine such conflict, and the proffer of a certified copy of the entry made by the said agent, shall give the said District Court full and complete jurisdiction to hear and determine said conflict; and upon the filing with the said Agent of a copy of the final judgment of said Court, he shall issue the certificate of purchase or other evidence of title, in accordance with said final judgment.

SEC. 2. Whenever any resident of this State desires to purchase any part of the one hundred and fifty thousand acres of land granted to the State for the use of an Agricultural College, he or she shall make an affidavit before any officer authorized to administer oaths, that he or she is a citizen of the United States (or if a foreigner, then that he has filed his intention of becoming a citizen), a resident of the State, of lawful age, that he or she desires to purchase said land, giving a description thereof by legal subdivisions, and that there are no improvements of any kind on said land other than those of the applicant; or if there be improvements other then his own, then he or she shall state that such improvements are the property of (giving his or her name), and have been upon the land for three months or over, and that the township has been sectionized and the plats of survey filed in the Land Office of the district in which the land is located, for three months or over, which application shall be forwarded to the said Land Agent of the University.

SEC. 3. This Act shall be in force from and after its passage.

CHAPTER XXIV.

An Act to provide for the preservation of the material of the Geological Survey of California.

[Approved March 27, 1874. Stats. of Cal. 1873–4, p. 694.]

ARTICLE 85.

SECTION 1. It shall be the duty of the State Geologist to deliver to the President of the University of California, at Berkeley, in this State, all instruments, accouterments, furniture, property, maps, books, drawings, manuscripts, notes, engravings, lithographic stones, woodcuts, field notes, and other material of every description and nature belonging or appertaining to the Geological Survey of California; such surrender and delivery to be made without delay.

ARTICLE 86.

SEC. 2. The Regents of the University of California shall safely keep and preserve, at the said University, all the property and material referred to in section one of this Act, until such time as the Legislature may direct otherwise.

ARTICLE 87.

SEC 3. The sum of five thousand dollars is hereby appropriated out of any money in the General Fund not otherwise appropriated, to pay the necessary cost of arranging, packing, transporting, and delivering the said property and material; and the Controller shall draw his warrant or warrants for such purpose, not to exceed said sum of five thousand dollars, when directed to do so by the State Board of Examiners, and the Treasurer shall pay the same.

ARTICLE 88.

SEC. 4. The Regents of said University shall keep on hand and offer for sale all volumes of reports and maps published by said Geological Survey; they may also, as soon as the present supply of reports and maps is exhausted, cause any portion of the same to be republished and sold at the prices now provided or that may hereafter be provided by law; *provided,* that said republication shall be done without cost to the State; *provided further,* that the proceeds of the sale of all such maps and reports, over and above the cost of publication, shall be paid in to the State Treasurer and by him credited to the School Fund of the State.

SEC. 5. This Act shall take effect immediately.

CHAPTER XXV.

[Approved March 30, 1874. Stats. of Cal. 1873–4, p. 902.]

ARTICLE 89.

Act appropriating eighty-four thousand dollars to the University.

CHAPTER XXVI.

An Act to regulate contracts on behalf of the State, in relation to erections and buildings.

[Approved March 23, 1876. Stats. of Cal. 1875–6, p. 427.]

ARTICLE 90.

SECTION 1. That in all cases where the Commissioners, Directors, Trustees, or other officer or officers, to whom is confided by law the duty of devising and superintending the erection, alteration, addition to, or improvement of any State institution, asylum, or other improvement, erected, or now being erected, or to be erected, by the State, such Commissioners, Directors, Trustees, or other officer or officers, before entering into any contract for the erection, alteration, addition to, or improvement of such institution, asylum, or other improvement, or for the supply of materials therefor, the aggregate cost of which erection, alteration, addition, or improvement, and materials therefor, exceed the sum of three thousand dollars, shall make, or procure to be made, a full, complete, and accurate plan or plans of such institution, asylum, or other improvement, or of any addition to, or alteration, or improvement thereof, in all its parts, showing all the necessary details of the work, together with working plans suitable for the use of the mechanics or other builders during the construction thereof, so drawn and represented as to be plain and easily understood; and, also, accurate bills, showing the exact amount of all the different kinds of materials necessary in the erection thereof, addition thereto, or in the alteration or improvement thereof, to accompany said plan or plans; and, also, full and complete specifications of the work to be done, showing the manner and style in which the same will be required to be done, giving such directions for the same as will enable any competent mechanic or other builder to carry them out, and afford the builders all needful information to enable them to understand what will be required in the erection, addition to, alteration, or improvement of such institution, asylum, or other improvement; and to make, or cause to be made, a full, accurate, and complete estimate of each item of expense, and the entire aggregate cost of such institution, asylum, or other improvement, or of any addition to, alteration, or improvement thereof, when completed.

ARTICLE 91.

SEC. 2. That such plans, drawings, representations, bills of materials, and specifications of work, and the estimates of the cost thereof, in detail and in the aggregate, as are required in the first section of this Act to be made, shall be, when made, submitted to the Governor, State Treasurer, and Secretary of State, for their approval, and if approved by them, a copy thereof shall be deposited and safely kept in the office of Controller of State.

ARTICLE 92.

SEC. 3. That after such plans, descriptions, bills of materials, and specifications and estimates, as are in this Act required, are made and approved, in accordance with the requirements of this Act, it shall be and is hereby made the duty of such Commissioners, Directors, Trustees, or other officer or officers to whom the duty of devising and superintending the erection, addition to, alteration, or improvement of such institution, asylum, or other improvement, as in this Act provided, to give or cause to be given public notice of the time and place when and where sealed proposals will be received for performing the labor and furnishing the materials necessary to the erection of such institution, asylum, or other improvement, or for the adding to, altering, or improvement thereof, and a contract or contracts, based on such sealed proposals, will be made; which notice shall be published weekly for four consecutive weeks next preceding the day named for the making of such contract or contracts, in the paper having the largest circulation in the county where the work is to be let, and in two daily papers having the largest circulation and published each in the Cities of San Francisco and Sacramento, and shall state when and where such plan or plans, descriptions, bills, and specifications can be seen, and which shall be open to public inspection at all business hours between the date of such notice and the making of such contract or contracts.

ARTICLE 93.

SEC. 4. That, on the day named in said public notice, said Commissioners, Directors, Trustees, or officer or officers, as aforesaid, shall proceed to publicly open said sealed proposals, and shall award such contract or contracts for doing the work and for furnishing materials for the same, to the lowest bidder, giving responsible bonds; *provided, always*, that no proposals shall be considered unless accompanied with a bond of said proposer, equal to ten per cent of his proposal, with sufficient **sureties**, conditioned that if said proposal shall be **accepted, the party proposing** will duly enter into a proper **contract, and faithfully** perform his or their contract or contracts, in accordance with said proposal, and the plan or plans, specifications, and descriptions, which shall be and are hereby made a part of such contract or contracts; *and provided further*, that such contract or contracts shall not be binding on the State until they are submitted to the Attorney-General, and by him found to be in accordance with the provisions of this Act, and his certificate thereon to that effect made; *and provided further*, that if in the opinion of such Commissioners, Trustees, Directors, or other officer or officers, the acceptance of the lowest bid or bids shall not be for the best interests of the State, it may be lawful for them, with the written advice and consent of the Governor, State Treasurer, and Secretary of State, to accept such proposal or proposals opened, as in their opinion may be better for the interests of the State, or reject all proposals and advertise for others in the manner aforesaid. All contracts shall provide that such Commissioners, Directors, Trustees, or other officer or officers, may, as hereinafter provided, and on the conditions stated, make any change in the work or materials.

ARTICLE 94.

SEC. 5. That no change of the plan or plans, descriptions, bills of materials, or specifications, which shall either increase or decrease the cost of said institution, asylum, building, or improvement, exceeding the sum of one thousand dollars, shall be made or allowed, after they are once approved and filed with the Controller of State, as herein required, until such proposed change shall have received the approval of the Governor, State Treasurer, and Secretary of State; and when so approved, the plan or plans of such change, with the description thereof, and the specifications of the work, and bills of material, shall be filed with the Controller of State, in the same manner as required before such change was made; and no allowance whatever shall be made for work performed or materials furnished under such change of plan or plans, or descriptions or specifications, or bills of materials, unless, before such labor is performed and materials furnished, a contract or contracts therefor is made in writing, which contract or contracts shall show distinctly the nature of such change, and shall be subject to all the conditions and provisions herein imposed upon the original contracts, and be subject also to the approval of the Attorney-General, as hereinbefore provided; *provided*, that all changes in the contract exceeding five hundred dollars shall be by contracts in writing, with full specifications and estimates, and shall become a part of the original contract, and shall be filed with the Controller of State, with the original contract; *and provided further*, that the amount of such change in the contract, plans, descriptions, bills of materials, or specifications, shall not, in the aggregate, increase the cost of construction of said institution, asylum, building, or improvement, more than three per centum of the original contract price or cost.

ARTICLE 95.

SEC. 6. That no contract or contracts shall be made for the labor or material herein provided for at a price in excess of the entire estimate thereof, in this Act required to be made, and the entire contract or contracts shall not, including estimates of expenses for architects and otherwise, exceed in the aggregate the amount authorized by law for such institution, asylum, building, or other improvement, or such addition to, or alteration, or improvement thereof, under the penalties of section ten of this Act hereinafter provided.

ARTICLE 96.

SEC. 7. At the time or times named in the contract or contracts made and filed with the Controller of State, or which has been previously made and filed with him, in accordance with the provisions of this Act, for payment to the person or persons with whom such contract or contracts had been made, it shall be and is hereby made the duty of the Commissioners, Directors, Trustees, or other officer or officers, to whom is confided the duty of superintending the erection of such institution, asylum, building, or improvement, or adding to, altering, or improving the same, to make or cause to be made a full, accurate, and detailed estimate of the various kinds of labor performed and materials furnished under such contract or contracts, with the amount due for each kind of labor and materials and the amount due in the aggregate, which estimate shall be based upon an actual measurement of the labor so performed and materials so furnished, which estimate shall, in all cases, give the amounts of the preceding estimate or estimates, and the amount of labor performed and materials furnished since the last estimate, which estimate or estimates so made, as in this Act required, shall be recorded in a book for that purpose to be provided and kept, or caused to be kept by the said Commissioners, Directors, Trustees, or other officer or officers, and a certified copy thereof, addressed to the Controller of State by the said Commissioners, Directors, Trustees, or other officer or officers, or by such person as they may designate for that purpose, be delivered to the contractor or contractors entitled thereto; *provided*, that upon all estimates of materials furnished and delivered, and not actually having entered into and become a part of said institution, building, or other improvement, there shall not be paid, until the same shall be incorporated into and become a part of said institution, building, or other improvement, exceeding fifty per centum of such estimated value.

ARTICLE 97.

SEC. 8. It shall be the duty of the Controller of State, on the receipt of such estimate, so certified and approved, to compare carefully the same with the contract or contracts under which labor was done or materials furnished, and if there had been any previous estimates, then with such estimates; and if, upon such comparison, he shall find such last named estimate in all respects correct, he shall number the same, place it on file, and have a record thereof made, and give to the person or persons entitled thereto, taking his or their receipt therefor, a warrant on the Treasurer of State for the amount shown ·by such estimate or estimates to be due, less the amount of ten per centum thereon, which shall be retained as an additional security for the faithful performance of his or their contract or contracts, and shall be forfeited to the State in the event of a failure of such contractor or contractors to conform in good faith to the terms and conditions of such contract or contracts; but when the labor to be performed and materials furnished under such contract or contracts, is performed and furnished, and a final estimate thereof made, the Controller of State shall include in the warrant or warrants for the amount of such last estimate the percentage retained on former estimates.

ARTICLE 98.

SEC. 9. The Treasurer of State shall pay the warrants issued by the Controller of State, under and by virtue of the provisions of this Act, placing the same on file, and keeping a register of the names of the person or persons to whom such warrants are paid.

ARTICLE 99.

SEC. 10. Any Commissioner, Director, Trustee, or other officer or person otherwise appointed, whose duty it is to superintend, in whole or in part, the erection of such institution, asylum, building, or improvement, or of adding to, altering, or the improvement thereof, or the making of the plans, descriptions, and specifications of the labor to be performed and materials to be furnished, as provided in this Act, and the estimates of the cost thereof, or the estimates of the amount of labor done and materials furnished from time to time, under and in accordance with the terms and conditions of the contracts in this Act authorized to be made, and the provisions of this Act, who shall, in the performance of the duty herein imposed upon him or upon them, knowingly make incomplete or fraudulent plans, drawings, bills of materials, specifications of work, or estimates of the cost thereof, or permit the work in any other manner than is prescribed in such plans, descriptions, and specifications, or with materials inferior to that required by such bills of materials, to the injury of the State; or shall knowingly make false estimates of the labor done or materials furnished, either in the quantity or the price thereof, to the injury of the State, or any contractor, or any agent of any contractor or contractors, who shall knowingly permit materials to be used or work to be done inferior to or in violation of the contract of such contractor or contractors, to the injury of the State, shall be deemed and held guilty of a felony, and, upon conviction thereof, thall be confined in the State Prison for not less than one year nor more than five years, and be liable to the State for double the amount the State may have lost, or be liable to lose, by reason thereof. ·

Article 100.

Sec. 11. It shall be the duty of the Attorney-General to have charge of and direct all the proceedings necessary to enforce the contracts authorized by this Act, and the provisions of this Act, against such person or persons as become liable to the penalties herein prescribed.

Article 101.

Sec. 12. Whenever, in the opinion of the Commissioners, Directors, Trustees, or other officers charged with the duty of devising and superintending the erection, alteration, addition to, or improvement of any State institution, asylum, building, or other improvement under this Act, or any law of this State, the work under any contract made in pursuance of this Act, or any such law, is neglected by the contractor or contractors, or that the same is not prosecuted with the diligence and force specified, meant, or intended in and by the terms of the contract, it shall be lawful for such Commissioners, Trustees, Directors, or other officers to make a requisition upon such contractor or contractors for such additional specific force, or for such additional specific materials, to be brought into the work under such contract, or to remove improper materials from the grounds, as in the judgment of such Commissioners, Directors, Trustees, or other officers said contract and its due and faithful fulfillment require; of which action of said Board or other officers due notice in writing, of not less than five days, shall be served upon such con-

tractor, or his or their agent having charge of the work.
And if such contractor or contractors fail to comply with
such requisition within fifteen days, it shall be lawful for
said Commissioners, Directors, Trustees, or other officers, with
the consent, in writing, of the Governor, Treasurer of State,
and Secretary of State, to employ upon such work the additional force, or supply the materials so specifically required
as aforesaid, or such part of either, as they may deem proper,
and to remove improper materials from the grounds; and it
shall be the duty of such Commissioners, Directors, Trustees,
or other officers, to make separate estimates of all such additional force or materials so employed or supplied as aforesaid, and which, being certified to by said Commissioners,
Directors, Trustees, or other officers, shall be paid by the
Controller of State the same as if made out agreeably to section seven of this Act, and the amount so paid shall be charged
against said contractor or contractors, and deducted from his
or their next, or any subsequent estimate; or the same, or
any part thereof, not paid as aforesaid, may be recovered by
action from such contractor or contractors, and their sureties.

ARTICLE 102.

SEC. 13. In all contracts made under the provisions of
this Act, there shall be a provision in regard to the time
when the whole, or any specified portion, of the work contemplated in said contract shall be completed, and also
providing that for each and every day the same shall be
delayed beyond such time or times, so named, the said contractor or contractors shall forfeit and pay to the State a sum
of money, to be fixed and determined in said contract, to be
deducted from any payment or payments due, or to become
due, to said contractor or contractors.

ARTICLE 103.

SEC. 14. All contracts now made, and not performed,
for the erection, alteration, addition to, or improvement of,
any State institution, asylum, building, or other improvement, shall, as far as practicable, be performed, completed,
and enforced and settled for under this Act, or may, by the
consent of the contracting parties, be made to conform to,
and proceed under, the provisions of this Act.

SEC. 15. All Acts and parts of Acts in conflict with the
provisions of this Act are hereby repealed.

SEC. 16. This Act shall take effect from and after its
passage.

CHAPTER XXVII.

An Act to provide a supply of water for the University, and for the Asylum for the Deaf, Dumb, and Blind.

[Approved April 1, 1876.   Stats. of Cal. 1875–6, p. 816.]

ARTICLE 104.

SECTION 1. Any of the springs and natural sources of water supply which are within a distance of one mile and a half from the extreme limits of the University grounds, together with so much of the lands on which the same are located as are necessary for the protection of said springs and sources of supply, and the right of way for a pipe or aqueduct over intervening lands to reach the same, may be condemned, in the manner hereinafter provided, for the use of the University and Deaf, Dumb, and Blind Asylum; and shall not be taken up or appropriated by any private corporation. Said springs and sources of water supply, and said lands, are hereby declared to be necessary for the use of the institutions above named, and such use is declared to be a public use.

ARTICLE 105.

SEC. 2. In order to effect such condemnation, a complaint shall be filed by the Attorney-General, in the name of the people of the State of California, against all owners or claimants of such springs, and of the lands on which the same are situated, and of the lands over which a right of way is sought, where the names are known, or can be conveniently ascertained, and against all unknown owners and claimants, designating them as "unknown owners" in said complaint. All the proceedings thereafter shall be had and taken under and in accordance with the provisions of title seven, part third, of the Code of Civil Procedure, except that it shall not be necessary, upon the trial, to show that said springs are necessary to the institutions aforesaid.

ARTICLE 106.

SEC. 3. Instead of a trial by jury, the District Court may, in its discretion, appoint three Commissioners or Referees, to appraise the value of said springs and lands, and the right of way to reach the same from the University grounds, over the lands between said springs and the grounds of the University

ARTICLE 107.

SEC. 4. Upon a judgment being rendered for the condemnation of said springs and lands, and right of way, and appraising the value thereof, and upon filing in said proceeding a written certificate by the Governor approving such valuation, the Controller shall draw his warrant upon the State Treasurer, in favor of the Treasurer of the Board of Regents, for the amount of such valuation, payable out of any moneys in the General Fund, and said Treasurer of the Board of Regents shall pay the amount forthwith into the Court in which such judgment is rendered, to be paid out, under the order of said Court, to the parties entitled thereto. When said amount is paid into Court, the title to said springs and land, and right of way, shall vest in the State for the use and benefit of the public institutions hereinbefore referred to.

SEC. 5. This Act shall take effect and be in force from and after its passage.

CHAPTER XXVIII.

[Approved April 3, 1876.　Stats. of Cal. 1875-6, p. 751.]

ARTICLE 108.

Appropriation of forty thousand dollars for construction of Mechanical Arts College.

CHAPTER XXIX.

An Act to consolidate certain funds, and to create therefrom a permanent endowment for the University of California, of which the interest only shall be used by the Board of Regents to meet current expenses.

[Approved March 19, 1878.　Stats. of Cal. 1877-8, p. 337.]

ARTICLE 109.

SECTION 1. That the entire principal sums which have been or may be hereafter realized from the several sources of income and endowment funds of the University of California, to wit, the principal sum derived from the sale of lands granted to the State of California by Act of Congress, approved July second, eighteen hundred and sixty-two, and amendments thereto, and the principal sum derived from the sale of the seventy-two (72) sections of land granted to the State of California for the use of a seminary of learning, by Act of Congress, approved March third, eighteen hundred and fifty-three, and the principal sum derived from the sale of the ten (10) sections of land granted to the State of California for public buildings, by said Act of Congress, approved March third, eighteen hundred and fifty-three, and the principal sum which the Treasurer of the State of California was directed, by Act of the Legislature, approved April second, eighteen hundred and seventy, to place to the credit of the University Fund, and which, being invested in the bonds of the State or of the United States, should yield an annual income of fifty thousand dollars, and the principal sum now remaining on hand derived from the sale of the real estate in Oakland, Alameda County, and State of California, known as the "Brayton property," shall be from time to time, as the same is realized, invested in stocks of the United States or of the State, or other safe stocks or bonds, yielding not less than five (5) per centum upon the par value of said stocks or bonds, and the money so invested shall constitute a perpetual fund, to be known and designated as the "Consolidated Perpetual Endowment Fund of the University of California," the capital of which shall remain forever undiminished; *provided*, that any moneys realized from said sources of income or endowment funds, or either of them, which have been heretofore invested according to law, may remain so invested; *and it is further provided*, that all such stocks and bonds as aforesaid shall be deposited in the State Treasury to the credit of said fund, and shall be kept separate and apart from all other funds by the State Treasurer, who shall pay over, from time to time, all interest, profits, income, or revenue, arising from such stocks or bonds, to the Treasurer of said University, upon the demand or order of the Regents of the University.

ARTICLE 110.

SEC. 2. That all interest, profits, or revenue, arising from or growing out of the said "Consolidated Permanent Endowment Fund of the University of California," shall be placed in the general fund of the University, and subject to disbursement to meet the current annual expenses of the University of California.

SEC. 3. That all Acts or parts of Acts in conflict herewith are hereby repealed.

CHAPTER XXX.

An Act to create Hastings College of the Law in the University.

[Approved March 26, 1878.   Stats. of Cal. 1877–8, p. 533.]

ARTICLE 111.

SECTION 1. That S. C. Hastings be authorized to found and establish a Law College, to be forever known and designated as " Hastings College of the Law." That the officers of said College shall be a Dean, Registrar, and eight Directors. That the Directors shall be Joseph P. Hoge, W W. Cope, Delos Lake, Samuel M. Wilson, O. P Evans, Thomas B. Bishop, John R. Sharpstein, and Thomas I. Bergin, of the Bar Association of the City of San Francisco, who shall, when vacancies occur, fill the same from members of said association or otherwise, and shall always provide for filling a vacancy with some heir or some representative of the said S. C. Hastings. That the Dean and Registrar shall be appointed by the Directors.

ARTICLE 112.

SEC. 2. Said College shall affiliate with the University of the State upon such terms as shall be for the welfare of the College and University, and shall be the Law Department of the University.

ARTICLE 113.

SEC. 3. The Faculty of the University shall grant diplomas to the students of the College, and the President shall sign and issue the diplomas.

ARTICLE 114.

SEC. 4. There shall be set apart for the use of the students of the College, some room or suitable hall at the University; and the Board of Supervisors of the City of San Francisco is authorized to supply a suitable hall in the City of San Francisco for the students and Directors.

ARTICLE 115.

SEC. 5. The Dean of said College shall be ex officio of the Faculty of the University, to be designated as such by the Directors of the College.

ARTICLE 116.

SEC. 6. The diploma of the students shall entitle the student to whom it is issued to a license to practice in all the Courts of this State, subject to right of the Chief Justice of the State to order an examination, as in ordinary cases of applicants without such diploma.

ARTICLE 117.

SEC. 7. This Act is passed upon the condition that S. C. Hastings shall pay into the State Treasury the sum of one hundred thousand dollars, and is never to be refunded, except as hereinafter provided.

Article 118.

Sec. 8. The sum of seven per cent per annum upon one hundred thousand dollars is to be appropriated by the State and paid in two semi-annual payments to the Directors of the College.

Article 119.

Sec. 9. The business of the College shall be to afford facilities for the acquisition of legal learning in all branches of the law; and to this end shall establish a curriculum of studies, and shall matriculate students who may reside at the University of the State, as well as students residing in other parts of the State.

Article 120.

Sec. 10. Professorships may be established in the name of any founder of such Professorships who shall pay to the Directors the sum of thirty thousand dollars.

Article 121.

Sec. 11. All the business of the College shall be managed by the Directors without compensation. And all officers acting, including the Dean and Registrar, shall be appointed by the Directors and removed by them.

Article 122.

Sec. 12. The Law Library Association of the City of San Francisco shall grant to the students the use of their library upon such terms and conditions as they may agree with the Directors of the College.

Article 123.

Sec. 13. The object of this Act being to grant a perpetual annuity for the support and maintenance of said College, should the State or any government which shall succeed it fail to pay to the Directors of said College the sum of seven per cent per annum, as above stipulated, or should the College cease to exist, then the State or its successor shall pay to the said S. C. Hastings, his heirs or legal representatives, the sum of one hundred thousand dollars, and all unexpended accumulated interest; *provided,* that such failure be not caused by mistake or accident, or omission of the Legislature to make the appropriation at any one session.

ARTICLE 124.

SEC. 14. That the Chief Justice of the Supreme Court of the State (or if there be no such other officer of the State or government) shall be the President of the Board of Directors, five of whom shall be a quorum to transact all business.

CHAPTER XXXI.

[Approved March 30, 1878. Stats. of Cal. 1877-8, p. 834.]

ARTICLE 125.

Act authorizing Regents to waive certain stipulations in contract for building Mechanic Arts College.

CHAPTER XXXII.

[Approved April 1, 1878. Stats. of Cal. 1877-8, p. 930.]

ARTICLE 126.

Act appropriating twenty-five thousand dollars, to be used conjointly with a like amount donated by H. D. Bacon, for construction of Library and Art Gallery.

CHAPTER XXXIII.

[Approved April 1, 1878. Stats. of Cal. 1877-8, p. 1008.]

ARTICLE 127.

Act appropriating ten thousand dollars to University Mechanic Arts College, and ten thousand dollars to University Agricultural College.

CHAPTER XXXIV.

An Act for the promotion of the viticultural interests of the State.

[Approved April 15, 1880. Stats. of Cal. 1880, p. 53.]

ARTICLE 128.

SECTION 8. And for the further promotion of viticultural interests, it shall be the duty of the Board of Regents of the

University of California to provide for special instruction to be given by the Agricultural Department of the University in the arts and sciences pertaining to viticulture, the theory and practice of fermentation, distillation, and rectification, and the management of cellars, to be illustrated by practical experiments with appropriate apparatus; also, to direct the Professor of Agriculture, or his assistant, to make personal examinations and reports upon the different sections of the State adapted to viticulture; to examine and report upon the woods of the State procurable for cooperage, and the best methods of treating the same; and to make analysis of soils, wines, brandies, and grapes, at the proper request of citizens of the State; also, to prepare a comprehensive analysis of the various wines and spirits produced from grapes, showing their alcoholic strength and other properties, and especially any deleterious adulterations that may be discovered. The Regents shall also cause to be prepared, printed, and distributed to the public, quarterly reports of the professor in charge of this work relating to experiments undertaken, scientific discoveries, the progress and treatment of the phylloxera and other diseases of the vine, and such other useful information as may be given for the better instruction of viticulturists.

ARTICLE 129.

SEC. 9. The Board of Regents of the University shall be authorized to receive and accept donations of lands suitable for experimental vineyards and stations, and shall submit in their next annual report an economical plan for conducting such vineyards, and for the propagation and distribution of specimens of all known and valuable varieties of grapevines.

ARTICLE 130.

SEC. 10. There is hereby appropriated for the purposes mentioned in this Act the sum of seven thousand dollars, to be apportioned as follows: For the necessary and contingent expenses of the Board of State Viticultural Commissioners, four thousand dollars, and for the University of California, three thousand dollars; and the State Controller shall draw his warrants upon the State Treasurer in favor of the Treasurers of the said Board of State Viticultural Commissioners and of the University of California for the amounts of four thousand and three thousand dollars respectively, as hereby appropriated, upon proper demand being made for the same; *provided*, that the said Board of State Viticultural Commissioners shall, in the month of December, submit to the Governor annual statements, duly verified by the oaths of the President and Treasurer, and attested by the Secretary of said Board, showing in detail the manner in which moneys received from the State have been expended, and also the amount remaining unexpended, together with an estimate of expenses for the ensuing year, beginning on the first day of July next thereafter.

CHAPTER XXXV.

[Approved April 9, 1880.   Stats. of Cal. 1880, p. 36.]

ARTICLE 131.

An Act amending Act of March thirteenth, eighteen hundred and seventy-four (See Chapter XXIV), concerning selection and sale of lands.

NOTE.—By this Act "Superior Court" is substituted for "District Court."

CHAPTER XXXVI.

[Approved April 9, 1880.   Stats. of Cal. 1880, p. 27.]

ARTICLE 132.

An Act to encourage the planting of jute.

CHAPTER XXXVII.

An Act concerning the Medical Department of the University of California.

[Approved March 3, 1881, p. 24.]

ARTICLE 133.

SECTION 1.   The Medical Department of the University of California shall hereafter be known and designated as the "Toland Medical Department of the University of California," and all degrees, diplomas, scholarships, and records of said department shall be made out, and all proceedings in connection therewith, shall be conducted in and by such name and designation.

SEC. 2.   This Act shall take effect from and after its passage.

CHAPTER XXXVIII.

An Act to appropriate money to reimburse the University of California for moneys heretofore appropriated to the Endowment Fund thereof, which moneys have by mistake been withheld therefrom and appropriated to other State purposes.

[Approved March 4, 1881. Stats. of Cal. 1881, p. 50.]

ARTICLE 134.

SECTION 1. The sum of forty-seven hundred and eighty five dollars is hereby annually appropriated to the University of the State of California, out of any moneys in the State Treasury not otherwise appropriated.

ARTICLE 135.

SEC. 2. This appropriation shall continue, and the said sum shall be annually paid to said University until the State elects to and does return to the Endowment Fund of said University the sum of seventy-nine thousand seven hundred and fifty dollars, heretofore appropriated, but by mistake withheld therefrom and used for other State purposes.

SEC. 3. This Act shall be in force from and after its passage.

CHAPTER XXXIX.

[Approved May 12, 1881. Stats. of Cal. 1881, p. 115.]

ARTICLE 136.

An Act making the following appropriations: Furnishing Bacon Art, and Library building, $10,000; for Mechanical and Mining Art College, $8,000; for Agricultural Department, $10,000.

CHAPTER XL.

An Act to amend an Act entitled an Act to create Hastings College of the Law, in the University of the State of California, approved March 26, 1878.

[Approved March 3, 1883.   Stats. of Cal. 1883, p. 26.]

ARTICLE 137.

The Act entitled an Act to create Hastings College of the Law, in the University of the State of California, is hereby amended so as to read as follows:

SECTION 1.   That S. C. Hastings be authorized to found and establish a law college, to be forever known and designated as "Hastings College of the Law." That the officers of said College shall be a Dean and Registrar. The Regents of the University shall have the same control of the College as they possess over the academic department of the University of California, except as hereinafter provided.

ARTICLE 138.

SEC. 2.   The Board of Regents, on recommendation of the Dean and Faculty of the College, shall grant diplomas to the students of the College, and the President shall sign and issue the diplomas.

ARTICLE 139.

SEC. 3.   There shall be set apart for the use of the students of the College some room or suitable hall in the buildings of the University at Berkeley, and the Board of Supervisors of the City of San Francisco shall supply a suitable hall in the City of San Francisco for the use of the College.

ARTICLE 140.   •

SEC. 4.   The Dean of said College shall be ex officio of the Faculty of the University, and entitled to attend meetings of the Board of Regents at all times when he shall have business of the College to lay before them, and to be heard on all questions affecting the College.

ARTICLE 141.

SEC. 5.   The business of the College shall be to afford facilities for the acquisition of legal learning in all branches of the law, and to this end it shall establish a curriculum of studies, and shall matriculate students who may reside at the University of the State, as well as students residing in other parts

of the State; *provided,* there shall always be in said College
a course of lectures upon the duties of municipal officers in
the City and County of San Francisco.

ARTICLE 142.

SEC. 6. Professorships may be established in the name of
any founder of such professorships who shall pay to the
Regents of the University the sum of thirty thousand
($30,000) dollars. The son of the founder, Robert P. Hast-
ings, shall be Dean of the College during his lifetime, and
after his death or resignation the Dean shall be elected by
the members of the highest appellate Court of the State of
California, which said Court shall appoint one of the male
heirs of the founder, if deemed capable and competent.
The Registrar, after the death or resignation of the present
incumbent, shall be elected by the Board of Regents.

ARTICLE 143.

SEC. 7. The object of this Act being to grant a perpetual
annuity for the support and maintenance of said College,
should the State or any government which shall succeed it
fail to pay to the Regents of the University the sum of seven
per cent per annum, as above stipulated, or should the College cease to exist, then the State or its successor shall pay to
the said S. C. Hastings, his heirs, or legal representatives, the
said sum of one hundred thousand ($100,000) dollars, and all
unexpended accumulated interest; *provided,* that such failure
be not caused by mistake, or accident, or omission of the
Legislature to make the appropriation at any one session.

ARTICLE 144.

SEC. 8. No part of the annuity herein provided for shall
be expended by the Regents of the University for any other
purpose than instruction; *provided, however,* that an amount.
not to exceed six hundred dollars per annum, may be used
from such annuity to pay for the services of the Registrar.

ARTICLE 145.

SEC. 9. The Dean, Acting Professors, Lecturers, Readers,
and other instructors, shall constitute the Faculty and Exam-
ining Board of the College.

SEC. 10. This Act shall take effect and be in force from
and after sixty days after its passage.

CHAPTER XLI.

An Act to provide for the better control and management of the several funds of the University of California, and for the investment and security of the same.

[Approved March 7, 1883.   Stats. of Cal. 1883, p. 54.]

ARTICLE 146.

SECTION 1.   The Regents of the University of California shall have the exclusive control and management of all the funds, endowments, and donations of the University of California, and are charged with the duty and responsibility of investing and reinvesting the same; *provided*, that said Regents shall deposit in the State Treasury for safe keeping such funds and securities as are now by law required to be there deposited.

ARTICLE 147.

SEC. 2.   The Treasurer of the State of California is hereby required to receive and safely keep all funds and securities deposited as herein provided in the State Treasury by the Regents of the University of California, subject at all times to the control and management of said Regents; and the State Treasurer shall deliver any or all of said securities and funds so deposited in the State Treasury to the Treasurer of the Regents of the University of California, upon presentation to him of a resolution of the said Regents indorsed by the Governor of the State demanding the same or any portion thereof.

ARTICLE 148.

SEC. 3.   The Regents of the University of California are authorized and empowered to invest and reinvest any or all the funds of the University of California in such manner and upon such security as they may deem best for the interest of the University of California; *provided*, that they shall in good faith respect all the conditions and limitations of such endowments and donations as have been made under conditions or limitations.

SEC. 4.   All Acts or parts of Acts in conflict herewith are hereby repealed.

SEC. 5.   This Act shall take effect from and after its passage.

CHAPTER XLII.

*An **Act** authorizing and empowering the Regents of the University of California to convey certain lands.*

[Approved March 9, 1883. Stats. of Cal. 1883, p. 62.]

ARTICLE 149.

SECTION 1. The Regents of the University of California are hereby authorized and empowered to reconvey to Henry D. Cogswell, of the City and County of San Francisco, all that certain lot, piece, or parcel of land heretofore conveyed to said Regents of the University of California in trust by said Henry D. Cogswell on the nineteenth day of May, eighteen hundred and seventy-nine, which said property is situate, lying, and being in the City and County of San Francisco, State of California, and more particularly described as follows, to wit: Commencing at a point on the easterly line of Front Street, distant sixty (60) feet northerly from the northeast corner of the intersection of Front and Jackson Streets; thence northerly along the said easterly line of Front Street sixty (60) feet to Clark Street; thence at right angles easterly and along the southerly line of Clark Street eighty-five (85) feet to and including the brick wall, and the land on which stands the wall, which now constitutes the rear or easterly wall of the building erected on the premises hereby conveyed; thence at right angles southerly and parallel with Front Street sixty (60) feet; thence at right angles westerly and parallel with Jackson Street eighty-five (85) feet to the easterly line of Front Street and point of commencement.

SEC. 2. This Act shall take effect immediately.

CHAPTER XLIII.

[Approved March 9, 1883. Stats. of Cal. 1883, pp. 72-80.]

ARTICLE 150.

Appropriating as follows: $10,000 for the Mechanical College; $8,000 for the Mining Art College; $15,000 for continuing the special investigations and operations of Agricultural Department; $5,500 for Physical Laboratory, to be expended under the direction of the Professor of Physics; $5,000 for Department of Engineering; $2,000 for continuing and completing the work of the Department of Viticulture; $1,800 for continuing the work of the Agricultural Laboratory;

$2,500 for furnishing the Bacon Library Building; $4,785 to reimburse the University.

CHAPTER XLIV.

[Approved March 9, 1883.   Stats. of Cal. 1883, p. 80.]

ARTICLE 151.

An Act making an appropriation of $11,000 for the purpose of protecting and improving the buildings and grounds of the University of California.

CHAPTER XLV.

An Act to authorize the Governor of the State of California to reconvey to the United States a part of the lands heretofore granted the State of California by Act of Congress of July second, eighteen hundred and sixty-two, and listed to the State of California, under the agricultural college grant of one hundred and fifty thousand acres.

[Approved March 13, 1883.   Stats. of Cal. 1883, p. 287.]

ARTICLE 152.

WHEREAS, Under and by virtue of an Act donating public lands to the several States and Territories of the United States for the benefit of agriculture and the mechanic arts, approved July second, eighteen hundred and sixty-two, and amendments thereto, the Regents of the University of California, acting under and in conformity with an Act of the Legislature of the State of California entitled "An Act to create and organize the University of California," approved March twenty-third, eighteen hundred and sixty-eight, did select as a part of said grant, certain lands which were duly listed to the State by the United States—and it now appearing that it is to the interest of the University of California to secure the cancellation of said selections, it is therefore necessary to reconvey to the United States said lands, and thereby secure the right to select other lands instead thereof.   Therefore

The People of the State of California, represented in Senate and Assembly, do enact as follows:

SECTION 1. The Regents of the University of California are authorized and required to report to the Governor of the

State of California a description of such of the lands granted to the State of California by authority of the Act of Congress of July second, eighteen hundred and sixty-two, and amendments thereto, and listed to the State of California, that should be reconveyed to the United States.

ARTICLE 153.

SEC. 2. Whenever the report provided for in the first section of this Act shall have been received by the Governor, he may and is authorized in the name and by the authority of the people of the State of California to grant and reconvey to the United States such lands as may be embraced and described in said report.

SEC. 3. This Act shall take effect and be in force from and after its passage.

CHAPTER XLVI.

Provisions of the Political Code of California.

[Adopted March 12, 1872; to go into effect January 1, 1873.]

ARTICLE 154.

SEC. 332. All officers, Boards of officers, Commissioners, Trustees, Regents, and Directors required by law to make reports to the Governor or Legislature, except the Controller of State, must send such reports to the Governor before the first day of October in the year eighteen hundred and eighty, and in every second year thereafter.

ARTICLE 155.

SEC. 333. The Superintendent of State Printing must print such reports before the last Monday in November next after the receipt thereof.

ARTICLE 156.

SEC. 334. There must be printed:
Of the report of the Regents of the University, twelve hundred copies.

ARTICLE 157.

SEC. 335. The reports printed must be delivered by the Superintendent of State Printing as follows:
To the Regents of the University, three hundred copies of their report.

ARTICLE 158.

SEC. 343. The number and designation of the civil executive officers are as follows: * * * twenty-two Regents of the University of California, * * *.

ARTICLE 159.

SEC. 353. The Governor, Lieutenant-Governor, Speaker of the Assembly, Superintendent of Public Instruction, President of the State Board of Agriculture, and President of the Mechanics' Institute of San Francisco, are ex officio Regents of the University of California. The appointment and terms of office of the other Regents are provided for in Chapter I, Title III, of Part III, of this Code.

ARTICLE 160.

SEC. 380. In addition to those prescribed by the Constitution, the Governor has the power and must perform the duties prescribed in this and following sections * * *. He may require any officer or Board to make special reports to him, upon demand in writing, * * *. He may issue arms and accouterments for the use of colleges, * * *.

ARTICLE 161.

SEC. 550. The geological and other specimens collected by the State Geological Survey, must, excepting such as may be required by the State Geologist to aid in the preparation of his report, be delivered over to the Regents of the State University, to be by them deposited in the cabinet of the same as the property of the University.

ARTICLE 162.

SEC. 996. An office becomes vacant on the happening of either of the following events before the expiration of the term:

1. The death of the incumbent;
2. His insanity, found upon a Commission of Lunacy issued to determine the fact;
3. His resignation;
4. His removal from office;
5. His ceasing to be an inhabitant of the State, or if the office be local, of the district, county, city, or township for which he was chosen or appointed, or within which the duties of his office are required to be discharged;
6. His absence from the State without permission of the Legislature beyond the period allowed by law;
7. His ceasing to discharge the duties of his office for the

period of three consecutive months, except when prevented
by sickness or when absent from the State by permission of
the Legislature;

8. His conviction of a felony, or of any offense involving
a violation of his official duties;

9. His refusal or neglect to file his official oath or bond
within the time prescribed;

10. The decision of a competent tribunal declaring void
his election or appointment.

ARTICLE 163.

SEC. 1385. The University of California (located in Alameda County) has for its object general instruction and
education in all the departments of science, literature, art,
industrial and professional pursuits, and special instruction
for the professions of agriculture, the mechanic arts, mining,
military science, civil engineering, law, medicine, and commerce.

ARTICLE 164.

SEC. 1386. There must be maintained in the University :

1. A College of Letters ;

2. A College or Colleges of Science, including Agriculture,
Mechanics, Mining, Engineering, Chemistry, and such other
specialties as the Board of Regents may determine ;

3. Colleges of Medicine and Law ;

4. Such other Colleges as the Board of Regents may establish.

ARTICLE 165.

SEC. 1387. The College of Letters must embrace a liberal
course of instruction in language, literature, and philosophy.

ARTICLE 166.

SEC. 1388. Each full course of instruction consists of its
appropriate studies and courses, to be determined by the
Board of Regents.

ARTICLE 167.

SEC. 1289. The President of the University is the executive head of the institution in all its departments, except as
herein otherwise provided.

ARTICLE 168.

SEC. 1390. He must, subject to the Board of Regents, give
general direction to the practical affairs of the several colleges, and in the recess of the Board of Regents may remove
any employé or subordinate officer not a member of any

Faculty, and supply for the time being any vacancies thus created; and until the Regents otherwise direct, he is charged with the duties of one of the professorships.

ARTICLE 169.

SEC. 1391. The immediate government of the several colleges is intrusted to their respective Faculties, each of which must have its own organization, regulate its own affairs, and may recommend the course of study and the text-books to be used.

ARTICLE 170.

SEC. 1392. Any resident of California, of the age of fourteen years or upwards, of approved moral character, may enter himself in the University as a student at large, and receive tuition in any branches of instruction at the time when the same are given in their regular course, on such terms as the Board of Regents may prescribe.

ARTICLE 171.

SEC. 1393. An admission fee and rate of tuition fixed by the Board of Regents must be required of each pupil, except as herein otherwise provided.   •

ARTICLE 172.

SEC. 1394. As soon as the income of the University shall permit, admission and tuition must be free to all residents of the State; and the Regents must so apportion the representation of students, according to population, that all portions of the State may enjoy equal privileges therein.

ARTICLE 173.

SEC. 1395. If approved by the Board of Regents, scholarships may be established in the University by any persons, for the purpose of private benefaction or of affording tuition in any course of the University free from the ordinary charges, to any scholar in the public schools of the State who may distinguish himself in study, according to the recommendation of his teachers, and who passes the examination required for the grade at which he wishes to enter the University.

ARTICLE 174.

SEC. 1396. The Board of Regents may affiliate with the University any incorporated college of medicine, law, or other special course of instruction, upon such terms as may be deemed expedient; and such college may retain the control of its own property, have its own Boards of Trustees, Faculties, and Presidents, respectively; and the students of such colleges recommended by the respective Faculties thereof may receive from the University the degrees of those colleges.

ARTICLE 175.

SEC. 1397. The examinations for degrees must be annual. Students who have passed not less than a year as residents in any college, academy, or school in this State, and who, after examination by the Faculty thereof, are recommended by them as proficient candidates for any degree in any regular course of the University, must be examined therefor at the annual examination; and, on passing such examination, may receive the degree and diploma for that course, and rank as graduates.

ARTICLE 176.

SEC. 1398. All students of the University who have been residents thereat for not less than one year, and all graduates thereof, may present themselves for examination in any course at the annual examinations, and, on passing such examination, may receive the degree and diploma of that course.

ARTICLE 177.

SEC. 1399. Upon such examinations each professor and instructor of that course may cast one vote, by ballot, upon each application for recommendation to the Board of Regents for a degree.

ARTICLE 178.

SEC. 1400. Graduates of the College of California, and of any incorporated college affiliated with the University, may receive the degrees from and rank as graduates of the University.

ARTICLE 179.

SEC. 1401. The Board of Regents may also confer certificates of proficiency in any branch of study upon such students of the University as upon examination are found entitled to the same.

ARTICLE 180.

SEC. 1402. The proper degree of each college must be conferred at the end of the course upon such students as, having completed the same, are found proficient therein.

ARTICLE 181.

SEC. 1403. The degree of Bachelor of Arts, and afterwards

the degree of Master of Arts, in usual course, must be conferred upon the graduates of the College of Letters.

ARTICLE 182.

SEC. 1404.   A system of moderate manual labor must be established in connection with the Agricultural College, upon its agricultural and ornamental grounds, for practical education in agriculture and landscape gardening.

ARTICLE 183.

SEC. 1405.   No sectarian, political, or partisan test must ever be allowed or exercised in the appointment of Regents or in the election of professors, teachers, or other officers of the University, or in the admission of students thereto, or for any purpose whatsoever; nor must the majority of the Board of Regents be of any one religious sect, or of no religious belief.

ARTICLE 184.

SEC. 1415.   The endowment of the University is:

1. The proceeds of the sale of the seventy-two sections of land granted to the State for a seminary of learning;

2. The proceeds of the ten sections of land granted to the State for public buildings;

3. The income derived from the investments of the proceeds of the sale of the lands, or of the scrip therefor, or of any part thereof, granted to this State for the endowment, support, and maintenance of at least one college where the leading object shall be, without excluding other scientific and classical studies, and including military tactics, to teach such branches of learning as are related to agriculture and the mechanic arts;

4. The income of the fund set apart by "An Act for the endowment of the University of California," approved April second, eighteen hundred and seventy, which is continued in force;

(5. Donations;)

6. The State of California, in its corporate capacity, may take by grant, gift, devise, or bequest, any property for the use of the University, and hold the same, and apply the funds arising therefrom, through the Regents of the University, to the support of the University, as provided in Article IX, section four, of the Constitution;

7. The Regents of the University, in their corporate capacity, may take by grant, gift, devise, or bequest, any property for the use of the University, or of any college thereof, or of any professorship, chair, or scholarship therein, or for the library, an observatory, workshops, gardens, greenhouses, apparatus, a Students' Loan Fund, or any other purpose

appropriate to the University; and such property shall be taken, received, held, managed, and invested, and the proceeds thereof used, bestowed, and applied by the said Regents, for the purposes, provisions, and conditions prescribed by the respective grant, gift, devise, or bequest;

8. The Regents of the University may invest any of the permanent funds of the University which are now or hereafter may be in their custody, in productive unincumbered real estate in this State, subject to the power of the Legislature to control or change such investment, excepting such as by the terms of their acquisition must be otherwise invested;

9. If by the terms of any grant, gift, devise, or bequest, such as are described in the preceding sixth and seventh subdivisions, conditions are imposed which are impracticable under the provisions of the Civil Code, such grant, gift, devise, or bequest shall not thereby fail, but such conditions shall be rejected, and the intent of the donor carried out as near as may be.

ARTICLE 185.

SEC. 1425. The University is under the control of a Board of Regents, consisting of twenty-two members; but the President of the University, for the time being, shall be a member of the Board of Regents by virtue of his office.

ARTICLE 186.

SEC. 1426. Sixteen members of the Board are appointed by the Governor, with the advice and consent of the Senate. Their term of office is sixteen years.

ARTICLE 187.

SEC. 1427. Six members of the Board hold by virtue of other offices, as provided in section three hundred and fifty-three.

ARTICLE 188.

SEC. 1428. Whenever a vacancy occurs in the Board, the Governor must appoint some person to fill it, and the person so appointed holds for the remainder of the term.

ARTICLE 189.

SEC. 1429. The Governor is President of the Board.

ARTICLE 190.

SEC. 1430. Seven members constitute a quorum of the Board.

ARTICLE 191.

SEC. 1431. The members receive no compensation.

ARTICLE 192.

SEC. 1432. The powers and duties of the Board of Regents are as follows:

1. To meet at such times and places as their rules may prescribe, or at the call of the President of the Board;

2. To control and manage the University and its property;

3. To prescribe rules for their own government and for the government of the University;

4. To adopt and prescribe rules for the government and discipline of the Cadets;

5. To receive, in the name of the State, or of the Board of Regents, as the case may be, all property donated to the University;

6. To choose a President of the University, the professors, and other officers and employés of the University, prescribe their duties, fix and provide for the payment of their salaries;

7. To fix the qualifications for admission to the benefits of the University;

8. To fix the admission fee and rates of tuition;

9. To appoint a Secretary and Treasurer, prescribe their duties, and fix and provide for the payment of their compensation;

10. To remove at pleasure any officer, professor, or employé of the University;

11. To supervise the general courses of instruction, and on the recommendations of the several Faculties, prescribe the authorities and text-books to be used in the several colleges;

12. To confer such degrees and grant such diplomas as are usual in Universities, or as they deem appropriate;

13. To establish and maintain a museum;

14. To establish and maintain a library;

15. To take immediate measures for the permanent improvement and planting of the University grounds;

16. To keep a record of all their proceedings;

17. Through the President of the University, to report to the Governor the progress, condition, and wants of each of the colleges embraced in the University; the course of study in each; the number of professors and students; the amount of receipts and disbursements, together with the nature, cost, and results of all important investigations and experiments, and such other information as they may deem important.

ARTICLE 193.

SEC. 1433. The entire income arising from the endowment is subject to the trusts at the disposition of the Board of Regents, for the support of the University

ARTICLE 194.

SEC. 1434. For the current expenditures of the University, specific sums of money must be set aside, out of the funds at their disposal, by the Board of Regents, which are subject to the warrants of the President of the Board, drawn upon the Treasurer of the University in pursuance of the order of the Board of Regents.

ARTICLE 195.

SEC. 1435. All moneys which may at any time be in the State Treasury, subject to the use of the Board of Regents, may be drawn therefrom by the President of the Board, upon the order of the Board in favor of the Treasurer of the University.

ARTICLE 196.

SEC. 1436. The Regents must cause to be constructed such buildings as are needed for the use of the University.

ARTICLE 197.

SEC. 1437. The plan adopted in the construction of buildings must provide separate buildings for separate uses, and so group all such buildings that a central building may bring the whole in harmony as part of one design.

ARTICLE 198.

SEC. 1438. The construction and furnishing of the buildings must be let out to the lowest responsible bidder, after advertisement for not less than ten days, in at least two daily newspapers published in the City of San Francisco; but the Regents may reject any bid, and advertise anew.

ARTICLE 199.

SEC. 1439. Until the University buildings are ready for use, the Regents may make temporary arrangements for buildings at Oakland.

6

ARTICLE 200.

SEC. 1449. A practical agriculturist, competent to superintend the working of the agricultural farm and to discharge the duties of Secretary of the Board of Regents, must be chosen by the Board as their Secretary

ARTICLE 201.

SEC. 1450. The Secretary must:

1. Reside and keep his office at the seat of the University;

2. Keep a record of the transactions of the Board of Regents, which must be open at all times to the inspection of any citizen of this State;

3. Have the custody of all books, papers, documents, and other property which may be deposited in his office;

4. Keep and file all reports and communications which may be made to the University appertaining to education, science, art, husbandry, mechanics, or mining;

5. Address circulars to societies and others soliciting information upon the latest and best modes of culture of the products adapted to the soil and climate of the State, and on all subjects connected with field culture, horticulture, stock raising, and the dairy;

6. Correspond with established schools of mining and metallurgy in Europe, and obtain information respecting the improvements of mining machinery adapted to California;

7. Correspond with the patent office at Washington, and with the representatives of the Government of the United States abroad, to procure contributions to agriculture from these sources; receive and distribute seeds, plants, shrubbery, and trees adapted to our climate and soils, for the purposes of experiment;

8. Obtain contributions to the museums and the library of the University;

9. Keep a correct account of all the executive acts of the President of the University;

10. Keep an accurate account of all moneys received into the treasury or paid therefrom;

11. Distribute the seeds, plants, trees, and shrubbery received by him and not needed by the University, equally throughout the State, to farmers and others who will agree to cultivate them properly, and return to the Secretary's office a reasonable proportion of the products thereof, with a statement of the mode of cultivation, and such other information as may be necessary to ascertain their value for cultivation in the State;

12. Publish from time to time in the newspapers of the State, free of charge, information relating to agriculture, the mechanic arts, mining, and metallurgy.

ARTICLE 202.

SEC. 1451. The Secretary holds office at the pleasure of and receives the compensation fixed by the Board.

ARTICLE 203.

SEC. 1461. The Academic Senate is composed **of the Faculties and Instructors** of the University.

ARTICLE 204.

SEC. 1462. The **Senate** must conduct the general administration of the University, regulate **the** general and special courses of instruction, receive and determine all appeals from acts of discipline enforced by the Faculty of any college, and exercise such other powers as the Board of Regents may confer upon **it**.

ARTICLE 205.

SEC. 1463. Its proceedings must **be** conducted according to rules of order adopted by it, and every person engaged in instruction in the University may participate in its discussions; but the right of voting is confined to the President and the Professors.

ARTICLE 206.

SEC. 1473. **The students of** the University must be **organized into a body known as the** "University Cadets."

ARTICLE 207.

SEC. 1474. The officers of Cadets, between and including the ranks of Second Lieutenant and Colonel, must be selected by the Chief Military Instructor, with the assent of the President **of** the University, and must be commissioned by the Governor.

ARTICLE 208.

SEC. 1475. The Adjutant-General of the State **must** issue such arms, munitions, accouterments, and equipments to the University Cadets as the Board of Regents may require and the Governor approve.

ARTICLE 209.

SEC. 1476. Upon graduating or retiring from the University, such officers may resign their commissions or hold the same as retired officers of the University Cadets, liable to be called into service by the Governor in case of war, invasion, **insurrection, or** rebellion.

Article 210.

Sec. 1477. The military instructor must make quarterly reports to the Adjutant-General of the State, showing the number, discipline, and equipments of the Cadets.

Article 211.

Sec. 2242. The State Geologist and Regents of the University may make up from duplicate specimens under their control, a geological cabinet for the use of the Asylum.

Article 212.

Sec. 3533. The Regents of the University may order the selection of the one hundred and fifty thousand acres of land granted to the State for the use of an Agricultural College, and dispose of the same at the price and in the manner fixed by them.

Article 213.

Sec. 3534. The Land Agent of the University, as the agent of the State, must select the lands according to the instructions of the Board, and issue certificates of purchase and patents to purchasers who comply with the conditions fixed by the Board; and the Regents must invest all moneys accruing from the sale of lands as they may deem best, subject to the conditions of the Act of Congress granting such lands.

Article 214.

Sec. 3535. All moneys, securities, or other properties arising from the sale of the seventy-two sections granted to the State for a seminary of learning, and from the sale of the ten sections granted to the State for the erection of public buildings, must be paid out of the State Treasury on the order of the Regents of the University

Article 215.

Sec. 3536. All persons who have purchased any portion of either of the grants mentioned in the preceding section, and who have not paid in full therefor, must be included in the delinquent list, and the District Attorney must proceed against such delinquents as provided in Sections 3547 and 3548, and the provisions of Sections 3548 to 3556, inclusive, are made applicable to such proceedings. If such lands revert to the State, they pass under the control of and may be sold by the Board of Regents of the University.

ARTICLE 216.

SEC. 172. PENAL CODE. Every person, who, within two miles of the land belonging to this State, upon which the State Prison is situated, or within one mile of the Insane Asylum at Napa, or within one mile of the grounds belonging and adjacent to the University of California, in Alameda County, or in the State Capitol, or within the limits of the grounds adjacent and belonging thereto, sells, gives away, or exposes for sale any vinous or alcoholic liquors, is guilty of a misdemeanor.

DIVISION FOUR—DECISIONS OF THE SUPREME COURT.

CHAPTER I.

ARTICLE 217.

Foltz vs. *Hoge et al.*

[54 Cal. 28.]

BY THE COURT:

Action for a mandate to compel the defendants, who are the Directors of the Hastings College of the Law, to admit the plaintiff as a student of the college. It is averred in the petition, and not denied in the answer, that the plaintiff is a citizen and resident of this State; that she is over the age of twenty-one years; that she is of good moral character; that she is entitled to practice as an attorney and counselor at law, and is now a regular practicing attorney of the Court in good standing; and that she duly made application for admission as a student in the college, and tendered the requisite fee, but that the Directors rejected her application, and refused to permit her to enter as a student of the college.

The answer avers that the college was founded by S. C. Hastings, under and by virtue of the Act entitled "An Act to create Hastings College of the Law in the University of the State of California," approved March twenty-sixth, eighteen hundred and seventy-eight (Stats. 1877-8, p. 533); that said Hastings paid into the State Treasury the sum of one hundred thousand dollars mentioned in the Act, and thereupon founded and established the "Hastings College of the Law," and that the same has since been managed by the Board of Directors mentioned in the Act. It admits that the defendants refused to permit the plaintiff to enter as a student of the college, but avers that they so refused "because they, in good faith, believed and determined that it was not wise or expedient, or for the best interest of the college, to admit any female as a student therein." It contains other averments respecting the power and discretion of the Board of Directors in the direction, management, and control of the college; but as they present only questions of law, they need not be further noticed at this time. The plaintiff moved for judgment on the pleadings, and the Court thereupon gave judgment that the peremptory writ of mandate issue, commanding the defendants to admit the plaintiff as a student in the college.

The question presented for decision is whether the Board of Directors can lawfully reject the plaintiff's application for admission as a student in the college, on the sole ground that she is a female?

The Act of March twenty-third, eighteen hundred and sixty-eight, to create and organize the University of California (Stats. 1867–8, p. 248) provides that "the Board of Regents may affiliate with the University, and make an integral part of the same, and incorporate therewith, any incorporated college of medicine, of law, or other special course of instruction now existing, or which may hereafter be created, upon such terms as to the respective corporations may be deemed expedient; and such college or colleges, so affiliated, shall retain the control of their own property, with their own Boards of Trustees, and their own Faculties and President of the same respectively," * * * (Sec. 8); and it is provided by the eleventh section, that such college, so affiliated, may retain its own property, to be vested in and held and managed by its own corporation. The eighteenth section provides that "the immediate government and discipline of the several colleges shall be intrusted to their respective Faculties, to consist of the President and the resident professors of the same, each of which shall have its own organization, regulate the affairs of its own college, recommending the course of study, and the text-books to be used, for the approval of the Board of Regents, and in connection with the President, as its executive officer, have the government of the students."

From those and other provisions of the Act, it appears that a complete scheme was devised for the affiliation with the University of a College of Law, and that the general features of the plan for the government of the college were prescribed.

The Act of 1878, to create the Hastings College of the Law, appointed a Board of Directors of the college, and provides for filling vacancies which may occur. It also provides, that the Board shall appoint the officers of the college; that the college shall affiliate with the University; that the Faculty (Regents?) of the University shall grant diplomas to the students of the college; that the Dean of the college "shall be ex officio of the Faculty of the University;" that the college "shall establish a curriculum of studies, and shall matriculate students who may reside at the University of the State, as well as students residing in other parts of the State;" and that "all the business of the college shall be managed by the Directors without compensation." The plan for the organization and government of the college, as presented by those provisions, does not materially differ from that which is contained in the Act to create the University; whatever differences there are being in the details, but not in the general plan.

It is contended by the defendants that the Act confers upon the Board of Directors absolute discretion in the matter of the admission of students, subject only to the supervision of a Court of chancery. Such discretionary power might have been granted, and could readily have been expressed in plain and unambiguous words; but the Act does not expressly grant such discretionary power; and if it is possessed by them, it is to be implied from the provisions and the general intent of the Act. Reliance is placed upon the provision that "all the business of the college shall be managed by the Directors, without compensation," as conferring discretionary power; but the purpose of the provision is to declare that Directors shall receive no compensation for their services. That is the obvious meaning of those words.

The provision that the college shall establish a curriculum of studies throws no light on the question; for if it be conceded that the power granted to the college to establish a curriculum of studies is not subject to the provision of the eighteenth section of the Act of 1868, above cited (to the effect that the course of study and the text-books recommended for the college is subject to the approval of the Board of Regents), that power might be exercised without regard to the power here claimed.

There is nothing in the general framework of the Act of 1878, nor in the nature or purpose of such a college, that requires that its Directors should have more enlarged powers over the admission of students than should be possessed by the Regents and the Faculty of the University, in respect to the admission of students at large.

It was, in our opinion, the intent of the Legislature that the college when established should affiliate with the University and be governed by the laws applicable to the University, except as otherwise provided, either in the Act of 1868 or the Act of 1878; that the University and the affiliated college should constitute one institution and be governed by the same laws, with only such special provisions as might be required for the harmonious operation of its different branches. That would seem to be the necessary result of the affiliation of a college with the University. Would not the provision in each Act, for the affiliation of the college with the University, be practically destroyed by construing the provisions of the Act for the organization of the college as conferring upon the Directors of the college, not only the management and control of its property, but also the absolute government of the college in all respects, except in the issuing of diplomas. An affiliation imports a subjection to the same general laws and rules that are applicable to the parent institution, with such special exception as may expressly be made and such as arise from the very nature and purpose of the affiliated institution. If this absolute power was intended to be conferred upon the Directors, the inquiry would be pertinent and suggestive why the Act should expressly give the control of the property of the college to the Directors (Sec. 8), or authorize the college to recommend the course of study and the text-books to be used to the approval of the Regents. If absolute discretionary power was intended to be vested in the Directors, why should particular power have specially been conferred? The inquiry suggests an argument of much force.

It is urged that no person can claim a strict legal right to be admitted to the college—that the very idea of a college implies the power to fix qualifications and limit the number of students. It must be conceded that no one has such strict legal right without any limitations or conditions; but on the contrary, the Directors may, as they should, exclude one whose moral character is bad, or who, by reason of tender years, has not sufficient capacity to study the law, or who applies for admission when the college already contains as many students as can advantageously be instructed therein, or who, for any sufficient reason, ought not to be admitted; but this does not tend to the conclusion that their discretion is unlimited—that the Directors are not subject to the laws applicable to the University.

If the absolute power claimed for the Directors is possessed by them, no reason can be suggested why they may not exclude every one who does not possess some qualification arbitrarily selected by them, such as nativity, time of residence in the State, or the like fanciful or accidental condition. They might thus exclude all except Indians, or those of foreign birth. The eighth section of the Act of eighteen hundred and seventy-eight, though not remarkable for its perspicuity, seems to establish as one of the qualifications of students that they must be residents of the State; and it contains one other provision which is very suggestive in this connection. It declares that the college "shall matriculate students who reside at the University of the State." That is to be construed as meaning students of the University. The only qualifications prescribed for students of the University are that they must be residents of the State, of the age of fourteen years or upwards, and of approved moral character. It is conceded that females are now, and for several years last past have been, admitted as students of the University; and the provision of section seventeen of the Political Code, that words used in the masculine gender comprehend as well the feminine gender, would seem to entitle females to enter the University as students at large.

Females are entitled by law to be admitted as attorneys and counselors in all the Courts of this State, upon the same terms as males. The college was founded for the purpose of affording instruction to those who desire to be admitted, as well as those who have been admitted, to practice as attorneys and counselors. It was affiliated with the University and thus became an integral part of it, and in our opinion became subject to the same general provisions of the law as are applicable to the University; and the same general policy which admitted females as students of the University opened to them as well the doors of the College of the Law.

Judgment affirmed. Remittitur forthwith.

CHAPTER II.

ARTICLE 218.

Berryman vs. *Perkins, Governor, etc.*

[55 Cal. 483.]

The fourth section of the Act of April 1, 1876, "to provide for a supply of water for the University and for the Asylum for the Deaf, Dumb, and Blind" (Stat. 1875–6, p. 316), authorizes the Controller to draw his warrants for the appraised value of property sought to be condemned, "upon a judgment being rendered for the condemnation of said springs and lands and right of way, and appraising the value thereof, and upon the filing in said proceedings of a written certificate of the Governor appraising [approving] such valuation."

The statute requires, as conditions precedent to the taking of the land and water for public uses, not only that the land shall be appraised by the Superior Court, a jury, or commissioners, but also that such appraisal shall be approved by the Governor. Until he shall concur with the appraisal the condemnation cannot be made operative. This necessarily involves an inquiry and ascertainment of the actual value of the property, and the employment of judgment and discretion on the part of the Governor. The power to determine whether the appraisal is correct is his and we cannot deprive him of his discretion or adjudicate the value for him. In all matters vesting in the sworn discretion of the person to whom a duty is confided by law, mandamus will not lie to control the discretion or determine the decision which is to be made. (High ex rem. 42; Moses on Mandamus, 82; Harpending v. Haight, 39 Cal. 208.)

It is not necessary to inquire whether the Governor might be compelled to make inquiry in respect to the value of the property, if it should be made to appear that he had refused to make such an inquiry. The application here is that he be compelled to issue his certificate approving the valuation.

CHAPTER III.

ARTICLE 219.

John Le Conte, President of the University of California, vs. The Trustees and Marshal of the Town of Berkeley.

[57 Cal. 269.]

THE COURT:

A writ of prohibition does not run to a ministerial officer. The acts sought to be prohibited were not judicial acts; therefore the writ of prohibition, which was issued in this case on the twenty-sixth day of August, 1879, was improperly issued.

Judgment reversed, and cause remanded.

CHAPTER IV.

ARTICLE 220.

The People of the State of California, Respondents, vs. The President and Trustees of the College of California, Appellants.

[38 Cal. 166.]

BY THE COURT:

This is an action to quiet the title of the State of California to a tract of one hundred and sixty acres of land, situate near the City of Oakland, on which it is proposed to erect the State University; and the only question for our decision on this appeal is whether or not the conveyance from the President and Trustees of the College of California to the State, under the facts stated in the agreed case, was and is operative in law to vest the title in the State. In other words, whether or not, upon the agreed facts, the President and Trustees of the college had the power in law to convey the land to the State, under the circumstances, and for the purposes disclosed in the record, or whether the transaction was *ultra vires*. The college was incorporated under the Act of April 20, 1850, entitled "An Act to provide for the incorporation of colleges" (Stats. 1850, p. 273), and the Act amendatory thereof, passed April 13, 1855 (Stats. 1855, p. 110). In defining the powers of the Trustees, it is provided in section seven that they shall have power "to receive and hold by purchase, gift, or grant, any real or personal property, provided that the yearly income of the college shall not exceed its necessary yearly expenses ten thousand dollars;" and "to sell, mortgage, release, and otherwise use and dispose of such property in such manner as they shall deem most conducive to the prosperity of the college." The General Corporation Act provides (section one) that every corporation, as such, shall have power "to hold, purchase, and convey such real and personal estate as the purposes of the corporation shall require, not exceeding the amount limited by law." Under these provisions it is quite evident the Trustees have an unlimited discretion in respect to the sale or other disposition of the corporate property, for the advancement of the interests of the college; and it is equally plain that so long as they act in good faith their discretion, in this respect, is absolute. They alone are to decide whether the proposed disposition of the property will be "most conducive to the prosperity of the college." There is no room for argument on this point. But it is suggested that the action of the President and Trustees of the College of California, in alienating its property, is not only not "conducive to the prosperity of the college," but is avowedly intended to terminate its existence, in order that its corporate property may be devoted to the building up of a new institution of learning, with a different name, and under a new management; that the conveyance of the tract in question to the State was in part execution of this general plan; and that when the State, through its authorized agents and officers, accepted the conveyance, it had notice of the intention and purpose of the Trustees in making it; that whilst the Trustees may make such disposition of the corporate property as they shall believe will conduce to the prosperity of the college, they have no power to destroy it by alienating its property, with the avowed intention to terminate its existence, and turn over its estate to another institution; and that the State, having taken the conveyance with notice of the unlawful purpose for which it was made, is not entitled to the aid of a court of equity, in order that it may thereby validate a transaction which has an incurable infirmity.

In the recent case of Miners' Ditch Company vs. Zillerbock (37 Cal. 543), we had occasion to examine with much care the power of a corporation over its corporate property; and we held that all corporations, capable of taking and holding property, have the *jus disponendi* as fully as natural persons, except in so far as they are restrained by statute; that under the general power, a corporation, unless restrained by statute, may dispose of the whole of its corporate prop-

erty for any lawful purpose, and that if it conveys its property for a purpose apparently lawful, and within the scope
of its powers, to a *bona fide* purchaser, without notice, the
transaction will be valid, as between the corporation and the
purchaser, even though the secret purpose of the corporation
was unlawful; that if the purchaser had notice of the
unlawful purpose, and if the contract was fully executed,
and the purchaser was let into the possession, the Court
would refuse its aid to enable the corporation to recover the
property, on the ground that "*in pari delicto potior est con-
ditio defendentis.*" The first point, therefore, to be ascertained in the case we are considering is, whether the conveyance from the President and Trustees of the college to the
State was in part execution or in furtherance of an unlawful
plan for the disposition of the corporate property of the
college. The agreed case shows that the President and
Trustees are actuated by the most laudable motives in the
disposition they proposed to make of the property. The
bona fides of the transaction is not open to suspicion; on
the contrary, it appears affirmatively that the President and
Trustees were actuated only by a praiseworthy desire to
build up an institution of learning commensurate with the
wants of the State, and capable of dispensing greater benefits to the public than could be anticipated from the College
of California. If their laudable purpose fail, it will be
solely because of a want of the lawful power to accomplish
it, and not because it is tainted with any moral wrong. It
is a question of power merely, and in that light we shall
consider it.

The Act for the incorporation of colleges provides no
method by which they may be disincorporated or dissolved.
But the general Corporation Act (Sec. 31) prescribes a mode
for dissolving trade corporations on the petition of the stockholders. This provision, however, can have no application to
a corporation for literary purposes having no stockholders,
and we are not aware of any statutory provision for dissolving a corporation of this character. But at common law both
municipal and private corporations may be dissolved by a
surrender of the franchise. In Angell and Ames on Corporations (Sec. 772), after announcing that some doubt has existed
in England touching the power of a municipal corporation to
surrender its corporate existence, the author concludes that
"by far the better opinion is, that where the surrender is duly
made and accepted, it is effectual to dissolve a municipal
body. In this country the power of a private corporation to
dissolve itself by its own assent seems to be assumed by all
Judges who touch upon the point." The authorities quoted
in support of the last proposition are Riddle vs. Proprietors
of Locks, etc. (7 Mass., 185); Hampsheir vs. Franklin (16
Mass., 86); McLeren vs. Pennington (1 Paige, 107); Enfield
Toll Bridge Company vs. Connecticut Railroad Company (7

Conn., 45); Slee vs. Blum (19 John., 456); Canal Company vs. Railroad Company (4 Gill & J., 1); Trustees, etc. vs. Zanesville C. & M. Company (9 Ohio, 203); Penobscot Boom Company vs. Sampson (16 Maine, 224); Mumma vs. Potomac Company (8 Peters, 281).

Chancellor Kent says: The better opinion would seem to be that a corporation aggregate may surrender and in that may dissolve itself; but then the surrender must be accepted by Government and be made by some solemn act to render it complete. (2 Kent's Com., 311.)

When the statute prescribes a particular method for dissolving a corporation, that method must of course be pursued; but our conclusion is, that in the absence of any statutory provision defining the mode, a corporation aggregate may surrender its franchise, by proper proceedings for that purpose. It is not necessary in this case that we should lay down any precise rule as to the particular method by which the surrender may be accomplished and rendered effectual. For the purposes of this decision it is sufficient for us to have ascertained that there is a method by which the College of California may surrender its franchise. It was and is for the President and Trustees to decide whether or not the public interest would be subserved by dissolving the corporation and devoting its property, after the payment of its debts, to the support of a new and kindred institution, to be established under more auspicious circumstances, and with a more liberal endowment. There are no stockholders to be consulted whose interests might need protection; and the plan proposed is to take effect only after all the debts of the college are paid. Under these circumstances it would be an extraordinary *casus omissus* in the law if the managers of a literary institution, without a sufficient endowment to render it effective, were compelled, against their convictions and judgments, to maintain it in its feeble, sickly condition, when, by a surrender of its franchise and devoting its property in aid of a new institution of learning, a great public good might be accomplished. We entertain no doubt whatever of the power of the President and Trustees of the college not only to surrender their franchise, but to transfer the corporate property, after the payment of debts, to the State for the use of the University. The end proposed to be accomplished by the President and Trustees was not only lawful and within the scope of their powers, but was eminently meritorious and conducive to the public interest.

The fact that a portion of the funds of the college were the result of voluntary donations to it can, in no degree, impair the power of the Trustees to surrender its franchise, and dispose of its property in the manner proposed. The donors must be presumed to have known the law, and must be held to have assented in advance to any lawful exercise of power in good faith by the President and Trustees in

respect to the corporate franchise and property. In addition
to this, the donations were absolute and unconditional. The
donors retained no interest, present or future, in the sums
donated, nor acquired thereby any interest whatever in the
corporate property, nor any right to control it. The donations
were voluntary offerings by patriotic citizens in aid of the
cause of education, and the management and disposition of the
fund was confided absolutely to the President and Trustees,
subject only to such restrictions and limitations as the law
imposed upon them; and, as we have seen, the law does not
prohibit them from dissolving the corporation, and applying
its funds, after payment of debts, towards the endowment of
another kindred institution. That the Trustees have the
power to surrender the franchise, after its debts are paid, is a
proposition which admits of no doubt; and if they should
do so, without having made any disposition of its property,
there being no stockholders or creditors, the personal property of the corporation would vest in the State. (2 Kent's
Com., 386; Angell and Ames on Corp., Sec. 195.) Such real
estate as remained undisposed of, or which had been acquired
by donation, would revert to the donors. But this rule would
not apply to real estate acquired by the corporation by a purchase for value. In such cases the vendor has no further
interest in the property or its application, and on a dissolution of the corporation, if there be no stockholders or
creditors, the title would vest in the State in the same manner as if it were personal property. This point was under
discussion in Bacon vs. Robertson (18 Howard U. S. R., 480),
and, in delivering the opinion of the Court, Mr Justice
Campbell says: "The acquisitions of real property by a trad-
ing corporation are commonly made upon a bargain and
sale, for a full consideration, and without conditions in the
deed, and no conditions are implied in law in reference to
such conveyances. The vendor has no interest in the appropriation of the property to any specific object, nor any
reversion where the succession fails." We are satisfied this
is the true rule. If the College of California, therefore, had
surrendered its franchise, owing no debts, all its personal
estate then remaining, and all its real property acquired by
purchase for value, would have vested, by operation of law,
in the State. It appears from the agreed statement that the
whole of the tract of one hundred and sixty acres in contest
was acquired by purchase for a valuable consideration, except
the fifteen acres conveyed by Pioche, and the ten acres conveyed by Blake; and the latter has expressly ratified the
conveyance to the State, while the former has conveyed to
the college by deed absolute, and released it from any obliga-
tion to appropriate the land to any particular use, which is
equivalent to a ratification of the conveyance to the State.
The President and Trustees, therefore, in conveying this
tract to the State, in anticipation of an actual dissolution of

the corporation, have only accomplished in advance a result which would have ensued by operation of law on a dissolution of the corporation, after the payment of its debts. The case shows that it yet retains property amply sufficient to meet the demands of its creditors, none of whom are here to complain of this transaction. On the whole, we see no error in the record.

Judgment affirmed.

CHAPTER V.

ARTICLE 221.

Ex parte Joseph McClain.

[61 Cal. 436.]

Application for discharge on writ of habeas corpus.

The petitioner was convicted of a misdemeanor for violating section one hundred and seventy-two Penal Code, and was adjudged to pay a fine of twenty-five dollars, in default of payment whereof he was restrained by the Sheriff. The section reads as follows: "Every person who, within two miles of the land belonging to this State upon which the State Prison is situated, or within one mile of the Insane Asylum at Napa, or within one mile of the grounds belonging and adjacent to the University of California, in Alameda County, or in the State Capitol, or within the limits of the grounds adjacent and belonging thereto, sells, gives away, or exposes for sale, any vinous or alcoholic liquors, is guilty of a misdemeanor."

This section was enacted prior to the adoption of the new Constitution and is unaffected by it.

The power to enact the law in question falls within that large class of powers belonging to the Legislature essential to the promotion, regulation, and preservation of the morals, health, prosperity, and general well-being of the people of the State. All power rests in the Legislature not prohibited by the Constitution of this State or the United States.

Under the late Constitution it was competent for the Legislature to prohibit the sale of vinous or alcoholic liquors within the limits specified in the section, if, in its opinion, the well-being of the youth being educated at the University, or the discipline and reformation of convicts, or the health of unfortunate insanes, would be thereby promoted or preserved.

Petitioner remanded.

CHAPTER VI.

ARTICLE 222.

TAXATION OF UNIVERSITY MORTGAGES.

Hollister vs. *Sherman.*

[10 Pacific Coast Law Journal, p. 666.]

The opinion of the Court is as follows:

We can see no difference as to ownership between property taken by the Regents of the University "by grant, gift, devise, or bequest" (Political Code, 1415, Subdivision 7), and other property administered by them. If any all such property is exempt from taxation. The mortgage to secure the money loaned by the Regents to plaintiff was not, therefore, subject to taxation. As the mortgage was assessed to the Regents of the University, the tax deed would show the assessment was void. The deed would cast no cloud upon plaintiff's title, since in an action brought upon it by the purchaser, the present plaintiff would not be called upon to introduce any evidence; but the purchaser must fail on his own showing. (Grimm vs. O'Connell, 54 Cal., 521.) Judgment and orders affirmed.

TITLE THREE.

PRIVATE DONATIONS.

7

TITLE THREE—PRIVATE DONATIONS.

CHAPTER I.

From the College of California to the State of California.

ARTICLE 223.

This indenture, made this twelfth day of February, A. D. one thousand eight hundred and sixty-eight, between the President and Board of Trustees of the College of California, a corporation organized and existing under the laws of the State of California, party of the first part, and the State of California for the uses of a University, of the second part:

WHEREAS, At a meeting of said President and Board of Trustees of the College of California, held in the City of San Francisco on the ninth day of October, A. D. one thousand eight hundred and sixty-seven, the following resolutions were by them adopted, viz. .

Resolved, That the President and Board of Trustees of the College of California hereby offer to donate to the State Board of Directors of the Agricultural, Mining, and Mechanical Arts College one hundred and sixty acres of land situated in the Township of Oakland, County of Alameda, said State, consisting of the lands lying between the two ravines or branches which unite to form Strawberry Creek, and known as the California College lands, as and for a site and grounds of said Agricultural, Mining, and Mechanical Arts College, and of an academical college or university.

Resolved—Second, That in making this offer of donation said President and Board of Trustees of the College of California are influenced by an earnest hope and confident expectation that the State of California will forthwith organize and put into operation, upon the aforesaid site and grounds, a University of California, which shall include a College of Mines, a College of Civil Engineering, a College of Mechanics, a College of Agriculture, an Academical College, all of the same grade and with courses of instruction at least equal to those of eastern colleges and universities.

Now, therefore, this indenture witnesseth that the said party of the first part, in conformity with the said resolutions, and for and in consideration of the sum of ten dollars, lawful money of the United States, to it paid by said party of the second part, at or before the ensealing and delivery of these presents, the receipt whereof is hereby acknowledged, and also for other good and valuable considerations, it hereunto moving hath granted, bargained, and sold, and by these presents doth grant, bargain, and sell, unto the said party of the second part and its assigns forever, all that certain tract, piece, or parcel of land situated, lying, and being in the Township of Oakland, County of Alameda, and State of California, bounded and described as follows, namely: Beginning at a point on the northeasterly part of plat No. 69 (sixty-nine), on the map hereinafter referred to, which point is also the center of Strawberry Creek, where the same is intersected by the center line of the northern branch of said creek, and is distant about two hundred and sixty feet southwesterly from the corner common to plats 69, 70, 79, and 81, on said map; and thence following the center of the northern branch of said Strawberry Creek in a northeastwardly direction to a point in said creek where the same would be intersected by a line drawn parallel with the northerly line of said plats 69 and 70, and distant therefrom, on a line drawn parallel with the easterly line of plat 81, one thousand and ten (1,010) feet; thence running north 80° 31' east three thousand five hundred and ninety-two (3,592) feet, to a point; thence at a right angle south 9° 30', east one thousand eight hundred and forty-five (1,845) feet, more or less, to a point where the same would be intersected by a line drawn through two stakes, marked respectively stake 23 and stake 24, and extended easterly in the same course; thence westerly along said course to the northwest corner of the abutment of a bridge over Strawberry Creek, on which said abutment is marked stake 23; thence along the westerly bank of said creek to a stake marked "No. 24," which, on a course south 80° 19' west, is one hundred and twenty-one (121) feet distant from said stake marked stake 23; thence along said westerly bank south 30° 20' west two hundred (200) feet to a stake marked 25; thence south 83° 30' west two hundred (200) feet to a stake marked 26; thence south 88° 30' west two hundred (200) feet to a stake marked "No. 27;" thence north 79° 15' west one hundred and eighty-nine (189) feet to a stake marked "No. 28;" thence north 85° 00' west thirty-six (36) feet to a stake on the steep bank of the creek marked No. 29; thence north 81° 30' west one hundred (100) feet; thence along the northern bank of the creek and along the fence standing thereon north 20° 20' west fifty-seven (57) feet; thence north 38° 15' west one hundred (100) feet; thence north 58° 00' west sixty-six (66) feet; thence north 74° 10' west one hundred (100) feet; thence north 53° 40' west two hundred (200) feet; thence north 16° 00' west one hundred and fifty-four (154) feet; thence north 53° 00' west two hundred and eleven (211) feet; thence south 61° 30' west one hundred and eighty-one (181) feet; thence north 89° 30' west one hundred feet; thence south 64° 10' west, crossing the creek, two hundred feet to a stake on the westerly line of plat No. 80, marked "40;" thence south 5° 30' east sixty-four (64) feet along said line of plat No. 80, to a point near the corner of Hillegas' orchard, to a stake marked "No. 41;" thence south 61° 30' west along said orchard fence eleven hundred and sixty-seven (1,167) feet, to a stake marked "No. 42;" thence south 69° 10' west along said fence six hundred and fifty-four (654) feet, to a stake marked "No. 43," on the south bank of the creek, and distant from the center line thereof sixteen (16) feet; thence along the fence north 87° 30' west eighty-six (86) feet, to a stake marked "No. 44;" thence north 81° 30' west one hundred and seventy-five (175) feet, to a stake in the fence thirty-four (34) feet from the center of the creek, on the line of the fence marked "No. 45;" thence along the south bank of the creek south 71° 00' west ninety (90) feet, to a stake on the south bank marked "No. 46;" thence along the south bank of said creek south 82° 30' west fifty (50) feet, to the east line of Dana Street, of the College Homestead Tract; thence along the east line of said Dana Street north 10° 10' west to center of said creek; thence along and following the center of the creek, in a westerly and northwesterly direction, to the point of beginning. Being portions of plats 69, 70, 71, 79, 80, 81, and 82, as the same are laid down, designated, and numbered on a map of the Ranchos of Vicente and Domingo Peralta, surveyed by Julius Kellersberger, and on file or of record in the County Recorder's office of Alameda County, containing one hundred and sixty acres of land, and being the same land and premises which are mentioned and contemplated in and by the said resolutions of said President and Board of Trustees, hereinbefore set forth; together with all and singular the tenements, hereditaments, and appurtenances thereunto belonging, or in anywise appertaining, and the reversion and reversions, remainder and remainders, rents, issues, and profits thereof, and also all the estate, right, title, and interest, property, possession, claim, and demand whatsoever, as well in law as in equity, of the said party of the first part, of, in, and to the above described premises, and every part and parcel thereof, with the appurtenances.

To have and to hold, all and singular, the above mentioned and described premises, together with the appurtenances, unto the said party of the second part and its assigns forever.

[Duly executed and recorded, Liber 30 of Deeds, page 163, Alameda County Records.]

CHAPTER II.

College of California to the Regents.

ARTICLE 224.

This indenture, made the first day of June, in the year of our Lord one thousand eight hundred and seventy, by and between the President and Board of Trustees of the College of California, a corporation duly incorporated under and by virtue of the laws of the State of California, acting herein by Horatio Stebbins, its President, and J. W Stow, its Secretary, hereunto duly authorized by resolution of said Board of Trustees as hereinafter set forth, party of first part, and the Regents of the University of California, a corporation duly incorporated under and by virtue of the laws of the State aforesaid, party of the second part, witnesseth: Whereas, at a meeting of the Board of Trustees of the party of the first part, held on the thirtieth day of May, A. D. 1870, the following resolution was duly adopted, to wit: Whereas, The President and Board of Trustees of the College of California is indebted in the sum of fifty-four thousand and fifty $\frac{40}{100}$ dollars, and the Regents of the University of California has assumed the said indebtedness and relieved the "President and Board of Trustees of the College of California" therefrom; and whereas, the President and Board of Trustees of the College of California desire to promote the educational plans and objects of the Regents of the University of California; now, therefore, it is resolved, That the President and Secretary of this Board be and they are hereby authorized and empowered, by good and valid deed, to donate and transfer and convey to the Regents of the University of California, and to its successors and assigns forever, all the following described property, to wit: 18 $\frac{25}{100}$ acres of land in plat No. 82, 64 $\frac{40}{100}$ acres of land in plat No. 80, 230 acres of land, more or less, in the mountain or undivided tract, and lots Nos. 1 to 11 inclusive in Block B, lot No. 49 in Block F and lots Nos. 20, 21, 23, 24, 26, 27, 28, 29, 31, and 32 in Block D, as laid down and designated upon the map of a portion of the Berkeley property, all of which lots, being twenty-two in all, being also portions of plot No. 80, also, Block No. 173, as laid down on Kellersberger's map of the City of Oakland, the same being all the lands now belonging to the President and Board of Trustees of the College of California, in trust, to sell, mortgage, or dispose of the same, or any part thereof, at such time or times, at such price or prices, and on such terms, as it shall deem best, and to give good and valid title to the purchaser or purchasers thereof without requiring the said purchaser or purchasers to look to the application of the purchase money paid or to be paid therefor, and out of proceeds thereof to retain and repay the advances made and to be made by it in the payment of the indebtedness aforesaid, and the balance of said proceeds to use, bestow, invest, and reinvest for its own uses and purposes, and until said sale, mortgage, or disposition of said property, to take, receive, hold, and in all respects manage the same as to it may seem best. Now, therefore, the party of the first part doth by these presents donate, transfer, and convey unto the party of the second part and to its successors and assigns forever, all those certain pieces or parcels of land situate, lying, and being in the County of Alameda, State of California, bounded and described as follows, to wit. First, commencing at the southeast corner of plot number eighty-two (82) as known upon the map hereinafter referred to, and running thence north 5° 30′ west fifteen (15) chains; thence south 80° 30′ west twelve (12) chains and sixty-eight (68) links; thence south 9° 30′ east fifteen chains, and thence north 80° 30′ east eleven (11) chains and sixty-three links to the point of beginning, containing eighteen $\frac{24}{100}$ (18 $\frac{24}{100}$) acres of land, and being a portion of plot number eighty-two (82) as designated and numbered on a certain map of the Ranchos of Vicente and Domingo Peralta, surveyed by one Julius Kellersberger and on file in the County Recorder's office in and for the said County of Alameda.

Second—Commencing at the northeast corner of plat number eighty (80) as designated and numbered on the said map of the said Kellersberger, and running thence south 5° 30′ east forty-three (43) chains and fifty (50) links, thence south 85° 30′ west six (6) chains and seventy (70) links, thence north 13° 30′ east two (2) chains, thence north 33° east seven (7) chains and sixty (60) links, thence north 13° 30′ west two (2) chains, thence north 82° west seven (7) chains and eighty-nine (89) links, thence south 50° 45′ west three (3) chains and forty-four (44) links, thence south 79° 30′ west two (2) chains and eighty-six (86) links, thence north 8° 45′ west two (2) chains and eighty (80) links, thence south 81° 15′ west six (6) chains and ten (10) links, thence north 8° 45′ west eight (8) chains and eighteen (18) links, thence north 29° 40′ west one (1) chain and seventy-nine (79) links, thence north 32° west five (5) chains and ninety-one (91) links, thence north 44° 15′ west four (4) chains and thirty-two (32) links, thence north 46° 15′ west two (2) chains and seventy (70) links, thence north 72° west one (1) chain and thirty-nine (39) links, and thence north 19° 30′ west one (1) chain and seventy-five (75) links, thence north 60° 15′ west one (1) chain and sixty-five (65) links, thence south 58° 15′ west two (2) chains and twenty-one (21) links, thence north 84° 30′ west seventy-five (75) links, thence north 40° 30′ west eighty-four (84) links, thence south 72° west three (3) chains and seventy-four (74) links, thence north 6° east one (1) chain and seventy-five (75) links, thence north 79° 30′ east two (2) chains and twelve (12) links, thence north **89° 45'** east two (2) chains and seventy-six (76) links, thence north **46° 45' east one** (1) chain and ninety-eight (98) links, thence south 64° 45' east **two** (2) chains and eighty-one (81) links, thence south 28° east one (1) chain and forty-eight (48) links, thence south 52° 45' east three (3) chains, thence south 75° 30' **east** one (1) chain and fifty-eight (58) links, thence south **44° 45'** east one (1) chain and twelve (12) links, thence south **59°** 15' east two (2) chains and fifty-eight (58) links, thence south 64° 30' east one (1) chain and seventy-seven (77) links, thence south 86° 30' east four (4) chains and fifty (50) links, thence north 89° 30' east **three** (3) chains and three (3) links, thence north 36° 30' **east** three (3) chains and three (3) links, thence north 86° 15' **east** one (1) chain and eighty-three (83) links, thence north **90°** 30' west twelve (12) chains and fifty-six (56) links, and thence north 80° 30' east **eleven** (11) chains and sixty-three (63) links, to the **point** of beginning, containing sixty-three $\frac{42}{100}$ ($63\frac{42}{100}$) of land, and being a portion of said plot number eighty (80).

Third—All those certain **lots** numbered **one** (1), **two** (2), **three** (3), four (4), five (5), **six** (6), seven (7), eight (8), nine **(9),** ten (10), and eleven (11), **in** Block B, lot number forty-**nine** (49), in Block F, and lots numbered twenty (20), twenty-one (21), **twenty-three (23),** twenty-four (24), twenty-six (26), twenty-seven (27), twenty-eight (28), twenty-nine (29), thirty-**one** (31), and thirty-two (32), in Block D, as designated and numbered on a certain map of a portion of the Berkeley property situated between the University of California and the State Deaf, Dumb, and Blind Asylum, Oakland, Alameda County, as laid out by Frederick Law Olmstead, and surveyed by W. F. Boardman, County Surveyor for the said County of Alameda, and filed for record in the County Recorder's office in and for the said County of Alameda, the **said** lots being twenty-two in all, and a portion of said plot number eighty (80), as designated on said map of Kellersberger.

Fourth—All the right, title, and interest of the party of the first part, of, in, and to **all** the undivided mountain land situate easterly of the **said** plats, numbered eighty (80) **and** eighty-two (82), as known and designated on the said map of the said Julius Kellersberger; the same being the undivided interest in lands not embraced in any of the numbered plots **upon** the said map of Kellersberger; said undivided interest supposed to be two hundred and thirty (230) acres of land more **or** less, and more particularly described **in a** certain **deed** bearing date November 6, **A. D.** 1858, made and exe-**cuted by** one John A. Bonneron **to one** Orrin Simmons, and **recorded** in the County Recorder's office in and for the County of Alameda, on March 21, A. D. 1859, in Liber H of Deeds, page **717,** and also in a certain other deed bearing **date** August 10, **A. D.** 1864, made and executed by the said **Orrin** Simmons and Hannah his wife, to the party of the first part herein, and recorded in the County Recorder's office aforesaid, on August 19, A. D. 1864, in Liber P of Deeds, page 687, to both of which said deeds, for greater certainty, reference is hereby made, together with all right, title, and interest, possession, claim, and demand, conveyed to the party of the first part herein by the said last above mentioned deed from the said Orrin Simmons and Hannah his wife, of, in, and to all that certain portion of the undivided mountain lands herein above referred to, which had been included and inclosed within a fence by the said Simmons, and was in the possession of and occupied by the said Simmons at the date of the execution and delivery by himself and wife of the said deed last above mentioned, and since then continuously has been and now is in the actual, notorious, and exclusive possession of and occupied by the party of the first part herein.

Fifth—All that certain other piece or parcel of land situate, lying, and being in the City of Oakland, County of Alameda, aforesaid, bounded and described as follows: On the north, by Thirteenth Street; on the east, by Webster Street; on the south, by Twelfth Street, and on the west by Franklin Street, being block number one hundred and seventy-three (173) as designated and numbered on a certain map of the said City of Oakland, made by the said Julius Kellersberger, and on file in the County Recorder's office in and for the County of Alameda, aforesaid; together with all and singular the tenements, hereditaments, and appurtenances thereunto belonging or in anywise appertaining, and the reversion and reversions, remainder and remainders, rents, issues, and profits thereof; and, also, all the estate, right, title, interest, property, possession, claim, and demand whatsoever, as well in law as in equity, of the party of the first part, of, in, and to the above described lands and premises, and every part and parcel thereof, with the appurtenances.

To have and to hold, all and singular, the above mentioned and described lands and premises, together with the appurtenances, unto the party of the second part and to its successors and assigns forever; in trust, however, for the several interests and purposes following, that is to say: In trust to sell, mortgage, or dispose of the said lands and premises, or any part thereof, at such time or times, and at such price or prices, and on such terms as it, the party of the second part, shall deem best, and to give good and valid title to the purchaser or purchasers thereof, without requiring the said purchaser or purchasers to look to the application of the purchase money paid or to be paid therefor, and out of the proceeds thereof to retain and repay the advances made or to be made by the party of the second part in the payment of the indebtedness mentioned in the resolution herein above set forth, and the balance of said proceeds to use, bestow, invest, and reinvest for its, the party of the second part, own use and purposes, and until such sale, mortgage, or disposition of said lands and premises to take, receive, hold, and in all respects manage the same.

[Duly executed and recorded, Liber 55 Deeds, p. 227, Alameda County **Records.**]

CHAPTER III.

College of California to the Regents.

ARTICLE 225.

This indenture, made this sixteenth day of October, in the year eighteen hundred and seventy-one, between the President and Board of Trustees of the College of California, a corporation created under the laws of California, party of the first part, and the Regents of the University of California, a corporation created by the laws of California, party of the second part, witnesseth: That, whereas, the said party of the first part, heretofore executed and delivered a certain deed of gift to the said party of the second part, bearing date the first day of June, in the year eighteen hundred and seventy, of certain real estate, upon certain considerations and trusts expressed in the said deed of gift, reference being had to the said deed of gift, for the full particulars thereof; and whereas, it was intended by the said party of the first part to embrace in the said deed of gift, and thereby convey to the said party of the second part, the real estate hereinafter described, but apprehensions are entertained that said intention has failed to be executed, because the title to such real estate was not, at the time of the execution and delivery of the said deed of gift, vested in the said party of the first part, and moreover, such real estate is in said deed of gift imperfectly and insufficiently described; now, therefore, in consideration of the premises, and particularly of the matters set forth in the said deed of gift, the said party of the first part doth by these presents donate, grant, transfer, and convey unto the party of the second part, its successors and assigns forever, all that certain piece and parcel of land situated in the City of Oakland, County of Alameda, and State of California, being the southwestern quarter of the College Block, so called, as laid down on Wartcher's official map of said city, and more particularly described as follows: beginning at a point forming the southwest corner of block one hundred and seventy-three, as laid down on Kellersberger's map of said city, and being, also, the northeast corner of Twelfth and Franklin Streets; thence running northerly along the line of Franklin Street two hundred and forty feet to a point where it would be intersected by the center line of Thirteenth Street if produced; thence easterly along said center line produced three hundred and forty feet to a point where the same would be intersected by the center line of Webster Street if produced; thence southerly along said last mentioned center line produced two hundred and forty feet to the north line of Twelfth Street; thence westerly along the north line of Twelfth Street three hundred and forty feet to the place of beginning; in trust, however, for the uses and purposes specified in the said deed of gift, together with all and singular the tenements, hereditaments, and appurtenances thereunto belonging, or in anywise appertaining, and the reversion and reversions, remainder and remainders, rents, issues, and profits thereof. And also all the estate, right, title, interest, property, possession, claim, and demand whatsoever, as well in law as at equity, of the said party of the first part, of, in, or to the above described premises, and every part and parcel thereof, with the appurtenances.

To have and to hold all and singular the above mentioned and described premises, together with the appurtenances, unto the said party of the second part, its successors and assigns, forever, in trust, however, for the uses and purposes and subject to the conditions and limitations set forth in the said deed of gift, and to none other or different.

In witness whereof, the said party of the first part has hereunto set its corporate seal, and has caused these presents to be signed by its President and Secretary in its behalf, on the day and year first above written, pursuant to a resolution of its Board of Trustees duly passed on that day and year.

The word "insufficiently" being written over an erasure in the phrase "deed of gift imperfectly and insufficiently described."

But nothing herein contained shall be held or construed to impose any liability upon the said party of the first part, or to give rise to any cause or causes of action against them, of any nature, either at law or in equity.

[Duly executed.]

CHAPTER IV.

College of California to the State.

ARTICLE 226.

This indenture, made the twenty-seventh day of November, in the year of our Lord one thousand eight hundred and sixty-nine, between the President and Board of Trustees of the College of California, a corporation duly formed and existing under the laws of the State of California, the party of the first part, and the State of California, represented by the Regents of the University of California, a corporation duly formed and existing under the laws of said State, the party of the second part, witnesseth: That the said party of the first part, for and in consideration of the sum of one dollar, lawful money of the United States of America, to it in hand paid by the said party of the second part, at or before the ensealing and delivery of these presents, the receipt whereof is hereby acknowledged, hath granted, bargained, and sold, and by these presents doth grant, bargain, and sell unto the said party of the second part, and to its successors and assigns forever, all the right, title, and interest of the said party of the first part of, in, and to all that certain tract, piece, or parcel of land situated, lying, and being in Oakland Township, in the County of Alameda, and State of California, bounded and described as follows, viz.: beginning at the corner common to plats numbers 69 (sixty-nine), 70 (seventy), 79 (seventy-nine), and 81 (eighty-one) of the ranchos of Domingo and Vicente Peralta, as the same are laid down and designated on the map of said ranchos made by Julius Kellersberger, and on file or of record in the County Recorder's office of said county, running thence south 5° 7' (five degrees seven minutes), east along the dividing line between said plats 69 (sixty-nine) and 70 (seventy) nine chains and ninety-two links (9.92) to a point, thence south 80° 30' (eighty degrees thirty minutes) west ten chains and thirteen links (10.13) to a point, thence north 5° 07' (five degrees seven minutes) west nine chains and ninety-two links (9.92) to a point in the dividing line between plats 69 (sixty-nine) and 79 (seventy-nine), thence along said last mentioned line north 80° 30' (eighty degrees thirty minutes) east ten chains and thirteen links (10.13) to the point of beginning: containing ten acres of land and being a portion of said plat number 69 (sixty-nine). Together with all and singular the tenements, hereditaments, and appurtenances thereunto belonging, or in anywise appertaining, and the reversion and reversions, remainder and remainders, rents, issues, and profits thereof; and, also, all the estate, right, title, interest, property possession, claim, and demand whatsoever, as well in law as in equity, of the said party of the first part, of, in, or to the above described premises, and every part and parcel thereof, with the appurtenances.

To have and to hold all and singular the above mentioned and described premises, together with the appurtenances, unto the said party of the second part, its successors and assigns forever.

[Duly executed and recorded December 3, 1869, in Liber 48 of Deeds, p. 441, Alameda County Records.]

CHAPTER V.

College of California to the State.

ARTICLE 227.

This indenture, made the twenty-sixth day of November, A. D. 1869, between the President and Board of Trustees of the College of California, a corporation organized and existing under the laws of the State of California, the party of the first part, and the State of California represented by the Regents of the University of California, a corporation duly formed and existing under the laws of said State, the party of the second part, witnesseth: That the said party of the first part, for and in consideration of the sum of twenty-four thousand six hundred dollars, lawful money to it in hand paid by the said party of the second part, at or before the ensealing and delivery of these presents, the receipt whereof is hereby acknowledged, hath granted, bargained, and sold, conveyed and confirmed, and by these presents doth grant, bargain, and sell, convey and confirm unto the said party of the second part, its successors and assigns forever, all those certain tracts, pieces, or parcels of land situate, lying, and being in the Township of Oakland, County of Alameda, and State of California, bounded and particularly described as follows:

First—Beginning at a point in the easterly line of plat number 69 (sixty-nine) of the ranchos of Vicente and Domingo Peralta, as said plat is laid down and designated on the map of said ranchos made by Julius Kellersberger, on file or of record in the County Recorder's office of Alameda County, distant south 5° 07' (five degrees seven minutes) east nine (9) chains and ninety-two (92) links from the northerly line of said plat number 69 (sixty-nine); thence north 80° 30' (eighty degrees thirty minutes) east seven (7) chains and fifty (50) links, more or less, to a point in the center of the southern branch of Strawberry Creek; thence down said branch of said creek in a northwesterly direction, following the center line thereof, to a point on the same where it is intersected by the said easterly line of said plat number 69 (sixty-nine); thence along said last mentioned line south 5° 07' (five degrees seven minutes) east seven (7) chains, more or less, to the place of beginning. Being a portion of plat number 70 (seventy) on said map.

Second—Commencing at a point in the dividing line between plats number 79 (seventy-nine) and 81 (eighty-one) on said map where the same is intersected by a line drawn through the center of the northern branch of said Strawberry Creek, thence in a southwesterly direction following the center of said northern branch of Strawberry Creek to a point where the same is intersected by the dividing line between plats

number 69 (sixty-nine) and 79 (seventy-nine) on said map,
running thence westerly along said last mentioned line to a
point therein distant thereon ten (10) chains and thirteen
(13) links westerly from the corner common to plats 69
(sixty-nine), 70 (seventy), 79 (seventy-nine), and 81 (eighty-
one) on said map, thence north 5° 7' (five degrees seven minutes) west fifteen (15) chains, to a stake, thence north 80° 30'
(eighty degrees thirty minutes) east to a point in the center
of the said north branch of Strawberry Creek, thence in a
southwesterly direction along and following the center line
of said north branch of Strawberry Creek to the place of
beginning. Being portions of plats numbers 79 (seventy-
nine) and 81 (eighty-one) on said map.

Said two tracts of land containing together thirty-one acres
and seventy-three hundredths of an acre of land; together
with all and singular the tenements, hereditaments, and
appurtenances thereunto belonging or in anywise appertaining, and the reversion and reversions, remainder and remainders, rents, issues, and profits thereof; and also all the estate,
right, title, and interest, property, possession, claim, and
demand whatsoever, as well in law as in equity, of the said
party of the first part of, in, or to the above described and
hereby granted and released premises, and every part and
parcel thereof, with the appurtenances.

To have and to hold all and singular the above mentioned
and described premises, together with the appurtenances,
unto the said party of the second part, its successors and
assigns forever.

[Duly executed and recorded in Liber 48 of Deeds, pp. 435-36-37, of the Alameda
County Records.]

CHAPTER VI.

Acceptance of donations from the **College of California.**

ARTICLE 228.

Resolved, That the Board of Regents take this occasion to
repeat the expression of their profound appreciation of the
far-seeing public spirit, devotion to learning, and the good
of the commonwealth manifested by the Trustees of the
College of California in the resolutions passed by their Board,
August, eighteen hundred and sixty-seven, to wit: "*Resolved,*
That the President and Board of Trustees of the College of
California hereby offer to donate and convey to the State
Board of Directors of the Agricultural, Mining, and Mechan-
ical Arts College one hundred and sixty acres of land in the
Township of Oakland, Alameda County, including the lands
between the two ravines, commonly known as the California

College Site, for the site and farm of the said State College.
Resolved, That in making this donation the College of California is influenced by the earnest hope and confident expectation that the State of California will forthwith organize and put into operation upon this site a University of California, which shall include a College of Mines, a College of Civil Engineering, a College of Mechanics, and College of Agriculture, and an Academical College, all of the same grade, and with courses of instruction equal to those of eastern colleges.
Resolved, That the President and Secretary of this Board be authorized to enter into a contract with the State Board of Directors of the Agricultural, Mining, and Mechanical Arts College to the effect that whenever a University of California shall be established as contemplated in the next preceding resolution, then the College of California will disincorporate, and, after discharging all its debts, pay over its net assets to said University;" and that we recognize in these resolutions the incipient germ of the State University.

Resolved, That in view of the important trusts prospectively confided to us by these resolutions, we do hereby signify to the Trustees of the College of California our sense of responsibility, and our purpose and intent to preserve, cherish, and carry forward to posterity these trusts in the same enlightened spirit in which they are confided to us.

Resolved, That for the purpose of simplifying our relations, and for the greater facility in the management of our affairs, we do hereby express to the Trustees of the College of California our readiness now to conclude the transaction by which their institution and its effects are to be transferred to the University.

Resolved, That the Regents will in case of these conclusive acts, carry forward without interruption, as classes in the University those now in the College of California, and such as may join them, in the buildings of the College of California until this Board shall be ready to receive those classes and students in the contemplated University buildings at Berkeley.

Resolved, That if the Trustees of the College of California are pleased to accept the proposal and stipulations made in these resolutions, we do hereby request them to signify the same to this Board, and to communicate their wishes concerning time, place, and occasion for that important transaction.

[Minutes, vol. 1, pp. 75, 76, 77, April 5, 1869.]

CHAPTER VII.

Hillegass and Wife to the College of California.

ARTICLE 229.

This indenture, made the fourth (4th) day of September, A. D. 1860, between William Hillegass and Eugenie Hillegass, wife of the said William, both of Oakland, in the County of Alameda and State of California, parties of the first part, and the President and Board of Trustees of the College of California, of the second part, witnesseth: That the said parties of the first part, for and in consideration of the sum of two thousand dollars, lawful money of the United States of America, to them in hand paid by the parties of the second part, the receipt whereof is hereby acknowledged; also, for and in consideration of the agreement made by the parties of the second part to erect, build, and maintain the College of California upon the ground hereby conveyed, or upon the college grounds contiguous thereto; also, for and in consideration of the agreement on the part of the parties of the second part to furnish to the parties of the first part, the amount of three hundred gallons per day of the water of the creek now running through the lands conveyed, provided the said creek be taken and used for college purposes, have remised, released, and quitclaimed, and by these presents do remise, release, and quitclaim, and by these presents do remise, release, and quitclaim unto the parties of the second part, all that certain tract, piece, or parcel of land situated in said Oakland Township and described as follows, to wit: Beginning at the point forming the southeast corner of the tract of land designated as plot number eighty-one (81) upon Julius Kellersberger's map of subdivisions of that part of the Rancho of San Antonio heretofore claimed by Domingo and Vincente Peralta; thence running south eighty and one half (80½) degrees west twenty and twenty-six hundredths (20.26) chains, to the point forming the northwesterly corner of plot number seventy-one (71); thence along the westerly line of said plot number seventy-one (71) south five and one half degrees (5½) east eleven and seventy-four hundredths (11.74) chains, to the point forming the northwesterly corner of the orchard of the parties of the first part; thence north sixty-eight and three fourths (68¾) degrees east three and thirteen hundredths (3.13) chains, to a point marked by a stake; thence north sixty-two (62) degrees east seventeen and eighty hundredths (17.80) chains, to a point on the westerly line of plat number eighty (80), thence along said westerly line of plat number eighty north five and one half (5½) degrees west five and fifty-six hundredths (5.56) chains, to the point of beginning, being a part of the plat designated upon said map as number seventy-one (71), and containing seventeen and thirteen hundredths (17.13) acres of land. Together with all and singular the tenements, hereditaments, and appurtenances thereto belonging, and the rents, issues, and profits thereof. It being understood that the trees bordering upon the creek on said premises are not to be cut down, destroyed, or in any way impaired, except for the purposes of building, and for roads or paths, or for the adornment and greater beauty of the land belonging to the parties of the second part: and it is agreed and understood that if the parties of the second part should fail to erect the contemplated College of California upon said premises, or upon the college grounds contiguous thereto, or if at any time after the same has been erected on said grounds, said college should be removed, or it should cease actual operation as a college, then this conveyance shall be void, and said land shall be redeeded to the parties of the first part or his heirs or assigns, on the payment to the parties of the second part the sum of two thousand dollars, and that the parties of the first part shall have six months after said abandonment to pay said sum of two thousand ($2,000). And it is further understood that the party of the first part reserves the right to take three hundred gallons of water per day from the creek running through the grounds hereby conveyed, and if the parties of the second part should turn the course of said creek and should not furnish to the party of the first part said amount of three hundred gallons per day, then the party of the second part shall dig and brick up a good and sufficient well for the party of the first part on that part of the ranch of the party of the first part to be by said party of the first part designated.

In witness whereof, the said parties of the first part hereunto set their hands and seals first above written the day and year.

WM. HILLEGASS,   [SEAL.]
EUGENIE HILLEGASS. [SEAL.]

[Recorded Liber T, pp. 189, 190, 191, Records of Alameda County.]

CHAPTER VIII.

Hillegass to the College of California.

ARTICLE 230.

This indenture, made the nineteenth day of February, A. D. 1868, between William Hillegass, of the County of Alameda, of the first part, and the President and Board of Trustees of the College of California of the second part, witnesseth: That

8

the said party of the first part, for and in consideration of the sum of one dollar, lawful money, to him in hand paid by the party of the second part, and the undertaking of the party of the second part to locate, or cause to be located, on the lands hereby conveyed, or on lands now or late of the party of the second part contiguous thereto, a State University, or State College, or College of California, hath granted, bargained, and sold, and by these presents doth grant, bargain, sell, and convey unto the said party of the second part all that certain piece or parcel of land situate, lying, and being in Alameda County, State of California, in Oakland Township, beginning at the southeast corner of plat No. 81, as the same is shown on map hereinafter mentioned, running thence south 81° 30′ west along the southerly line of said plat twenty chains and twenty-six links (20.26), to the northwesterly corner of plat No. 71; thence along the westerly line of said plat No. 71 south 5° 30′ east eleven chains and seventy-four links (11.74), to the point forming the northwesterly corner of the orchard of the party of the first part; thence north 68° 45′ east three chains and thirteen links (3.13), to a point marked by a stake; thence north 62° east seventeen chains and eighty links (17.80), to a point in the westerly line of plat No. 80; thence along said westerly line north 5° 30′ west to the point of beginning, being part of the plat designated on Julius Kellersberger's map of subdivision of the ranchos of Domingo and Vicente Peralta, by the number 71 (seventy-one), and containing seventeen and thirteen one hundredths acres of land, for the uses and purposes of the said university or college, subject to the conditions and agreements contained in a deed from the party of the first part and his wife to the said party of the second part, dated September 4, 1860, and recorded in said county in Liber T of Deeds, page 189, etc., except the condition to establish on or near said lands the College of California.

To have and to hold the same to said party of the second part, its successors or assigns, so long as the same shall continue to be used for the purposes of a college.

This conveyance is made subject to the condition that said land shall be used for the purpose of a university or college only and be a part of the grounds of such university or college, and that the alienation thereof by the college corporation to which said lands may be conveyed by the party of the second part, or the removal of the college or university which it is intended to establish on or near said lands to some other locality and the subjection of said lands to other uses than to the uses and purposes of college grounds, shall work a forfeiture of the estate hereby granted, and that the said land shall thereupon become again the property of the party of the first part, his heirs and assigns, and he shall have the same estate therein which he would have had if this conveyance had not been made.

In witness thereof the party of the first part hath hereunto set his hand and seal the day and year first above written.

[Duly executed. Recorded in Liber 43 of Deeds, p. 108, Records of Alameda County.]

CHAPTER IX.

Blake to the University of California.

ARTICLE 231.

Articles of agreement made and entered into the twenty-eighth of August, A. D. 1869, between George M. Blake, of Oakland, Alameda County, State of California, of the first part, and the Regents of the University of California, a corporation duly formed and existing under the laws of said State, of the second part. Whereas, heretofore the President and Board of Trustees of the College of California donated to the State of California, for the uses of a State University, a certain tract of land in the Township of Oakland, in the County of Alameda, in said State, particularly described in the deed of conveyance thereof to said State, of record in the Recorder's office of said county; and whereas, the State of California, represented by the said party of the second part, hath undertaken to locate upon said donated land, establish, and maintain a State University, embracing the several colleges described in section two of an Act of the Legislature of said State, entitled "An Act to create and organize the University of California," approved March 23, 1868; and whereas, the said party of the first part is the owner of that certain tract of land in said township, county, and State hereinafter particularly described, adjoining said first mentioned tract on the westerly and southwesterly sides thereof; and whereas, the said mentioned tract of land hereinafter described is necessary to be had by the said State, represented by said party of the second part, for the uses of said State University; and whereas, the said party of the first part is desirous of fostering and encouraging the establishment and maintenance of a State University upon said lands, in which shall be merged and included the Mining and Agricultural Colleges heretofore existing in said county, and the objects of instruction of which said colleges shall be taught in said university as branches of the courses of instruction thereof; and has, at the request of the party of the second part, agreed that if the said State of California shall establish, erect, and maintain a State University, embracing the said Mining and Agricultural Colleges, on the lands so donated to the State by the said President and Board of

Trustees of the College of California, within the period of three years from the date of these presents, that he will, on request, donate to the said party of the second part, and to the State of California, represented by said party of the second part, for the uses of said university, the said tract of land hereinabove mentioned and hereinafter described, and will convey the same to said party of the second part, and to said State, for the uses of said university, upon the conditions hereinafter expressed. Now this agreement witnesseth, that the said party of the first part, for and in consideration of the premises, and of the sum of one dollar, lawful money of the United States, to him in hand paid by the said party of the second part, the receipt whereof is hereby acknowledged, hath undertaken and agreed, and doth hereby covenant and agree, to and with the said party of the second part, that if the said State of California shall establish, erect, and maintain a State University, embracing the said Mining and Agricultural Colleges, on the said lands so donated to said State as aforesaid, within the period of two years from the date of these presents, he will, and his heirs, executors, administrators, and assigns shall, on request of said party of the second part, convey, free of incumbrance by him or them made, done, created, or suffered, and execute, acknowledge, and deliver to the said party of the second part, and to the State of California, represented by said party of the second part, for the use of said university, a good and sufficient conveyance of all that certain tract, piece, or parcel of land situate, lying, and being in Oakland Township, Alameda County, and State of California, bounded and described as follows, viz.: Beginning at a point forming the southwesterly corner of the tract of land designated as plot eighty-one (81), upon Julius Kellersberger's map of subdivision of that part of the rancho of San Antonio heretofore claimed by Domingo and Vicente Peralta; thence running south five and one half (5½) degrees east, and nine and ninety-two hundredths (9.92) chains, to a point marked by a stake upon the dividing line between the plots marked upon said map as numbers sixty-nine (69) and seventy (70), thence south eighty and one half (80½) degrees west ten and thirteen one hundredths (10.13) chains, to a point marked by a stake; thence north five and one half (5½) degrees west nine and ninety-two (9.92) chains, to a point on the dividing line between said plot number sixty-nine (69) and plot number seventy-nine (79); thence along said last mentioned dividing line north eighty and one half (80½) degrees east ten and thirteen hundredths (10.13) chains, to the point of beginning, being part of said plot sixty-nine (69), and containing ten (10) acres of land, with the tenements, hereditaments, and appurtenances thereunto belonging or in anywise appertaining. But such conveyance shall be subject to the following conditions, viz.:

First—That the said above described tract of land shall during all coming time be used *only* for the purposes of the said State University;

Second—That said above described tract of land shall not at any time be sold or in any way encumbered;

Third—That the said California College grounds on which it is proposed to locate the said State University shall be used for no other purpose, and shall not be sold or transferred to any other person or body corporate;

Fourth—That whenever said State University shall be removed from said California College grounds, or sold, or transferred to any other person or body corporate, or shall cease as a State University, then the above described lands shall revert to the said George M. Blake, his heirs and assigns. The said party of the first part expressly reserves to himself the exclusive use and occupation of the said ten acres of land above described, without let or hindrance, until the necessary buildings are erected for, and the State University shall be actually established and in active operation on said college grounds.

In witness whereof the said party of the first part hath hereunto set his hand and seal, and the said party of the second part hath caused these presents to be subscribed by its President and Secretary, and its corporate seal to be hereunto affixed, the day and year first above written.

Signed, sealed, and delivered in the presence of J. Temple as to signature of H. H. Haight.

H. H. HAIGHT,
President Board Regents.

ANDREW J. MOULDER,
Secretary Board Regents.

Seventh—That no person, or body corporate, shall either directly or indirectly receive any money or other consideration (except myself) for the said ten acres, or any part thereof, or for the procuring of this donation, or for any conveyance from me of the said land.

Witness my hand and seal this eighth day of November, 1869.

GEORGE M. BLAKE.

[Recorded Liber 48, p. 425, Records of Alameda County.]

ARTICLE 232.

SAN FRANCISCO, April 1, 1873.

To the President and Board of Regents of the University of the State of California:

GENTLEMEN: I take pleasure in presenting to you a deed to ten acres of land for the use and benefit of the State University. This tract of land is adjoining to and ought to be a part of the University site, and believing that this land will be a great convenience, and as I hope, a lasting benefit to the University, I freely offer the same to you as its representatives.

Trusting that you will accept this offering, made in behalf of the educational interest of this State.

I remain yours,

GEO. M. BLAKE.

ARTICLE 233.

I, George M. Blake, of Oakland, Alameda County, State of California, in performance of the terms on my part of a certain agreement, made and entered into by me with the Regents of the University of California, dated August 28, 1869, and recorded in the County Recorder's office of Alameda County, December 3, 1869, in Liber No. 48 of Deeds, at pages 425, etc., do hereby grant to the Regents of the University of California, a corporation duly formed and existing under the laws of the State of California, all that real property situated in Oakland Township, Alameda County, and State of California, bounded and described as the same is particularly bounded and described in the said agreement, and being part of plot number (sixty-nine) 69, as shown on Julius Kellersberger's map of subdivision of Vicente and Domingo Peralta's portion of the Rancho San Antonio, said portion of said plot containing ten acres. This grant is made upon and subject to all the conditions expressed in the said foregoing agreement; except, that I hereby agree that the said grantee has become entitled to this conveyance, and to the use and occupation of the said tract of land, by the terms of said agreement.

In witness whereof, I have hereunto set my hand and seal this first day of April, in the year one thousand eight hundred and seventy-three.

GEO. M. BLAKE.

Sealed and delivered in the presence of—

T. I. THIBAULT.

[Duly executed and recorded, Liber 89 of Deeds, page 353, Records of Alameda County.]

ARTICLE 234.

Resolved, That the acknowledgments of this Board are hereby tendered to Geo. M. Blake, Esq., of Oakland, for his most acceptable donation made this day to the University of California, of a tract of ten acres of land adjacent to the University site at Berkeley, and that he be informed that the Board accepts this tract with a high appreciation of the generosity of the donor in thus contributing to the welfare of the University.

CHAPTER X.

The University Medal Fund.

ARTICLE 235.

We, the undersigned, desirous of furnishing a stimulus for the development of the best talent in the University, hereby agree to subscribe fifty dollars ($50) each to a fund to be invested, and the proceeds annually applied to the purchase of a gold medal, of suitable design, to be awarded to the most distinguished graduate of each year. April, eighteen hundred and seventy-one.

H. H. Haight, S. F. Butterworth, Andrew J. Moulder, Henry Durant, Wm. C. Ralston, Wm. Watt, J. Mora Moss, Edward Tompkins, John W. Dwinelle, F L. A. Pioche, A. A. Cohen, D. O. Mills, Barron & Co., P. H Canavan, Haggin & Tevis, Richard P. Hammond, A. S. Hallidie, H. M. Newhall, Wm. Norris, A. Hayward, Charles Mayne, Wm. Alvord, Edmond L. Goold, L. L. Robinson, John S. Hager, H. A. Lyons, Wm. Burling, John Benson, Lafayette Maynard, E. L. Sullivan, J. Friedlander, Louis Sachs, Wm. A. Woodward, John B. Felton, Samuel Merritt, S. B. McKee, Thomas Findley, Wm. Sharon, Wm. M. Lent.

NOTE.—The entire sum now amounts to $2,925 ,77.

CHAPTER XI.

Tompkins' Endowment.

ARTICLE 236.

To the Regents of the University of California:

The business between California and Asia is already very great. Its future is beyond any estimate that the most sanguine would now dare to make. The child is now born that will see the commerce of the Pacific greater than that of the Atlantic. It is carried on with people of whose language we are wholly ignorant, and in all the vast transactions that it involves, we are dependent upon native interpreters, whose integrity will not become more reliable as the magnitude of their temptations shall increase. It is therefore of the utmost consequence for California that the means shall be provided to instruct our young men, preparing for lives of business activity, in the languages and literature of Eastern Asia. It is the duty of the University to supply this want. It can only be done by a well organized department of Oriental languages and literature, and every day that it is delayed is an injury to the State. Fully believing that it is to become not only an important but a leading department of the new education that our peculiar circumstances demand, I have hoped that it might be my privilege to endow the first professorship specially devoted to it. The wish has not brought with it the necessary means and the money for the purpose is not within my control, but I have property that I can spare without wrong to any claim upon me, and rather than longer postpone an object that I deem so important, I venture to make you the following proposition:

I have prepared, and now offer for your acceptance, a deed of about forty-seven acres of land, with good title and free from incumbrance, at the junction of Broadway and University Avenue, Oakland, upon the following terms and conditions:

You shall forthwith establish, and as soon as practicable, fill a professorship of Oriental Languages and Literature in the University of California, with the same salary as the other regular professorships.

You shall take possession of the land conveyed by me, and sell the same as rapidly as it can be done judiciously, until you shall have sold the whole, or enough thereof to produce the sum of fifty thousand dollars in gold coin. All the money so realized shall be set apart as an Endowment Fund for said professorship. It shall never be mixed with other funds of the University, or loaned in whole or in part to any other fund, or to the University itself, in any manner or on any pretext whatsoever. It shall be kept invested in mortgage securities upon unincumbered productive real estate within the limits of the present County of Alameda. If the income shall exceed the salary of the professor, the surplus shall be added to the principal, to provide as far as possible for the time when the rates of interest will be lower than they now are.

My consent in writing, or that of my legal representatives, if I shall not be living, shall be necessary to any sale of said land, or any part thereof, within five years from this date: after that time no such consent shall be necessary to any sale or sales not exceeding in the aggregate the said sum of fifty thousand dollars.

Whenever said sum of fifty thousand dollars shall have been realized from said land, either in money or in obligations or securities, and there shall remain any surplus, either of land or money or securities, such excess shall be conveyed or paid to me, my legal representatives or assigns, it being my intention to give for the endowment of said professorship the sum of fifty thousand dollars, if said land shall produce that sum, and no more.

The salary of said professor, until the same can be paid from the income of said endowment fund, and all expenses of the execution of this trust or of the investment or reinvestment of the fund, shall be paid by the Regents, and no money thus paid, whether for salary or expenses, shall be deducted from said fund, or the subsequent income thereof, it being the intention hereof that neither said fund or the current income thereof shall ever be diminished by any claim for advances made on its account, on any pretext whatsoever. If said professorship shall not be kept up, or the conditions hereinbefore stated shall not be complied with, said land, or so much thereof as has not been sold, and the proceeds of all that has been sold, shall forthwith revert to me, my heirs or assigns, and shall be conveyed or payed over by said Regents without delay.

As a recognition of the debt of humanity to the great and good man now honoring our State with his presence, the said professorship shall be known as the "Agassiz Professorship of Oriental Languages and Literature."

As the department thus organized will at first not be fully employed, I hope that it may also be utilized for the education of such young men as may come here for that purpose from Asia, upon such terms and under such restrictions as the Regents may prescribe. As a lover of California, I feel deeply the humiliation of seeing them pass by us in almost daily procession to the other side of the continent, in search of that "intellectual hospitality" that we are not yet enlightened enough to extend to them, and yet more that I cannot impose this as a condition of this trust without danger of injury to the great interests that I most earnestly desire to promote.

I repeat the expression of my regret that it is not in my power to simplify this trust by the direct payment of the necessary money. Desiring to place it beyond contingency by completing it during my own life, and to make such return as I am able for the kindness and prosperity by which I have been blessed in California, I have decided to postpone it no longer, but of such as I have, of that freely to give. I humbly pray that in the coming time the Agassiz Professor-

ship may be an instrument of great good to those for whose
benefit it is designed.

OAKLAND, September 18, 1872.

EDWARD TOMPKINS.

ARTICLE 237.

This indenture, made the eighteenth day of September,
A. D. one thousand eight hundred and seventy-two, between
Edward Tompkins, of Oakland, Alameda County, California,
party of the first part, and "The Regents of the University
of California," party of the second part, witnesseth: That the
said party of the first part, for and in consideration of the
sum of one dollar, lawful money of the United States of
America, to him in hand paid by the said party of the second
part, at or before the ensealing and delivery of these presents,
the receipt whereof is hereby acknowledged, has granted,
bargained, sold, conveyed, and confirmed, and by these
presents does grant, bargain, sell, convey, and confirm unto
the said party of the second part, and to its successors and
assigns forever, all that certain piece or parcel of land lying
upon both sides of Broadway, in Oakland, bounded northerly by the Peralta Reservation, so called, easterly by lands
of Flint and Magher, southerly by the old road leading
from Oakland to Hayes Valley, and westerly by University Avenue, containing about forty-seven acres of land,
more or less, being the same premises formerly owned and
occupied by Richard Comerford, and known as the "Comerford Ranch." This conveyance is made subject to the right
of E. M. Birdsall to remove the buildings occupied by him,
to all the rights of the public to the use of Broadway and
University Avenue, and to certain conditions this day agreed
upon between the parties hereto, and that are expressed in
the minutes of the proceedings of the meeting of the said
Board of Regents, held this day, together with all and singular the tenements, hereditaments, and appurtenances
thereunto belonging, or in anywise appertaining, and the
reversion and reversions, remainder and remainders, rents,
issues, and profits thereof; and also, all the estate, right,
title, interest, property, possession, claim, and demand whatsoever, as well in law as in equity, of the said party of the
first part, of, in, or to the above described premises, and
every part or parcel thereof, with the appurtenances.

To have and to hold, all and singular, the above mentioned
and described premises, together with the appurtenances,
unto the said party of the second part, its successors and
assigns forever.

In witness whereof, the said party of the first part has

hereunto set his hand and seal the day and year first above written.

Signed, sealed, and delivered in the presence of—

EDWARD TOMPKINS.

[Duly executed and recorded in Liber 85 of Deeds, p. 313, Records of Alameda County.]

ARTICLE 238.

Resolved, That the Regents accept the conveyance of land in Oakland, this day made to them by Edward Tompkins, upon the terms and conditions in the communication from said Edward Tompkins, accompanying said deed, expressed, and that as evidence of such acceptance, the Secretary deliver to said Edward Tompkins a copy of such conditions, and of this resolution duly certified, and that he affix the corporate seal thereto.

CHAPTER XII.

The will of F. L. A. Pioche.

ARTICLE 239.

I give and bequeath to the University of California, known by the name of "Board of Regents of University," an establishment situate and about to be founded in the County of Contra Costa, State of California, all the paintings, sketches, engravings, drawings, and objects of art belonging to me, and which at the time of my death will be found (at the time of my death) at my house in San Francisco, at New Almaden, or elsewhere in the State of California. I also give and bequeath to said University all the books and various works, composing my library at San Francisco, and at New Almaden, as also everything that constitutes my mineralogical, geological, and conchological collection in San Francisco, State of California.

These collections are partially classed, and a catalogue is partially made. I desire that they should be placed in a special portion of the buildings erected or to be erected for the said University, and that the room or place reserved for them be open to the public freely, and at fixed and frequent periods, as is the case with the museums in Europe, so that students and patrons of the arts and sciences may there instruct themselves and increase the sphere of their studies and their knowledge of facts that may be of use to hasten the progress and development of this country. In order the better to facilitate the execution of this wish of mine, I make a donation of five thousand dollars, which will be paid by my testamentary executors to the Treasurer of the said University, in gold coin of the United States, and placed at the disposal of the Regents and Trustees, to cover the first cost for arranging and preserving them—the objects composing the bequest and present made by me to the University of California.

If, in opposition to my wish, and all that I am allowed to suppose, the Regents and Trustees of the University were to refuse to accept and preserve, in whole or in part, the divers objects, and principally certain objects of art, books, or paintings, in my collections, I request my testamentary executors to take them back and send them to France, and so hold them at the disposal of my brother, Leopold Pioche, whose name, surname, and residence are already mentioned. (Article 17 in this testament.)

[Will admitted to probate San Francisco, **June, 1872.**]

Article 240.

Pioche Collection—Paintings.

1. St. Martin.   French school, by **Arnout Picornet, 1387.**
2. Adoration by the Kings.   German **school.**
    Landscape by P. J. Glauber.
    Figures by G. Lairesse, 1646.
3. Portrait of a lady of the court of Louis XIII, represented by the artist in the character of Judith having killed Holofernes.   French school, 1630.
4. Scene in the Market.   Flemish school, 1610.
5. Daphnis and Chloe.   Italian school, by Antonio **Allegri,** called Corregio, 1494.
6. A Ride on the Beach.   **Dutch school,** miniature painted on wood.
7. Ascension of the **Virgin.**   Spanish school, painted on copper, **1650.**
8. A Concert.   **French school, time of** Henry IV, 1600.
9. The Walking **of the Queen.**   French school, by François Besson, 1850.
10. Group of Quails and Pistols.   **French school,** San Francisco, by Sidonie Petetin, 1861.
11. Portrait.   Pastel painting, French **school, time of Louis** XV.
12. Fortune of **War.**   Italian school, Francis Albani, 1578.
13. Flowers.   French school, San Francisco, Sidonie Petetin, 1861.

14. Cupids on the Playground. French school, by J. Vander Star, called Stella, 1596.
15. Scene in a Village. French school, by Faustin Besson, 1850.
16. Visions of St. Francis Xavier. German school, by J. W. Bumgartner, 1712.
17. Head of Christ. Russian school. Enamel (taken from a church at Sebastopol during the Crimean War), by E. R. Megerditsch, 1470.
18. Christ in the Grotto. German school, by J. W. Bumgartner, 1712.
19. Relics. Russian school. Oil painting, ornamented and covered up by silver chiselings, by C. F. F. Ivanowitch, 1765.
20. Travel through Egypt. Flemish school, by Paul Bril, 1556.
21. Portrait of Mary Stuart, Queen of Scotland. English school. Miniature on ivory, painted from life, by the portrait painter of Queen Elizabeth, Nicholas Hilliart, 1577.
22. Bathers. French school, by François Boucher, 1704.
23. Relics. Russian school. Oil painting, ornamented and covered up by silver chiselings, by C. F. F. Ivanowitch, 1765.
24. Cupido and Galatheo. French school, by Nicholas Poussin, 1594.
25. Slaughtered Cattle. Flemish school, by David Teniers, 1582.
26. Landscape. French school, by Claude Geléc, called Le Lorrain, 1600.
27. Head of Christ. Russian school. Oil painting, ornamented and covered up by silver chiselings, by C. F. F. Ivanowitch, 1765.
28. Adoration by the Kings. German school, by Albert Durer, 1471.
29. Vision of St. Anthony of Padona. Spanish school, by Bartholomew Esteban Murillo, 1618.
30. Portrait. Dutch school, by Van Ryn Rembrandt, 1607.
31. Cupido. Italian school, by Guido Reni, 1575.
32. Judas Kissing Christ. Italian school, by the first painter of the Italian school, Jean Cimabue, 1249.
33. Relics. Russian school, oil painting covered up and ornamented with silver chiselings, by C. F. F. Ivanowich, 1765.
34. A Slut with her Puppies. American school, painted from life by George G Butler, 1867.
35. Landscape. English school.
36. Return Home of a Guilty Daughter. French school, pen drawing with sepia, by P. A. Ville, 1768.
37. Bouquet. French school, San Francisco, by Sidonia Petetin, 1861.

38. Huntress Diana. French school, Pastel painting, time of Louis XV.
39. Marine; Sea Fight. French school, 1617.
40. Flora. French school, Pastel painting, time of Louis XV.
41. Virtue and Vice. German school, by C. V. Mannelich, 1817.
42. Christ on Mount Olivet. French school, San Francisco, by Sidonia Petetin, 1862.
43. Portrait. Flemish school, 1620.
44. Bunch of Asparagus (panel). French school, 1750.
45. Annunciation of the Virgin. French school, by Eustache de Lueur, 1617.
46. Fowls and Kid Hiding from a Bird of Prey. Flemish school, by Eugene Verboeckhöven (senior), 1798.
47. "On Deck;" Marine. Flemish school.
48. Portrait of Frederick the Great. German school, painted on wood for a snuff box.
49. A Battlefield. German school, by Geo. P. Rugendas, 1666.
50. Flowers. Italian school, by Pissani, 1780.
51. St. Francis Xavier Italian school, 1700.
52. Venus discovered by a Satyr while watching over the sleep of Cupid. Italian school.
53. Moses and Pharaoh's Daughter. Italian school, by P. P. Rubens, 1577.
54. Battle of Constantine. French school, original crayon sketch by Horace Vernet, 1835.
55. The Bride of the Village. French school, engraved by Cochin Tardieu from the original painting by Watteau, 1765.
56. Sailing for Cythera; steel engraving. French school, engraved by Cochin Tardieu from the original painting by Watteau, 1765.
57, 58, 59, 60, 61, 62, 63. Anatomical Studies from Life. Italian school, by Ferranti, 1718.
64. F. L. A Pioche. Medallion, by Mezzara.

CHAPTER XIII.

Dr. Toland to the Regents of the University of California.

ARTICLE 241.

SAN FRANCISCO, March 3, 1873.

To the Board of Regents of the University of California

I am authorized to inform you, that at a meeting of the Trustees of the Toland Medical College, held this day, it was voted with entire unanimity, and with the hearty concurrence of the Faculty, including Dr. Toland, the founder, that the President and Secretary be authorized, on behalf of the Board, to make a deed and legal conveyance of all the property of the college to the Regents of the University. The proper conveyance will be executed and delivered on our receiving from you an intimation of your acceptance of the trust.

Hoping that the prosperity of the University, in one of its legitimate departments, as well as the cause of sound medical education, may be promoted by the proposed transfer, I have the honor to be, very respectfully, your obedient servant,

IRA P. RANKIN, Secretary.

ARTICLE 242.

SAN FRANCISCO, March 4, 1873.

Professor D. C. Gilman, President of the University of California:

DEAR SIR: I herewith inclose a communication from the Board of Trustees of the Toland Medical College, which you will be good enough to present to the Board of Regents of the University of California, and with it my assurance that the chief donor, Dr H. H. Toland, has expressed to me in writing his cordial assent to this action of the Board of Trustees. In addition to the real property, the gift will include all and every description of property, such as books, preparations, models, instruments, and such other apparatus as belong to the college.

With much respect, I remain yours, etc.,

R. BEVERLEY COLE, Dean.

ARTICLE 243.

This indenture, made the fourth day of March, one thousand eight hundred and seventy-three, between the President and Board of Trustees of "The Toland Medical College," a corporation duly incorporated under and by virtue of the laws of the State of California, the party of the first part, and "The Regents of the University of California," a corporation duly incorporated under and by virtue of the laws of the State of California, the party of the second part, witnesseth: That the said party of the first part, for and in consideration of the sum of one dollar, lawful money of the United States of America, to it in hand paid by the said party of **the second part**, at or before the ensealing and delivery of **these** presents, the receipt whereof is hereby acknowledged, has granted, bargained and sold, conveyed and confirmed, and by these presents does grant, bargain and sell, convey and confirm unto the said party of the second part, and to its successors **and** assigns forever, all that certain lot, **piece**, or parcel of land situate, lying, **and** being in **the** City and County of San Francisco, State **of** California, bounded and particularly described as follows, **to** wit: Commencing at a point on the easterly line of Stockton Street, distant eighty (80) feet northerly from the northeast corner of Chestnut and Stockton Streets, running thence northerly along the said line **of** Stockton Street forty-two and one half (42½) feet to an alley **or** small street called Pfeiffer Street; thence at right angles easterly along the southerly line of said Pfeiffer Street **one** hundred and thirty-seven and a half (137½) feet; thence **at** right angles southerly parallel with Stockton Street **along** the westerly line of another alley, **or** what is known **as** "Bellevue Place," one hundred and **twenty**-two and **a half** (122½) feet to the northerly line of **Chestnut** Street; **thence** at right angles westerly along **the said** northerly **line of** Chestnut Street fifty-seven and one **half** (57½) feet, thence **at** right angles northerly parallel with **Stock**ton Street eighty (80) feet; and thence at right angles westerly parallel with Chestnut Street eighty (80) feet to Stockton Street and point of commencement, being a portion of fifty vara lot numbered fourteen hundred and ninety-three upon the official map of the City and County of San Francisco, there being eighty feet square taken from the said fifty vara on the northeast corner of Stockton and Chestnut Streets; also fifteen feet off of the northern end on Pfeiffer Street aforesaid; the remainder of said fifty vara being the land conveyed by this deed. Together with all and singular the tenements, hereditaments, and appurtenances thereunto belonging or **in** anywise appertaining, and the reversion and reversions, remainder and remainders, rents, issues, and profits thereof ; and also all **the** estate, right, title, interest, property, possession, claim, **and** demand whatsoever, as well in law as in equity, of said party **of** the first part, of, **in, or** to the above described premises, **and every** part and parcel thereof, with the appurtenances.

To have and to hold all and singular the above mentioned and described premises, together with the appurtenances, unto the said party of the second part, its successors, heirs, and assigns forever.

ARTICLE 244.

Resolved, That the Board of Regents have heard with satisfaction the proposal to transfer the property of the Toland Medical College to the University of the State, and that they accept with readiness this unconditioned gift.

Resolved, That a committee be appointed by the Chair to receive the formal transfer of this property, and that said committee be requested to present to the Board at the next meeting a plan for the promotion of medical instruction in the University.

Resolved, That the Board hereby record their grateful appreciation of the praiseworthy munificence of Dr H. H. Toland of San Francisco, in his liberal endowment of a school of medicine, and that they receive the gift which is made in his name with the belief that by it the University of California will be enabled in an efficient manner to maintain the department of medicine.

CHAPTER XIV.

ARTICLE 245.

Deed between H. D. Cogswell and the Regents of the University of California.

This indenture, made the nineteenth day of May, in the year of our Lord eighteen hundred and seventy-nine, between Henry D. Cogswell, of the City and County of San Francisco, State of California, the party of the first part, and the Regents of the University of California, an institution duly created, organized, and existing under the laws of the State of California, and by said laws placed under the charge and control of a Board of Directors, known and styled as the Regents aforesaid, the parties of the second part, witnesseth: That the said party of the first part, for and in consideration of the sum of five dollars, to him in hand paid by the said parties of the second part, the receipt whereof is hereby acknowledged, hath bargained and sold, and by these presents doth bargain and sell forever unto the said parties of the second part and their successors, all that certain lot, piece, or parcel of land, situate, lying, and being in the City and County of San Francisco, State of California, and particularly described as follows, to wit: commencing at a point on the easterly line of Front Street, distant sixty (60) feet northerly from the northeast corner of the intersection of Front and Jackson Streets, thence northerly along said easterly line of Front Street sixty (60) feet to Clark Street, thence at right angles easterly and along

9

the southerly line of Clark Street eighty-five (85) feet to and including the brick wall and the land on which stands the wall which now constitutes the rear or easterly wall of the building erected on the premises hereby conveyed, provided that said wall now is and shall remain forever a party wall between the premises hereby conveyed and the lot of land with its appurtenances lying to the east of the said premises, and if and when the said building is increased in height as hereinafter provided, the rear or easterly wall thereof, so far as built up to a greater height, shall also constitute a party wall between the said premises and the said lot to the east thereof, without being chargeable to the latter for any part of the cost of erecting it, thence at right angles southerly and parallel with Front Street sixty (60) feet, thence at right angles westerly and parallel with Jackson Street eighty-five (85) feet to the easterly line of Front Street and point of commencing. Together with all and singular the hereditaments and appurtenances thereunto belonging or in anywise appertaining; and the reversion and reversions, remainder and remainders, rents, issues, and profits thereof, and also all the estate, right, title, interest, claim, or demand whatsoever of him, the said party of the first part, either in law or in equity of, in, and to the above bargained premises and every part and parcel thereof.

To have and to hold all and singular the said hereinbefore granted and demised premises, with the appurtenances, unto the said parties of the second part and their successors forever, upon the trusts, nevertheless, and to and for the uses, interests, and purposes hereinafter limited, described, and declared, to wit:

First—Until the improvement and enlargement of the building erected on said premises, to be made as hereinafter mentioned, the said parties of the second part shall at all times and continuously, in consideration of this conveyance, demise, let, and furnish unto the "Cogswell Dental College of the University of California," all and singular the second story of the brick building situated in said premises as it now exists, or so much thereof as the Faculty of said Dental College may require, except the portion thereof which is demised to said party of the first part by an indenture or lease of even date with these presents, to be used by said Dental College for the purpose thereof, and subject to such changes or alterations in the arrangement and partitioning of the said rooms as the Faculty of the said Dental College may deem it proper to make; *provided*, that when the said parties of the second part shall have made and completed the said improvement and enlargement for the said building, as hereinafter mentioned, then and thenceforth they shall demise, let, and furnish unto the said "Cogswell Dental College" one entire story in the said building for the exclusive use and purposes of the said college, said story to be selected by the Faculty of said college, and if the said parties of the second part in their discretion should deem it advisable, they shall furnish the said Dental College, gratuitously, with so much more room in the said building, beside the said story thereof, as they shall deem needful for its uses and purposes.

Second—That the parties of the second part shall use all proper efforts to rent or demise all the rest and residue of the said building, including the stores on the first floor thereof, to suitable tenants, for the highest and best rents that can be obtained therefor, and that after paying out of said rents the necessary expenses connected therewith, and with the maintenance and preservation of the said building, they shall employ the remainder, to wit: the net amount thereof, as an accumulation fund, which fund and interest thereof, if they shall be able to obtain interest on the same or any portion of it, shall be kept augmenting until it has attained an amount or aggregate sum sufficient to enable the said building to be improved and enlarged by the addition of three new brick stories thereto; that is to say, two full stories and such third story or half story as shall be afforded by a mansard roof, which shall by them be placed on said building, and the said improvement and elevation, and any corresponding improvement in the portion of the building already erected, shall be made in such form and with such regard to finish, quality, and character of ornament as shall seem to the said parties of the second part best adapted to further and fulfill the purposes of the party of the first part in the creation of the said trust; *provided*, that the stone tablet, with the inscription, "Cogswell's Building, 1859," shall be permanently retained upon and constitute a visible portion of said building.

Third—That it may be at all times lawful and proper for the said parties of the second part, in order to facilitate and expedite the aforesaid enlargement and improvement of said building, to hypothecate and pledge the future rents thereof, as well those arising from the said building in its present form, as those which may ensue from the new portions of said building so to be superadded as and for a means of securing and paying for the cost of the said improvement, by obtaining a loan of money sufficient for that purpose, to repay which loan, with interest, said rents may be by the parties of the second part pledged and hypothecated; and in case said loan is effected it shall be the duty of the parties of the second part to repay the same, with the interest thereof, out of the first net rents received by them, and before employing the said rents or any part thereof, for any of the other trusts herein created and specified; *provided*, that the said party of the first part, H. D. Cogswell, shall have the first option or choice of making the said loan and taking the said security therefor.

Fourth—After the building has been enlarged and completed as aforesaid, the said parties of the second part shall provide and furnish in perpetuity one entire story thereof to the said Dental College, and so much more of the room therein as they may deem needful, and as hereinbefore specifically provided.

Fifth—All the rest and residue of the said building, except that portion thereof which is demised to said party of the first part by an indenture of lease of even date with these presents, shall be let and rented by the said parties of the second part to suitable tenants for the highest and best rents that can be obtained therefor, and out of the net receipts from the said rents, after paying the necessary expenses connected therewith, and when said receipts become sufficient for that purpose, up to which period they shall be accumulated, if necessary, so as to constitute a fund in furtherance of the same object, they shall be appropriated by the said parties of the second part to the payment of a monthly amount or sum of $300, or $3,600 per annum, for the establishment and maintenance of a Chair in the said University, which it is the further object of these trusts to create and endow, to be known and designated as the "Cogswell Chair of Moral and Intellectual Philosophy," and said sum shall be so appropriated in perpetuity or so long as the said parties of the second part shall be enabled to realize the same from the sources aforesaid.

Sixth—After appropriating the rents of the said premises as aforesaid, the parties of the second part shall appropriate such further net proceeds as shall result therefrom, one half to the said Dental College, for the uses and purposes thereof, and one half to the said parties of the second part, to be used in and under their discretion, as a means of contributing to the support and maintenance of such students in the said University as, from their lack of pecuniary ability, are incapable of supporting themselves during the period of a collegiate course, and who would otherwise for such reason be unable to obtain the benefit of an education in the said University; *provided*, that when such further net proceeds amount to the sum of $600 per annum, the one half thereof, namely, $300, is to be appropriated to the said Dental College as aforesaid; then and thereafter all the increase of the said net proceeds over and above the said sum of $600 shall be appropriated by the said parties of the second part to the full extent to which the amount thereof may increase at any time hereafter to the same object as that hereinbefore last above mentioned, to wit: to the support or maintenance of such students as, from their said lack of pecuniary ability, are incapable of supporting themselves during the period of a collegiate course, and who would otherwise, for such reason, be unable to obtain the benefit of an education in the said University, which fund last mentioned shall be known and designated as the "Cogswell Students' Relief Fund;" *and provided further*, that if at any time hereafter, in the discretion of the said parties of the second part, it shall be deemed desirable to use the said net proceeds over and above the said $600, or any part of said net proceeds, for the purposes of said Dental College, either to pay for the services or salary of professors or lecturers, or to render the tuition in said College free and gratuitous, or for both of said objects, it shall and may be lawful for them so to do, and these trusts are upon the express condition that they may exercise, at all times, the said discretion, and so appropriate the said proceeds, or any part thereof, it being the wish of the said party of the first part that the said Dental College should be brought, by the parties of the second part, to as high a degree of character, scholarship, standard of tuition, and efficiency as exists in any similar institution.

Seventh—That the said premises hereinbefore conveyed, and their extension and enlargement and the accumulation derived therefrom, shall constitute three several endowments by the said party of the first part, Henry Daniel Cogswell, and Caroline Elizabeth, his wife, namely, an endowment for the said Dental College, an endowment for the said Chair of Moral and Intellectual Philosophy, and an endowment for the said Students' Relief Fund, to the creation of which several endowments the party of the first part and his said wife are prompted by their desire to aid the cause of dental science and the cause of education.

Eighth—That the said parties of the second part shall and will keep the building erected upon said premises, and any addition, improvement, or enlargement made thereon as aforesaid, insured against loss by fire to an amount equal to two thirds of the value of the said building, exclusive of the foundations thereof, consisting of the piles and capping which constitute the same, out of said fund.

Ninth—That in case the said parties of the second part should sell or mortgage the premises hereinbefore conveyed, or any part thereof, this conveyance and transfer shall thereafter be considered and be null and of no effect, and the property hereby conveyed shall revert to and become the property absolutely of the party of the first part, or his legal representatives.

Tenth—That the estate hereby conveyed, and the net proceeds thereof, shall constitute the sole and only fund and source from which the said trusts shall be sustained, and the said endowments supported, and the moneys required therefor obtained; and the said parties of the second part shall not be liable in their individual or corporate capacity, nor shall the said University be liable to advance any further or other moneys, or become in any respect chargeable for any expense or charge whatever connected with the said trust.

In witness whereof, the said party of the first part has

hereunto set his hand and seal the day and year first above written.

HENRY D. COGSWELL.

Signed, sealed, and delivered in presence of—

CAROLINE E. COGSWELL.

And the said parties of the second part, in pursuance of a resolution of the said Board of Regents, passed on the nineteenth day of May, 1879, and set forth in the Book of Records of the said Board, have caused these presents to be sealed with the corporate seal, signed by the President, and attested by the Secretary of the said Board the day and year first above written.

[Duly executed, recorded in the Records of the County of San Francisco, Deeds 953, page 1.]

ARTICLE 246.

Resolved, That the Board of Regents of the University of California do hereby accept the donation of Dr. H. D. Cogswell upon the terms embraced in his deed, and authorize the execution of a certain lease between the Regents of the University of the State of California and Henry D. Cogswell and Caroline E. Cogswell, and that the Hon. William Irwin, Governor of the State of California, and President of said Board of Regents, be and is hereby authorized and empowered to sign, on the part of the Regents of the University of the State of California, said deed and lease, and that the corporate seal be affixed, and duly attested by the Secretary of said Board of Regents.

ESTABLISHMENT.

The College was organized by the adoption of the following resolutions:

Resolved, 1. That the Board of Regents of the University of California, in conformity with the terms of the deed executed by H. D. Cogswell, establish a Dental College, to be designated the "Cogswell Dental College," in which complete courses of instruction must be given in the theory and practice of dentistry, consisting of such appropriate studies and lectures as may be determined by the said Board of Regents.

2. That the following Chairs be established in said College, to be filled by the Board of Regents, by the election of competent professors and instructors, as soon as may be practicable, namely:

(1.) A Chair of Operative Dentistry.

(2). A Chair of Mechanical Dentistry.

(3.) A Chair of Regional Anatomy and Surgery.

Also, in connection with the "Medical Department" of the University of California, the following Chairs

(a). A Chair of Anatomy

(b). A Chair of Physiology.

(c). A Chair of Chemistry.

(d). A Chair of Surgery.

Also, such other Chairs, under appropriate designations, as the said Board of Regents may hereafter see fit to establish in said College.

3. That the Board of Regents will confer the Degree of "Doctor of Dental Surgery," at the end of the prescribed course, upon such students as, having completed the same, are found proficient therein.

4. That the compensation of the professors and instructors in said College, as well as other expenses of the same, are to be paid from the tuition fees of the students and the Special Endowment Fund of said College, in such manner as the said Board of Regents may determine.

5. That the said College be organized in accordance with the several "requirements" of the donor, herewith submitted:

REQUIREMENTS OF THE DONOR IN RELATION TO THE ESTABLISHMENT OF THE "COGSWELL DENTAL COLLEGE."

1. That twelve (12) free scholarships be granted to the donor, or his legal representatives, he or they nominating the candidates for such scholarships, who, when found properly qualified, shall receive tuition in all branches of study required for the proper degree in the "Cogswell Dental College," free from all charge for the same.

2. That the Faculty of said College shall, as soon as practicable, organize a system "of free dental operations," for a class of persons who may be adjudged unable to pay for the same, to be kept open at such hours at said College as may be arranged by the said Faculty. This is not intended to prevent the exaction of small charges for necessary supplies, sufficient to cover the actual cost of material used, for themselves and others not able to pay anything.

3. That when "Cogswell Contingent Fund," as provided in the deed, becomes available, it shall be used—first, in small temporary loans to indigent and meritorious students in said college, of approved moral character. and frugal habits; and second, in providing proper appliances for instruction.

4. That qualified females shall be received as students in the said college upon the same terms as males.

5. That no person of proper qualifications and of good moral character and habits shall be refused admission or

graduation in said college, on account of nationality, color, politics, or religion.

(Signed:)   H. D. COGSWELL.

CHAPTER XV.

ARTICLE 247.

The James Lick Trust.

OFFICE OF THE BOARD OF TRUSTEES OF THE
"JAMES LICK TRUST,"
SAN FRANCISCO, November 1, 1875.

To the Regents of the University of California:

GENTLEMEN: I am instructed by the Board of Trustees of the "Lick Trust," to inform you that you are one of the beneficiaries of the Trust.

The terms of the Trust in your favor are to be found in the following extract from the Trust Deed, viz.:

"*Third*—To expend the sum of seven hundred thousand dollars ($700,000) for the purpose of purchasing land and constructing and putting up on such land as shall be designated by the party of the first part, a powerful telescope, superior to and more powerful than any telescope ever yet made, with all the machinery appertaining thereto and appropriately therewith, or that is necessary and convenient to the most powerful telescope now in use or suited to one more powerful than any yet constructed; and also a suitable observatory connected therewith. The parties of the second part hereto and their successors shall, as soon as said telescope and observatory are constructed, convey the land whereupon the same may be situated, and the telescope, observatory, and all the machinery and apparatus connected therewith, to the corporation known as the 'Regents of the University of California;' and if after the construction of said telescope and observatory, there shall remain of said seven hundred thousand dollars in gold coin any surplus, then said parties of the second part shall turn over such surplus to said corporation, to be invested by it in bonds of the United States, or of the City and County of San Francisco, or other good and safe interest-bearing bonds, and the income thereof shall be devoted to the maintenance of said telescope and the observatory connected therewith, and shall be made useful in promoting science; and the said telescope and observatory are to be known as 'The Lick Astronomical Department of the University of California.'"

I am further instructed to say, that Mr. Lick has selected as the site of the observatory, a section of land belonging to the United States, situated on Mt. Hamilton, in Santa Clara County, California. We desire to have your coöperation in attaining the title through the State grant to you.

We shall be pleased to hear that you accept the donation; and also in what manner and to what extent you are authorized or feel disposed to assist in carrying out the views of the beneficent donor.

I have the honor to be, very respectfully, your obedient servant,

RICHARD S. FLOYD,
President of the Board of Trustees of the Lick Trust.

———

OFFICE OF THE REGENTS OF THE . }
UNIVERSITY OF CALIFORNIA. }

Captain Richard S. Floyd:

DEAR SIR: Your communication as President, and on behalf of the Board of Trustees of the Lick Trust, addressed to the Regents of the University of California, in which you informed them that they were beneficiaries of the Trust whereby James Lick appropriated a fund of seven hundred thousand dollars to the construction of a telescope superior to any yet produced, and an observatory, both of which when completed with their machinery and apparatus, and the land whereon they shall be located, he directed said Board of Trustees to convey unto said Regents, was officially considered by them, and on behalf of the University of California, this munificent donation of Mr. Lick was unanimously accepted.

We are instructed by the Regents to offer you, and (through you) the Board of Trustees of the James Lick Trust, their thanks for the courteous manner in which you have notified them of this trust and solicited their acceptance of the gift of Mr. Lick. In contemplation of the magnitude and splendor of this large endowment, it was deemed advisable besides their recognition (through yourselves) of his noble benefaction, to make a further and personal acknowledgment to Mr. Lick, expressive of their thankfulness for his donation and appreciative of its value.

We are also instructed to inform you, that the Regents will coöperate with your Board in attaining the title to the lands designated in your communication, through the grant to them, and are cordially disposed to assist in carrying out the views of the beneficent donor, within the limits of their authority and influence, the manner and extent of which coöperation we are empowered to arrange by personal communication with you and your colleagues.

We are, sir, your obedient servants,

WM. T. WALLACE,
J. WEST MARTIN,
JOS. W. WINANS,
Special Committee.

SAN FRANCISCO, December 7, 1875.

———

OFFICE OF THE BOARD OF REGENTS OF THE }
UNIVERSITY OF CALIFORNIA. }

James Lick, Esq.:

HONORED SIR: The Board of Trustees of the Lick Trust, through their President, Captain Richard S. Floyd, have officially notified the Regents of the University of California, that so soon as the telescope, which you have designated as "one superior to and more powerful than any telescope ever yet made,"—and its observatory—for the construction and equipment whereof you have created a Trust Fund of seven hundred thousand dollars—shall have been completed, the said Trustees are directed by the terms of such trust to convey the said "telescope, observatory, and all the machinery and apparatus connected therewith," together with the land wherever the same may be situated, to the corporation known as the Regents of the University of California, to be by them made perpetually useful in promoting science, and to be known as "The Lick Astronomical Department of the University of California."

In response to this act of spontaneous and almost unparalleled munificence, whereby the interests of science, through one of its most exalted departments, may be enabled to attain, upon the shores of the Pacific and in one of the youngest States of the Republic, a higher advancement than has ever yet been reached by the oldest and most enlightened nations of the globe, the Regents of the University have delegated to us the duty of announcing their acceptance of this splendid gift and their appreciation of the noble purpose of its author.

From an endowment so exceptionally grand and massive the advantages which must result to the cause of science in the future are incalculable. Not only will it impart its luster to our State and to our country, but we may reasonably anticipate that its beneficent effects, and improved facilities for research into the mysteries of nature, will confer their influence and benefits on all mankind.

To you, sir, whose desire for the promotion of learning has prompted, whose intelligence has planned, and whose bounty has provided resources for the construction and maintenance of this stupendous work, belongs, and has been freely manifested, the gratitude of a whole community.

Among those public benefactors, of whose bright examples our country yields so many instances, your name will ever hold a prominent and honored place.

While the Regents tender you their thanks for having made the University of California the recipient of your magnificent donation, they assure you that they will faithfully endeavor to realize its highest aims, and consummate the scientific objects of its founder.

JOS. W. WINANS,
WM. T. WALLACE,
J. WEST MARTIN,
Special Committee.

San Francisco, December 7, 1875.

CHAPTER XVI.

Gifts of H. D. Bacon.

Article 248.

San Francisco, November 23, 1877.

To the Board of Regents of the University of California:

Gentlemen: As the result of an accumulation of many years, I have a valuable collection of works of art, sculpture, and paintings, and a library of several thousand volumes of standard and miscellaneous works, selected with much care.

For some years I have been considering how I could best bring them into the service of the public, and my mind is pretty well settled into the conviction that, through the instrumentality of the University of California, the object sought could be most surely realized.

California has decided that the University shall be the highest type of excellence in everything pertaining to education in the most advanced branches of mathematics, physics as connected with chemistry, mining and agriculture, etc., history and literature; and it seems to me the basis of the institution is broad enough to embrace instruction in the so called fine arts.

At the present time, when it is doubtless of the utmost importance that the State should contribute liberally to the establishment upon the most substantial basis of the arts and sciences tending to the most rapid development of the great natural resources of its agricultural and mining, I have supposed it would neither be prudent nor wise to ask for large appropriations from its treasury, to make provision for a costly structure in which a large collection of books and works of art could be conveniently and safely deposited, or to provide for the books and works of art; and yet, under proper conditions, it has seemed to me, the State would even now coöperate in beginning such a provision.

I have also supposed that your Board, if, upon a careful examination of the subject, you should regard it judicious and proper, would assume the responsibility of setting apart and devoting to it ample and properly located grounds for the complete structure, upon which to commence the erection of a building designed to meet, ultimately, the necessity of a repository for a vast library, and galleries for the exhibition of the æsthetic arts. In this connection I have thought it not unlikely that, at an early day, the San Francisco Art Association, if agreeable to your Board, might desire to become auxiliary to the University, and whether so or not, what it has done and is doing for the advancement of art, together with the increasing number of artists on this coast, who are rapidly advancing to eminence and the front rank in their profession, would soon do much in adorning the walls of the proposed structure with specimens of the choicest works, and that, too, without cost to the University.

California is not only increasing in wealth in an unparalleled degree, and with it her citizens are very much disposed to liberality in securing the best works of art; and with a noble structure in which to deposit such things, very many would esteem it a privilege to contribute to the education of a correct and refined taste not only of students, but the public generally. The library, under similar influence, would grow into great usefulness, and at a moderate cost to the University or State.

Cost is not always a safe criterion to judge of the value of things, and most often is this the case when applied to what, by courtesy, are called works of art; but as I wish to get a starting point in submitting my views to your consideration; and as I do not rely alone upon my own judgment as to the money value or excellence of the works of art and books which I am considering, I do not anticipate adverse criticism from the well informed, when I place a value of fifty thousand dollars (they have cost me much more) on that portion which I design embracing in what follows.

My plan is that, if we can agree upon a method of organization of a library and art gallery in connection with the University, to contribute to it a large part of my books and works of art, together with twenty-five thousand dollars in money; provided the State will appropriate a like sum at the next meeting of the Legislature, to be used conjointly in erecting the first subdivision of the building to be dedicated to the aforesaid purposes.

If this fifty thousand dollars could be devoted almost exclusively to the structure, there would be secured, probably, a subdivision which would meet requirements until the State would feel at liberty to make further appropriations for needed enlargements from time to time. And as we have in California architects who have given evidence of much genius, I cannot doubt there would be such a spirit of emulation among them to provide the University plans, specifications, and estimates, and without cost to it, as that the fifty thousand dollars could practically be used in the structure alone. I do not think I have anticipated too much from our architects; architecture being one of the highest branches of art, there would be ample motive to secure success in the competition, as he who attained it would indelibly fix and enshrine his name with, and be almost the first to contribute to this endowment.

It may be urged that the State will not appropriate funds for such a purpose. It is not my province or purpose to urge that it should; but I think we have reason to believe that the State not only now has, but in the future will have, an increasing pride in the prosperity and greatness of the University. If it has not already accomplished all that was originally hoped from it, it has certainly done very much to elevate the standard of education, and has stimulated all classes of our citizens to closer thought and observation of systems of education which are being pressed upon public attention and the leading educators of the day, and out of this activity of mind and investigation, under the guidance of your Board and the able Faculty of the University, in a short time the best of these systems will be selected and crystallized in the most useful forms. Soon, too, we shall begin to feel the beneficent effects of the noble endowments of Lick for the promotion of science, and under such influences our Legislatures will feel that money contributed to advance and educate its sons and daughters is far preferable to expenditures in punishing and repressing crime, the fruits, most often, of ignorance. Our State, too, owing to the wise provisions of its Constitution, and perhaps the governing desire of its citizens, is almost free of debt, and without burdening itself with taxation can easily promote the intellectual advancement of its citizens. But this argument is unnecessary, and perhaps lacking in good taste.

If you regard the suggestion worthy of consideration, I shall take pleasure in conferring with a committee of your Board, or otherwise, on the subject.

I remain, very respectfully, your obedient servant,

H. D. BACON.

Reply of the Regents.

ARTICLE 249.

SAN FRANCISCO, December 13, 1877.

Henry D. Bacon, Esq.:

DEAR SIR: Your letter of the twenty-third of November was presented to the Board of Regents of the University to-day, at an adjourned meeting, by Regent Martin. It was received with deep interest and admiration. We know not which most to admire, the spirit or manner of it. It was referred to us, the undersigned, as a special committee, to acknowledge the receipt of it, to pay you the respects of the Board, and to ask your pleasure to give the committee an early opportunity to meet you.

It is not within the scope of this correspondence for us to express the satisfaction we feel at your intelligent views and honorable acts, neither to enlarge upon the various interesting points suggested in your letter. The committee only wish to offer you the grateful acknowledgments of the Board and request you to appoint an early day when you will receive them.

We are your obliged fellow-citizens,

HORATIO STEBBINS,
J. WEST MARTIN,
GEORGE DAVIDSON,
J. W. WINANS,
JOHN LE CONTE.

Donations of H. D. Bacon.

ARTICLE 250.

La Conception, after Murrillo, by Commatty
Beggar Boy, after Murrillo, by Commatty.
Toast to the Vintage of 1834, after Louis Gross Claude, by Commatty.
Three Yosemite views, by Shapleigh.
One Hetchy-Hetchy, by Shapleigh.
Susannah at her Bath, by Jacoby.
Yosemite Winter Scene, by Bierstadt.
Death of Wallenstein, by a Scallaim Pelotzschove.
Kœnig Zu (Bavaria), by Gebhardt.
Ariadne statue, after Danneker.
Genius of America, or Abolition of Slavery, by John Halbig of Munich.
Bathing Nymphs, by John Halbig of Munich.

Standard Library, elegant bindings.

NOTE—First cost of the foregoing was about $60,000, and the same were insured by Mr. Bacon.

CHAPTER XVII.

Donation of Michael Reese.

ARTICLE 251.

"I give and devise to the corporation known as the Regents of the University of California fifty thousand dollars, to be by them invested in the founding and maintaining a library, to be known and called the Reese Library of the University of California."—[Will of Michael Reese.

That the library to be formed by virtue of the bequest of the late Michael Reese be general in its character, and that the same shall include judiciously selected works pertaining to literature, science, and the arts. The principal shall remain as an invested fund and the interest only shall be used for the purchase of books.—[Order of the Board.

ARTICLE 252.

The library shall be known as the Reese Library of the University of California.

ARTICLE 253.

A tablet has been placed in the library with the following inscription:

"To

"MICHAEL REESE,

"*In commemoration of his liberality in donating to the library fifty thousand dollars.*"

CHAPTER XVIII.

Donation of A. K. P. Harmon—The Harmon Gymnasium.

ARTICLE 254.

OAKLAND, January 20, 1879.

To the honorable the Board of Regents of the University of California:

GENTLEMEN: Some four months since it was suggested to me by Mr. George C. Edwards that if I felt so inclined I could do for the young men at the University that which would be of much profit and pleasure to them, and probably acceptable to the ruling authorities, if I would construct on the University grounds a building to be used as a gymnasium, and on extra University occasions as an auditorium. Upon this suggestion, and upon the realization of the fact that there were many reasons why the University stood in the immediate need of a building for these purposes, I caused plans to be drawn for such a building.

The structure, as then considered, met the approval of those members of your honorable Board, and other gentlemen to whom the plans were shown. The tender of such a building having been accepted by the Board, and a very accessible site chosen, work was immediately commenced, and the building pushed to as speedy a completion as good construction would permit. The only changes from the original plans that have been made were by way of improvement, particularly the putting in of a gallery with permanent seats, and the construction of a movable platform.

The building is completed, and I herewith have the honor of presenting the same to the University of California, through you, its very worthy Board of Regents. I also herewith present to you insurance policies, duly receipted, and to the amount of ten thousand dollars on the building and fixtures, for three years.

My hope is that the building will confer the benefits which the many friends of the enterprise predict. It has been constructed particularly for the young men—present and to come. In the fact of the annual change of a portion of the students, I see an element which will tend to perpetuate interest and diffuse benefits.

In turning over the keys to the University authorities, I impose no conditions whatever. I hope, however, that the property will be well preserved, and that the prime object of its construction, viz.: for a gymnasium, will not be lost sight of. It is earnestly recommended that the young men be cautioned with regard to violent exercise. It is also recommended that the students organize themselves into an association, properly officered and governed by a suitable set of by-laws, in order to secure a certain reasonable amount of exercise from each of its members, in order to better protect the property from injury, and in order to prevent the room from becoming a general lounging room.

It is hoped that the young men will secure the services of an excellent instructor entitled to their respect. With such an instructor the weaker parts of the body may be built up, and liability to falls or strains much lessened.

It is hoped that a portion of the apparatus will be gotten by the young men, with particular reference to the ladies, and that suitable hours be assigned to them for the cultivation of symmetry and strength.

Feeling assured that the building just constructed will satisfy a very decided want at the University.

I remain, gentlemen, yours most respectfully,

A. K. P. HARMON.

NOTE.—Said gift was attended by policies of insurance on the same for $10,000 for three years.

ARTICLE 255.

The thanks of the Board were voted to Mr. Harmon for his useful and generous **gift,** and the Secretary was instructed to express the same.

CHAPTER XIX.

S. C. Hastings endowment for the support of the Hastings College of the Law.

ARTICLE 256.

The conditions of this endowment are contained in Chapter XXX, of Division III, Title II, Article III.

ARTICLE 257.

The Secretary was instructed to communicate to Hon. S. C. Hastings, the founder of the Law School, the recognition by the Board of the donation that constitutes the endowment.

CHAPTER XX.

From D. O. Mills.

ARTICLE 258.

SAN FRANCISCO, March 28, 1873.

D. C. Gilman, Esq., President of the University of California:

MY DEAR SIR: It affords me much pleasure to present, through yourself, to the University of California, a collection of the ores, minerals, fossil animals and plants, of the State of California, together with some of the stone implements of the early inhabitants; a collection which has been brought together during several years past by an enthusiastic and skillful collector, Mr. C. D. Voy. It includes several thousand specimens, which are labeled and catalogued.

Displayed in connection with the collections of the Geological Survey of the State, it is my hope such may have a tendency to quicken the interest of the students of the University in the study of the mineral and geological resources of California, and alike contribute to the advancement of scientific research.

I am, my dear sir, very truly yours,

D. O. MILLS.

ARTICLE 259.

Resolved, That the thanks of the Regents be hereby extended to D. O. Mills, Esq., for his munificent purchase and gift of the cabinet of ores, minerals, and fossils, made by Mr. C. D. Voy, the value of which is now very great, while it will continue to increase as the sciences of geology and mineralogy advance, and it becomes more and more difficult to bring together such collections, illustrative of the resources and structure of California.

Resolved, That the remembrance of this benefaction be perpetuated by placing with the specimens when they shall be arranged at Berkeley, an inscription fitly acknowledging the generous source from which they were received.

CHAPTER XXI.

Contributions through Professor Carr—(1873).

ARTICLE 260.

Contributions which have been made to the University through Professor E. S. Carr.

ARTICLE 261.

From the Wood Preserving Company, San Francisco, a complete set of the materials used, with specimens illustrating their effects upon timber.

(For Technological Cabinet.)

ARTICLE 262.

From the Pacific Stone Company, San Francisco, complete set of materials used, and specimens of the work.

(For Technological Cabinet.)

Article 263.

Alvarado Beet Sugar Company, complete set of specimens. (For Technological Cabinet.)

Article 264.

Union Iron Works, San Francisco, fifty specimens of iron from Europe, Australia, and the Eastern States; a most valuable collection.

Article 265.

Also, from the same company, a complete battery of five stamps, including the latest improvements, valued at $750. (For Metallurgical Laboratory.)

Article 266.

From H. D. Dunn, acting Japanese Consul, a large and beautiful specimen of amber, formerly owned by a Japanese Daimio.

Article 267.

OF PLANTS.

From S. Nolan, proprietor of Belle View Nurseries, duplicates of his entire collection. (For the Arboretum and Botanic Garden.)

Article 268.

From I. N. Hoag, Secretary State Agricultural Society, Sacramento, a collection of eight species of mulberry, for same.

Article 269.

From Robert Williamson, Sacramento, twenty rare and valuable deciduous trees.

Article 270.

From L. Sanderson, San José, specimen plants and bundle of cuttings of basket willow, for hedge.

Article 271.

From Dr. J. Strentzel, Alhambra Gardens, Martinez, California, one dozen each of fig and pomegranate trees.

ARTICLE 272.

SAN FRANCISCO, February 18, 1873.

Professor Ezra S. Carr:

DEAR SIR: We take great pleasure in presenting to the University of California, as a contribution to the Metallurgical Department of the School of Mines, a complete battery of five stamps, including the latest improvements, and ask you in our behalf, to bring the matter before them. The battery awaits the order of the University.

H. J. BOOTH & CO.

CHAPTER XXII.

From the Mechanics' Institute of San Francisco.

ARTICLE 273.

SAN FRANCISCO, March 30, 1873.

D. C. Gilman, Esq., President University of California:

DEAR SIR In behalf of the Mechanics' Institute, I have the pleasure of presenting to the University of California a collection of native minerals, woods, grasses, and fibers, principally selected from the different districts of Japan by order of the Japanese Government, and by said Government forwarded to the Mechanics' Institute Industrial Exhibition of 1871 The Mechanics' Institute prizes the above mentioned collection—*first*, because of the source of the gift, and secondly, its intrinsic value; yet, while valuing it so highly, the Society believes that it will be of more benefit to the State and the people thereof if deposited with the University of California, and by it placed in its Museum, than if it were placed in the Cabinet of the Mechanics' Institute; and at the same time it will be, perhaps, more pleasing to the donor. I have the honor to be your obedient servant,

A. S. HALLIDIE, President.

ARTICLE 274.

SAN FRANCISCO, March 29, 1873.

Memorandum of minerals, etc.:

Two boxes, in trays, containing specimens of minerals from various districts of Japan.

One box containing specimens of timber and wood of Japan.

Four boxes samples of coals.

Above selected and forwarded by Japanese Government, and presented to Mechanics' Institute, 1871.

Two packages China grass.

One package bleached sea-weed.

One package China paper

One package vegetable tallow.

One package China cotton in the seed.

CHAPTER XXIII.

From Michael Reese.

ARTICLE 275.

SAN FRANCISCO, March 28, 1873.

To President Gilman:

SIR: I understand that the library of my distinguished countryman, Dr. Lieber, is for sale in New York for five thousand dollars. I inclose you a draft for the amount. You will please present the library to the University of the State of California. I wish the University and yourself the greatest success.

I am, with great respect, your obedient servant,

MICHAEL REESE.

Resolved, That the Regents return their grateful acknowledgments to Michael Reese, Esq., for his generous purchase of the library of Dr. Francis Lieber, of New York, and that they assure him of their belief that this collection of books will not only be an interesting memorial of his distinguished countryman, but will quicken the study of political and social science in the University and will suggest to others the advantage of buying like special collections of books accumulated by scholars during long lives of literary activity.

Resolved, That the President of the University cause to be inserted in the Lieber books a suitable label which shall indicate, briefly, the origin of the collection and the name of the donor

CHAPTER XXIV.

Wells, Fargo & Co.'s Express.

ARTICLE 276.

UNIVERSITY OF CALIFORNIA, ⎫
  BERKELEY, December 1, 1873. ⎬

Mr. J. J. Valentine, Gen'l Supt. W. F. & Co.'s Express, San Francisco:

DEAR SIR: The University of California has only recently entered upon its new site at Berkeley, taking possession of two large and commodious buildings provided by the State. Here are spacious and handsome rooms for museums and cabinets. Can you not through your widely extended agencies help us to fill them with such objects as will illustrate the resources, the natural productions, and the Indian history of this country? We shall be especially glad to receive such specimens as these:

1 Minerals, ores, fossils, and metallurgical products.

2. Specimens of the native plants, of the woods, timber, and peculiar vegetation of any region.

3. Specimens of rare insects, fishes, shells, birds, and animals.

4. Indian antiquities, skulls, weapons, stone implements, dresses, and other illustrations of aboriginal life.

5. Books, pamphlets, photographs, and maps.

Full directions will be given to any one interested in making collections, and every object received will be gratefully acknowledged to the donor, if the source of the gift is known, and will be accordingly entered on the University records. Specimens should be distinctly labeled, especially as to the place from which they were originally taken.

The University of California belongs to the State, and is free from sectarian character. It is absolutely free in tuition, and open to students—young men and women—from any State or country; it is devoted to the higher education, literary or scientific, and especially interested in the Pacific Coast.

Your kind cooperation will be most serviceable, and will be gratefully appreciated.

   Yours, very respectfully,

     D. C. GILMAN,
   President of the University of California.

Wells, Fargo & Co.'s Express.

ARTICLE 277.

GENERAL SUPERINTENDENT'S OFFICE, ⎱
SAN FRANCISCO, December 5, 1873. ⎰

To Agents and Employés Wells, Fargo & Co.:

GENTLEMEN: The accompanying letter from Prof. D C. Gilman, President University of California, explains itself. There is probably not one of the six hundred places at which this company is represented, which will not at one time or another afford opportunities for securing desirable articles for contribution, at no expense or trouble to an agent, clerk, or messenger, but which will undoubtedly be invested with much interest, and possibly prove of great value in a collection such as the University of California should and undoubtedly will secure, sooner or later

In bespeaking and hoping for your sympathy with and interest and coöperation in accomplishing the object set forth, you are not obligated officially or personally to subject yourselves to inconvenience or discomfort in any particular; but we have such a favorable opinion of the intelligence of the company's employés as to believe there will be a very general interest manifested and coöperation vouchsafed.

It is not expected that a general or important collection will be secured immediately, nor will spasmodic effort effect much. What is most desirable will be, to post this and the letter referred to in a conspicuous place in your office, and from time to time secure such offerings as will undoubtedly be tendered by all classes of men; for there is no walk in which knowledge—which is power—has not earnest votaries.

> " By knowledge we do learn ourselves to know,
> And what to man and God we owe."

Whenever any article is obtained, pack it securely, and address " University of California, Berkeley, California," way-billing it by express to Berkeley, *free*, inclosing, by letter to the University, any information relating to the thing sent.

Very respectfully, yours,

JNO. J. VALENTINE,
General Superintendent.

The special thanks of the Board were returned for this generous offer.

CHAPTER XXV.

Article 278.

On motion, it was ordered that the thanks of the Regents be returned to the following donors for their valuable gifts:

Article 279.

From John H. Carmany, Esq., the original manuscript of the poem of "The Heathen Chinee," by Bret Harte, and the proof sheets of the same with some important corrections.

Article 280.

A most valuable gift from C. E. Watkins, Esq., of fifty large photographic views of California and Oregon.

Article 281.

From several friends of the University, $500 for the purchase of brass instruments to be used by the military band formed among the students.

Article 282.

From a gentleman in Oakland, the sum of $100 to be expended among indigent students.

Article 283.

From C. H. Hawks, Esq., of New York, the "Colonial Records of Massachusetts and Plymouth," in 16 quarto volumes (a costly and valuable set).

Article 284.

From Messrs. James Anthony & Co. the forty-fifth volume of the "Sacramento Union."

CHAPTER XXVI.

Article 285.

Mr. Dwinelle, on behalf of Messrs. Wm. Alvord, S. F. Butterworth, Wm. C. Ralston, I. Friedlander, L. L. Robinson, Tiburcio Parrott, William Sharon, Oliver Eldridge, William Norris, and John W. Dwinelle, presented to the Regents for their acceptance a portrait of Louis Agassiz, painted from life during his recent visit to San Francisco. (February, 1873.)

Article 286.

Resolved, That the Secretary transmit to Messrs. Wm. Alvord, S. F. Butterworth, Wm. C. Ralston, I. Friedlander, L. L. Robinson, Tiburcio Parrott, Wm. Sharon, Oliver Eldridge, William Norris, and John W Dwinelle, their thanks for the present to the University of the portrait of Louis Agassiz, the distinguished naturalist.

Resolved, That we accept this graceful and appropriate gift and will cause it to be placed in the Library of the University.

CHAPTER XXVII.

Article 287.

Resolved, That the thanks of the Board be presented to Hon. F. Billings for his munificent gift of a portrait of Bishop Berkeley, painted by Weir from Smybert's original; and that the Board assure him of the special pleasure which it gives them to receive this interesting memorial as we take possession of the site which bears the name of Berkeley. (July, 1873.)

CHAPTER XXVIII.

On motion, the Secretary was instructed to return the thanks of the Regents, for their generous donations, to the following gentlemen:

Article 288.

Henry Edwards—An Herbarium, comprising 1,000 specimens of Australian plants.

Article 289.

William Sharon—Sets of the "San Francisco Bulletin," the "Sacramento Union," and the "San Francisco Herald;" also, "Evening Picayune" for 1851.

Article 290.

James Anthony—A set (nine volumes) of the early series of the "San Francisco Chronicle."

Judge S. J. Field—One hundred valuable volumes.

CHAPTER XXIX.

ARTICLE 291.

Resolved, That the Regents gratefully acknowledge the subscriptions of William H. Raymond, Esq., for educational purposes; Charles W. Howard, Esq., and Henry D. Bacon, Esq., for the purchase of educational apparatus and diagrams greatly needed by the University in two departments of study; to S. F. Butterworth, Esq., for his gift of a bound series of the "New York Daily Times," from its beginning till the close of the war; the unsolicited transfer of Japanese minerals and products from the Mechanics' Institute to the University; the valuable gift of minerals and ores made by Louis Janin, Esq.; and the present to the metallurgical collections of a five stamp battery from Messrs. H. J. Booth & Co., of the Union Iron Works. (1873.)

CHAPTER XXX.

ARTICLE 292.

Voted, that this Board hereby expresses its grateful appreciation of the generosity of an anonymous donor who has given his check for the sum of $1,316, for the payment of bills incurred in the purchase of a press, type, and other printing materials for the use of the students at Berkeley, and that the President of the University, in conveying to the donor this expression of thanks, assure him that the Board rejoice that the means are thus provided to enable such students as desire it to become acquainted with the "art preservative of all arts." (1874.)

CHAPTER XXXI.

W. T. Garratt.

ARTICLE 293.

List of articles presented to the University by W. T. Garratt, November 23, 1878:
One Hooker's steam pump.
One upright steam pump.
One hydraulic ram.
One Gates' patent self oiler.
Two steam syphons.
One steam whistle.

Two injectors.
One indicator for ship.
One combined water gauge and gauge cocks.
Numerous large and small pipe fittings.
One Garratt's self-feeding oil cup.
One garden angle valve.
One Eddy's valve.
One angle check valve.
One self-closing basin cock.
Two hydraulic nozzles.
One perpendicular check valve.
One brass ball gauge cock.
One automatic air valve.

ARTICLE 294.

Resolved by the Regents of the University of California, That the Board recognize the generous spirit of Mr. W. T. Garratt, of San Francisco, and especially thank him for his recent valuable and useful gift of numerous mechanical examples and parts of apparatus for instructional purposes in the mechanical classes of the University.

Resolved, That the foregoing be spread on the minutes, and a copy of the same communicated to Mr. Garratt by the Secretary.

CHAPTER XXXII.

Portrait of ex-Governor Haight.

ARTICLE 295.

SAN FRANCISCO, November 18, 1878.

We, the undersigned, agree to pay to W. Cogswell, or order, the sum set opposite our names, for the purchase of the portrait of ex-Governor H. H. Haight, to be presented to the University of California, located at Berkeley. Price of portrait and frame, $450:

J. Mora Moss, $100; D. O. Mills, $100; Thos. W. Blythe, $100; Alfred A. Cohen, $50; Freeborn & Eastland, $50; J. West Martin, $25; W. W. Crane, Jr., $25.

CHAPTER XXXIII.

Mrs. G. B. Grayson Crane.

ARTICLE 296.

The Secretary read a letter from Mrs. G. B. Grayson Crane, through W. C. Bartlett, Esq., Trustee, conveying to the University the unpublished work of her late husband, Colonel A. J. Grayson, on the ornithology of Mexico, with 163 colored plates, in two volumes, and the MSS. text in one volume, subject to the condition that if ever Mrs. Grayson Crane shall desire to publish the same, she shall have liberty to withdraw said volumes, and to deposit in lieu thereof the copy of same as published.

On motion, the gift was accepted, and the thanks of the Board tendered to the donor.

CHAPTER XXXIV

D. O. Mills' Donation.

ARTICLE 297.

426 CALIFORNIA STREET, }
SAN FRANCISCO, July 7, 1881. }

To the Board of Regents of the University of California:

GENTLEMEN: My interest in the institution over which you preside, and a desire to contribute to the benefit and support of good learning, prompt me to propose to you the establishing of a permanent foundation in the nature of a trust fund, of which the income shall be applied to the maintenance, in the University of California, of a Professorship of Intellectual and Moral Philosophy and Civil Polity.

The sole condition that I shall impose upon this trust and foundation is that the income only shall be devoted exclusively to the support of this professorship, and that any surplus shall be added to the original fund.

While I propose to commit this trust to the keeping of the Regents of the University, confiding in their wisdom to direct it to the promotion of the studies to which it is dedicated, and to the steady increase of human thought and progress, and would limit it by no narrow boundaries of transient opinion, I desire to record my views as to the nature of this professorship, and the character of man who should be called upon to discharge its duties.

The studies included under the general title pertain especially to man, his intellectual, moral, and social being, and can never cease to hold a high place in human learning, nor to have a great influence on human welfare. In the widest and most liberal meaning they underlie laws, manners, and religion, and in effect form the public opinion of the world; and their teacher should not be one who merely resorts to them, takes them up, or incidentally adopts them, but one of philosophic spirit who shall devote his life to this appropriate field of influence and noble labor. To such a man this professorship offers opportunities limited only by his own genius and devotion.

For the above purpose, I inclose herewith my check for the sum of seventy-five thousand ($75,000) dollars, and will be obliged if the Board will signify to me their acceptance of the trust.

Hoping that this may result to the advantage of the State and to the University.

I remain, gentlemen, very respectfully,

D. O. MILLS.

ARTICLE 298.

Resolved, That the Regents of the University of California do accept with the liveliest emotions and the heartiest gratitude, the munificent gift of seventy-five thousand ($75,000) dollars from D. O. Mills, upon the conditions expressed in his letter received this day, to establish a Professorship of Intellectual and Moral Philosophy and Civil Polity in this University.

Resolved, That in recognition of the living interest and broad views of the donor, the professorship thus endowed shall bear the name and title of the Mills Professorship of Intellectual and Moral Philosophy and Civil Polity, and that the wishes of Mr. Mills shall be consulted in the appointment of the first professor.

Resolved, That the Finance Committee be instructed to confer with Mr. Mills upon the best means of investing the above endowment fund.

CHAPTER XXXV.

McMillan & Co.

ARTICLE 299.

Regent Ashburner, of Library Committee, read a note from McMillan & Co.'s agent, in New York, Mr. George P. Brett, announcing the forwarding of certain volumes,

McMillan's series of "Classical Authors," as a present to the University Library.

The thanks of the Board were voted to the givers.

CHAPTER XXXVI.

From Mrs. Mark Hopkins.

ARTICLE 300.

Judge J. S. Hager, Chairman Library and Museum Committee, Board of Regents, University of California:

DEAR SIR: I take pleasure in presenting to the University of California the historical painting by Emmanuel Leutze, entitled "Washington at Monmouth."

MRS. MARK HOPKINS.

SAN FRANCISCO, April 14, 1882.

ARTICLE 301.

SAN FRANCISCO, April 17, 1882.

Mrs. Mark Hopkins:

DEAR MADAM: It gives me great pleasure to acknowledge your note presenting to the University of California the historical painting, by Leutze, of "Washington at Monmouth." At the next meeting of the Regents of the University the Committee on Library and Museum will have the honor to report your very valuable donation; and it will then be the agreeable duty of the Board, officially, to make suitable responsive acknowledgment of your munificent liberality.

Allow me, on behalf of the Committee on Library and Museum, to express our obligations and thanks for the great and valuable addition made, through your preference and generosity, to the Art Gallery of the University, and to convey to you, personally, assurance of our great respect.

JOHN S. HAGER,
Chairman of Committee on Library and Museum.

ARTICLE 302.

Resolved, That the Regents tender to Mrs. Mark Hopkins their acknowledgments and thanks for the very valuable and magnificent contribution she has made to the Art Gallery of the University, in her donation of the original painting by Leutze of "Washington at Monmouth," and that in commemoration of her generous liberality, a suitable tablet be affixed to the painting, bearing the following inscription:

"WASHINGTON AT MONMOUTH,
"BY LEUTZE.
"*Presented by Mrs. Mark Hopkins.*"

CHAPTER XXXVII.

Charles Mayne's donation.

ARTICLE 303.

SAN FRANCISCO, July 31, 1883.

Hon. John S. Hager, Regent of the University of California:

DEAR SIR: Permit me through you to present to the University of California two original oil paintings, named respectively "Summer" and "Winter," the joint work of J. B. Klombeck (one of the best landscape painters) and of Eugene Verboeckhoven (one of the best animal painters), as by their certificates attached thereto is fully verified. They were purchased by me from the artists themselves, with one of whom I am personally acquainted. This donation is intended as a contribution to the Art Gallery of the University, and if in any degree it shall be of assistance in the cultivation or development of a taste for art, I shall be satisfied and abundantly rewarded.

Very respectfully,

CHARLES MAYNE.

ARTICLE 304.

Resolved, That the Board of Regents accept with great pleasure from Charles Mayne, Esq., as a contribution to the Art Gallery of the University, two original oil paintings, denominated respectively "Summer" and "Winter," the joint work of J. B. Klombeck and Eugene Verboeckhoven, and hereby tender to him the acknowledgments and thanks of the Board for his liberal and very valuable donation.

CHAPTER XXXVIII.

Donations to the Library.

ARTICLE 305.

The following have made, from time to time, valuable donations to the University Libraries: Rev. A. C. Ager, Hon. Thomas Beck, Hon. Newton Booth, Charles S. Capp, Hon. H. F. Page, H. D. Bacon, Mrs. H. D. Bacon, John T. Best, I. N. Choynski, Henry Holt & Co., New York, Mrs. J. M. Page, Professor P. Pioda, Dr. J. D. B. Stillman, Lieut. Col. R. S. Williamson, L. Bachman, A. B. Elfelt & Co., I. Glazier, Adam Grant, Miss Mary Hawley, Neustadter Bros., William Scholle, Louis Sloss & Co., Ign. Steinhart & Co., Levi Strauss & Co., Alexander Weill, Hon. D. C. McRuer, Hon. A. A. Sargent, Hon. Alexander Del Mar, Col. W G. Boyle, Hon. John B. Harmon, Hon. Stephen J. Field, Sir Redmond Barry, Melbourne, United States Bureau of Education, Coast Survey, Hydrographic Office, Naval Observatory, Dr. G F. Verbeck, George E. Whitney, Rev. S. H. Willey, Hon. Horace Davis, Smithsonian Institution, F. E. Abbott, J. C. Abbott, D. Appleton & Co., W. D. Armes, Yezaburro Arrow, Boston Publishing Library, H. J. Bowditch, M. D., Brazillian Geological Commission, Joaquin Garcia Condé, Mexican Consul, Hon. J. T. Farley, C. H. Dwinelle, Harvard Observatory, E. W. Hilgard, John S. Hittell, Prof. John Le Conte, Monseñor Roque Cocchia, Prof. W. T. Welcker, Dr. H. C. Garrow, Herman Snow, Very Rev. O. M. Comerford, Prof. George H. Cooke, Hon. John S. Hager, George T. Marye, Jr., Gen. W. S. Rosecrans, Josiah Royce, Departments of United States Government, F. J. Vassault, Wells, Fargo & Co., through J. J. Valentine.

British Association, Etc.

ARTICLE 306.

April 23, 1883, ordered:

The Council for the British Association for the Advancement of Science, having, on the application of Professor William Ashburner, granted to the Library of the University of California the annual volume of the reports, etc., of said association; therefore be it

Resolved, That the thanks of the Board of Regents of the University of California are hereby tendered to the British Association for the Advancement of Science for the annual reports of the association.

CHAPTER XXXIX.

Portrait of George Bancroft.

ARTICLE 307.

September 5, 1882, it being reported to the Board of Regents by Regent Stebbins, that Mr. George Bancroft, through him, had presented a copy of his portrait by Richter to the University, it was voted that the following minutes be entered upon the records and a copy sent to Mr. Bancroft by the Secretary: "The Board of Regents of the University of California offer Mr. Bancroft their sincere thanks for a copy of his portrait by Richter, and assure him of their great respect, and congratulate him and themselves upon his distinguished and honorable labors to perpetuate the history and renown of our common country. The portrait of Mr Bancroft shall be placed in the Library and Art Gallery among the permanent archives of the University."

CHAPTER XL.

The Donation of the Class of 1883.

ARTICLE 308.

SAN FRANCISCO, March 26, 1883.

To Mr. W. W. Deâmer, Chairman, and Earle A. Walcott, Jerome Newman, Ida D. Benfey, and Abbie M. Fulton, Committee on Library Memorial of the Class of 1883, University of California:

At a meeting of the Board of Regents, held on Tuesday, the sixth of March, I was instructed to convey to your class the sentiments of the Board in view of the gift of books presented by you to the Library of the University.

The Regents understand your gift to be an expression of the grateful regards you feel towards the University at which you have been educated, united with an honorable desire that these regards shall be preserved in the name of the class perpetually. They wish to convey to you their admiration of the motives that inspire your conduct, and their appreciation of so substantial a contribution to the permanent value of the library.

They, also, wish to express the hope and the belief that such an example of intellectual and moral gratitude and enthusiasm will be contagious, and that the legacies of suc-

11

ceeding classes will form a chain of unbroken remembrance and grateful feeling through generations to come.

HORATIO STEBBINS,
For the Regents of the University.

CHAPTER XLI.

Article 309.

Regent Reid presented a communication from E. W. Hilgard announcing the presentation of a botanical collection, embracing twenty-one hundred species of plants, chiefly European, by J. A. Bauer, of San Francisco. (May, 1882.)

CHAPTER XLII.

Article 310.

Regent Reid presented a communication from C. H. Dwinelle, of the College of Agriculture, announcing a donation of a collection of beetles from Cutler Paige of Berkeley, class of '82, Captain J. M. McDonald of San Francisco, and Matthew Cooke of Sacramento. The price paid by the above donors was $400. On motion, the gift was accepted, and the Secretary was instructed to return the thanks of the Board. (May, 1882.)

CHAPTER XLIII.

Article 311.

Regent Reid read a letter from Instructor Christy announcing donations of the following articles by J. B. Randol, of the New Almaden Quicksilver Mining Company: One model Hinckley shaft roasting furnace, one model Schroeder shaft roasting furnace, one model each of the Jeffries, the Page, the Page improved, the Neich, and the Donaldson shaft roasting furnace. (May, 1882.)

CHAPTER XLIV.

Nine hundred Photographs by John S. Hittell.

ARTICLE 312.

The following extracts from letters of Mr. Hittell will indicate his purpose in this donation:

"It is highly desirable that California should have a comprehensive collection of photographs representing the most notable statues, buildings, public monuments, and pictures of the world, open to the people and conveniently accessible to them. The University of the State seems to be the best place for it, and since, so far as I know, others have neglected to do anything for an object so desirable, I shall make a beginning with some photographs of statuary. * * * The list which I already have comprises a majority of the best works of antiquity. In most cases the examination of a good photograph is almost as satisfactory as that of the original statue. I have selected the 'normal' size—about eight by ten inches—as the most suitable—large enough to show distinctly all the chief merits and not so large as to be inconvenient for handling. * * * I suggest that after you shall have received all that I send, you shall print a little catalogue with a note at the bottom requesting Californians traveling abroad to furnish any notable works not in the collection.

"As the stock increases my estimate of the value which will be placed on it by the public rises. There are large collections of drawings and engravings in public galleries and museums, but none of photographs, and I imagine that yours will be found attractive to the people and so interesting to those who love and appreciate art that it will be copied elsewhere.

"My gift has no conditions attached to it, but I feel justified in expressing a hope that it will be made accessible to the public in the most convenient manner. * * * If such a collection is desirable and valuable, then it should be exhibited in such a manner that additions can be made to it every year, for there is much new work of merit.

"The magnitude of the collection makes it important that it should be exhibited on desks and not in books, which latter, if I correctly anticipate the public curiosity to see the photos, would give very inadequate accommodation and besides would lead to rapid deterioration from very frequent handling.

"The class whose convenience and interest should be first consulted in reference to the arrangement and exhibition should be the general public, who should be attracted and attached to the University so that they will willingly and liberally sustain it. * * * Whether there is any divergence between their convenience and that of art students I do not know, but if so, I would sacrifice the latter, who are relatively few." (August, 1884.)

CHAPTER XLV.

The following donations have been received by the several departments of the University :

ARTICLE 313.

Charles Mayne, Esq., of San Francisco, in October, 1875, presented bronze busts by Barbienne, of Paris; copies from originals in the European museums, representing Solon, Socrates, Hippocrates, Homer, and Franklin.

ARTICLE 314.

In 1876, Henry Janin, Esq., a model of the New Almaden Quicksilver Mine.

ARTICLE 315.

Miss Mary A. McConnell—Several oil paintings.

ARTICLE 316.

D. Sutter presented a set of Swiss coins, a 5 franc, standing posture, wanting only to make it complete. They are as follows, viz.: One 5 franc, silver, sitting position; two 2 franc, silver, one sitting and one standing position; two 1 franc, silver, one sitting and one standing position; two 20 centimes, bronze; two 5 centimes, bronze; one 2 centimes, copper; one 1 centime, copper, and twenty-six miscellaneous copper and bronze coins.

ARTICLE 317.

Louis Janin—A selection of choice minerals.

ARTICLE 318.

Dr. W. Newcomb—A collection of Peruvian pottery.

ARTICLE 319.

S. F. Martin, Oakland—The eggs of forty-four species of California birds, numbering ninety-seven specimens.

ARTICLE 320.

Mme. R. S. Jaffa presented one hundred and one examples of medical herbs or their properties, illustrative of English practice, and found in the British Pharmacopœia. Also, Marks, a botanical companion to the British Pharmacopœia.

ARTICLE 321.

E. B. Rogers—A collection of coins numbering one hundred and twelve examples; among which are Sardinian, Portuguese, Spanish, English, Mexican, Italian, Republic of Peru, Chinese, Japanese, British American, British Indian, Prussian, Austrian, German, and Lombardo-Venetian. Also, a consecutive set of Confederate scrip, from 50 cents to $100, and a coupon of bond.

ARTICLE 322.

C. D. Voy—One large tree, fifteen feet high, of the *Yucca brevifolia* (Engl.); three of the same, six feet high; large sections of the wood of the same, from which paper is manufactured; all the above from the Mohave Desert, California; specimens of fiber in the various stages of the process of manufacture, from the tree to the brown pulp for ordinary wrapping paper, and the whitened pulp for the finer grades of paper, with numerous samples of paper made from the same. A beautiful collection of polished woods—most of the specimens are about twelve inches square—from California, Mexico, South Pacific, New Zealand, China, India, and numerous other localities, well arranged, with printed labels giving description of the same; also a fine collection of cones and seeds of trees indigenous to the Pacific Coast. Four specimens of bread fruit (*Artocarpus incisa*), from Tahiti, South Pacific; one owl, two fish, interesting specimens from San Francisco Bay and Flint Island, South Pacific. One box of rich silver ores, Arizona.

ARTICLE 323.

Angus Mackay, Esq., Commissioner from Queensland to the Centennial Exposition, presented a large series of tin ores from and a map of Queensland.

ARTICLE 324.

Mrs. E. Mack—A massive and valuable specimen of silver ore from Mono County, California.

ARTICLE 325.

Henry Tripp, Esq., Mazatlan, Mexico, presented a valuable working model of a locomotive.

ARTICLE 326.

Judge S. C. Hastings presented surveying and assaying apparatus, the bequest of his son, the late Marshall Hastings.

ARTICLE 327.

Adolph Mailliard, Esq., of San Rafael, presented a valuable set of one hundred and eighty-four military maps of France and Belgium, formerly used by Jerome Bonaparte, King of Spain.

ARTICLE 328.

Howard Stillman—Forty-six coins and one medal. Among them seven of silver (two of which were Roman), and the remainder copper or bronze.

ARTICLE 329.

J. J. Rivers has presented each of the departments of the Museum with many valuable specimens.

ARTICLE 330.

N. C. Carnall—A collection of implements from the South Pacific Islands, including a large wooden spear, three javelins, bow and six arrows, and a large wooden sword.

ARTICLE 331.

Hon. L. B. Mizner—A collection of wooden articles manufactured by the Alaskan Indians, comprising one finely carved wooden tray, two horn scoops, a hollow carved four legged figure representing a beaver, carving representing a water bird, kneeling figure bound as a prisoner, figure with two heads, upright figure, mask with perforated lip, mask with crown, compound figure of bear and bird, large upright figure with two heads, its base being another head.

ARTICLE 332.

Mrs. Charles Webb Howard, on behalf of several ladies, June 4, 1877, presented costly Gothic chair for the President, hair cushion in plush, and loose cover; also, President's gown.

ARTICLE 333.

The General Government has supplied the University with a complete set of standard weights and measures, and they are now on deposit in the Bacon Art and Library building.

CHAPTER XLVI.

ARTICLE 334.

German Library of the University of California.

Donations of money, books, and pictures to September 25, 1884:

Armes, W. D. _____Oakland
Aronstein, Dr. A._____San Francisco
Bates, Miss C. _____ Berkeley
Barkhaus, F. W. and D._____San Francisco
Burk, Fred. _____Oakland
Baum, J._____San Francisco
Brandenstein, J._____San Francisco
Bachman, S. _____San Francisco
Boyson, Dr. J. T._____San Francisco
Brown, M. _____San Francisco
Bancroft, A. L. & Co._____San Francisco
Bauer, J. C. _____San Francisco
Crist, G. F._____Oakland
Chabot, A._____ Oakland
Collection by A. Schwabacher_____San Francisco
Collection by Humboldt Savings Bank_____San Francisco
Collection by L. Lothammer and Chs. Schmidt__Sacramento
Cash from a friend_____
Cohn, Dr. David_____San Francisco
Duerr, Chas. _____Suñol
Duisenberg, Chas._____San Francisco
Dwyer, J. J _____San Francisco
Directors of the **General German Benevolent** Society_____
_____San Francisco
"Eintracht" Verein_____San Francisco
Fife, W. C._____San Francisco
Fisher, P. M._____ Oakland
Freud, Isaac _____San Francisco
Freud, Richard J._____San Francisco
Gutte & Frank_____San Francisco
Hansen, Mrs. Chas._____San Francisco
Hecht Bros. & Co._____San Francisco
Heller, Moses _____San Francisco
Hittell, Mrs. Theo. H. _____San Francisco
Jarboe, John R. _____San Francisco
King, M. G. _____Oakland
Kirchhoff. Theo. _____San Francisco
Kohler, Chas. _____San Francisco
Kohl, Wm. _____San Francisco
Kohler & Chase_____San Francisco
Kruse, Edw. _____San Francisco

Lincoln, Jerome B.	San Francisco
Mayrisch, Rud.	San Francisco
McClain, Jos.	Berkeley
Mandelbaum, F.	San Francisco
Miller, Albert	Oakland
Meyer, Daniel	San Francisco
Meinecke, Chas.	San Francisco
Michelsen, N.	San Francisco
Meek, Harry W.	San Lorenzo
Moffitt, Jas.	Oakland
Mayne, Chas.	San Francisco
Nussbaumer, Emil	Oakland
Nussbaumer, G. L.	Oakland
Niebaum, Gust.	San Francisco
Niehaus, E.	Berkeley
Nickals, W. N.	Berkeley
Platschek, Jul.	San Francisco
Putzker, Albin	Berkeley
Putzker, Mrs. C.	Berkeley
Roeding, F.	San Francisco
Rohte, Emil	San Francisco
Richter, Dr C. M.	San Francisco
Regensburger, Dr. J.	San Francisco
Rosenstirn, Dr. J.	San Francisco
Renken, H.	Oakland
Sachs, Louis	San Francisco
Scholle, Albert	San Francisco
San Francisco Turn Verein	San Francisco
Schmiedell, Henry	San Francisco
Slate, F., Jr.	Berkeley
Sohst, J. F. W.	Oakland
Sloss, Louis & Co.	San Francisco
Schussler, Herm.	San Francisco
Spreckles, Claus	San Francisco
Spreckles, Peter	San Francisco
Stern, Louis	San Francisco
Stern, Sig.	San Francisco
Taber, T. W.	San Francisco
Tannhauser & Co.	San Francisco
Trenkle, Dr. E.	San Francisco
Von Hoffman, Dr.	San Francisco
Wachs, A. N.	Oakland
Weiss, Jacob	San Francisco
Werthenner, E.	San Francisco
Wieland, John	San Francisco
Wolleb, Edw.	San Francisco
Wormser, Isaac	San Francisco
Wyttenbach, E.	Berkeley
Zeile, Fred. W.	San Francisco

TITLE FOUR.

MISCELLANEOUS.

TITLE FOUR—MISCELLANEOUS.

CHAPTER I.

Articles of Incorporation.

ARTICLE 335.

STATE OF CALIFORNIA—DEPARTMENT OF STATE.

I, H. L. Nichols, Secretary of State of the State of California, do hereby certify that the annexed is a true, full, and correct copy of certificate of incorporation of the Regents of the University of California, now on file in my office.

Witness my hand and the great seal of State, at office, in Sacramento, California, the nineteenth day of October, A. D. 1871.

[SEAL.]

H. L. NICHOLS,
Secretary of State.

ARTICLE 336.

This is to certify that pursuant to the provisions of an Act of the Legislature of the State of California, entitled "An Act to create and organize the University of California," approved March 23, A. D. 1868, the undersigned, Henry H. Haight, Governor of the State of California, William Holden, Lieutenant-Governor, and O. P. Fitzgerald, State Superintendent of Public Instruction, three of the persons indicated in and by such enactment as Trustees and Directors of the corporation thereby directed to be created, have associated ourselves together for the purpose mentioned in and by said enactment, and to form a corporation for such purposes, by the name and style designated in and by said enactment, which is "The Regents of the University of California."

The names of the members of said Board and the terms of service of appointed and honorary members are as follows:

ARTICLE 337.

State of California, City and County of San Francisco, ss.

On this twelfth day of June, A. D. one thousand eight hundred and sixty-eight, **before** me, Henry Haight, a Notary **Public** in and for said **city** and county, duly commissioned and sworn, personally appeared the within named H. H. Haight, Governor, William Holden, Lieutenant-Governor, and O. P. Fitzgerald, Superintendent of Public Instruction of the State of California, personally known **to me to** be the individuals described in and who executed the annexed instrument, and they severally acknowledged to me that they executed the same as said officials, freely and voluntarily, and for the uses and purposes therein mentioned.

In witness whereof I have hereunto set my hand and affixed my **official seal,** the day and year in the certificate above written.

[Seal.]   HENRY HAIGHT, Notary Public.

Indorsed:

The **Regents of** the University of California. Certificate of Incorporation and Record of Classification **of** the eight members appointed by Governor, and honorary members.

Filed: June 18, 1868, in the office of the Secretary of State.

H. L. NICHOLS, Secretary of State.
By LEN. B. HARRIS, Deputy.

ARTICLE 338.

City and County of San Francisco, ss.

John S. Bugbee, of said city and county, being duly sworn, deposes and says:

That on the thirtieth day of May, 1868, he served the annexed notice upon Wm. Holden, William Watt, C. F. Reed, Lawrence Archer. Samuel L. Merritt, S. B. McKee, John W. Dwinelle, and C. T. Ryland, by depositing in the Post Office in the City and County of San Francisco, on said day, eight copies of the said notice, each inclosed in an envelope, duly stamped with a United States postage stamp, and directed to each of said persons respectively, at their respective **places of** residence, as follows, viz.:

Hon. William Holden, Lieutenant-Governor, San Quentin, Marin County, Cal

William Watt, Esq., **Grass Valley, Nevada County, Cal.**

C. F. Reed, Esq., President **State Agricultural Society,** Knight's Landing, Yolo County, Cal.

Hon. **Lawrence Archer,** San José, Santa Clara County, Cal.

Samuel L. Merritt, Esq., Oakland, Alameda County, Cal.

Hon. S. B. McKee, Oakland, Alameda County, Cal.

John W. Dwinelle, Esq., Oakland, Alameda County, Cal.

Hon. C. T Ryland, Speaker of the Assembly, San José, Santa Clara County, Cal.

That at the time above mentioned communication by mail existed between the City and County of San Francisco and the several **cities** and places **to** which said envelopes were directed.

And deponent further says that he also served said notice **upon** Horatio Stebbins, on the first day of June, 1868, in the

City and County of San Francisco, by delivering to and leaving with a member of the family of said Stebbins, at his residence in said San Francisco, during his absence therefrom, on said last mentioned day, a copy of said notice inclosed in an envelope directed to Rev. Horatio Stebbins, San Francisco, California.

And deponent further says that he also personally served said notice, in the City and County of San Francisco, on the said first day of June, 1868, on A. S. Hallidie, Richard P. Hammond, O. P. Fitzgerald, and John T. Doyle, by delivering to and leaving with each of said four last mentioned persons respectively, on said last mentioned day, and in said city and county, a copy of said notice addressed to each of them respectively.

JOHN S. BUGBEE.

Subscribed and sworn to before me, this eighth day of June, 1868.

HENRY S. HAIGHT,
Notary Public.

NOTICE.

ARTICLE 339.

SAN FRANCISCO, May 28, 1868.

SIR: The first meeting of the Regents of the State University will be held at the office of Messrs. Haight & Temple, No. 510 Jackson Street, San Francisco, on Tuesday, June 9, 1868, at 11 o'clock A. M. As it is very desirable that all the Regents be present at the organization of the Board, you are particularly requested to attend the meeting.

Yours respectfully,

H. H. HAIGHT,
Governor, etc.

CHAPTER II.

Agreements of affiliation with Colleges.

ARTICLE 340.

HASTINGS COLLEGE OF THE LAW.

[See Title II, Division III, Chapters XXX and XL.]

Resolved, That the institution known as the Hastings College of Law shall be affiliated with the University of California, and made an integral part of the same, and incorporated therewith, upon the following terms and conditions, which are hereby made a part of such affiliation and incorporation:

First—The Directors of said college named in the Act of the Legislature which organized it, approved March 26, 1878, shall have authority to fill vacancies in their Board when the same occur, as prescribed in the said Act, subject to the approval of the Board of Regents of said University, except in so far as qualified by the next section.

Second—Hon. S. Clinton Hastings, as founder of said college, and his legal representatives, shall always be entitled to have the appointment from his heirs or representatives of one of said Directors, without such appointment being subject to the approval of said Board of Regents.

Third—The Faculty of said college shall have the authority to present to said Board of Regents the names of such students of said college as they recommend for diplomas, and the said Board of Regents shall issue diplomas to said students, subject to the right of said Regents to refuse the same for cause.

Fourth—As soon as practicable, there shall be set apart for the use of the students of said college some room or suitable hall at the University.

Fifth—The present Dean of said college, the Hon. S. Clinton Hastings, shall, during his lifetime, have a seat in the Academic Senate of said University, be a member thereof, and have a vote therein.

Sixth—The said college shall be subject to the dominion of the said Board of Regents in all matters pertaining to its management and welfare.

Seventh—The number and duties of the professors of said college shall be prescribed, and the business of said college managed, by said Board of Directors, subject to the approval of said Board of Regents.

[Resolution of Regents, August 7, 1879.]

ARTICLE 341.

THE TOLAND MEDICAL COLLEGE.

Resolved, That a college is hereby created and organized which shall be known and designated as the Medical Department of the University of California.

Resolved further, That the several professors in said Medical Department shall be elected by the Regents, and shall hold their office upon the same terms as the other professors of the University.

Resolved further, That the Faculty of Medicine shall have the power to determine the qualifications for the admission of students, and in lieu of salary, to charge such fees as they see proper; to make such regulations not inconsistent with the organic Act, for the preservation of order and for the management of the internal affairs of the Medical Department, as they may deem best, and to determine the course of study.

Resolved further, That the Regents of the University will establish a Board, to be known as the Board of Medical Examiners of the University of California, and will annually appoint the members of said Board, whose duty it shall be to examine all students applying for a medical diploma, as well from the Medical Department of the University, as from other medical colleges. The Regents of the University will confer degrees upon such students of medicine as may be recommended therefor by the Faculty of their respective colleges, and whom the Board of Medical Examiners shall report entitled thereto, and upon none others.

[Resolutions of Regents, April 1, 1873.]

That the Board of Regents adopt, as a standard of examination, study, and graduation in the Medical Department of the University, one not lower than that of the University of Pennsylvania, or of the Medical Department of Harvard University.

[Resolution of Regents December 31, 1877.]

ARTICLE 342.

THE COLLEGE OF PHARMACY.

Resolved, That the following be the basis on which the California College of Pharmacy is affiliated with the University:

In accordance with the organic act of the University of California, the California College of Pharmacy is hereby affiliated with the University upon the following basis:

The College will maintain its own Board of Trustees, and will continue to hold its own property, as if this affiliation had not been agreed upon. The College will also appoint its own professors and establish its own course of instruction, subject to the general approbation of the Regents of the University. The University will confer the degree of Graduate in Pharmacy upon candidates recommended by the Board of Examiners of the College, and approved by a committee to be appointed by the Regents. This agreement may be canceled by mutual consent at any time, or by the withdrawal of either party to it, after twelve months' notice to the other party.

[Resolution of Regents June 2, 1873.]

Article 343.

DENTAL COLLEGE.

First—That a Dental Department be established in connection with the Medical Department of the University, and that the same be organized with a Professor of the Principles and Practice of Operative Dentistry.

A Professor of Dental Pathology and Therapeutics.

A Professor of Dental Art and Mechanism.

A Professor of Physiology.

A Professor of Chemistry.

A Professor of Anatomy.

A Professor of Surgery.

Second—That all the chairs be filled upon the recommendation of the Medical Faculty, subject to the approval of the Board of Regents.

Third—That the appointment of all demonstrators and clinical instructors be left entirely with the Dental Faculty.

Fourth—That after the organization of the Dental Department, all vacancies shall be filled in the same manner as is at present done in the Medical Faculty.

[Report of Committee adopted by Regents September 7, 1881.]

CHAPTER III.

Form of Application for Degrees.

Article 344.

[*Official.*]

UNIVERSITY OF CALIFORNIA,
[Name of College or Course,]
, 188–.

President ———:

Dear Sir: In accordance with a vote of ———, passed ———, 188–, the following named students, who have satisfactorily completed the required course of study and passed the necessary examinations, are hereby recommended to the honorable Board of Regents for the degree of ———.

Attest,   ——— ———, Dean.

[SEAL.]

12

CHAPTER IV.

Form of Diplomas.

ARTICLE 345.

Gubernatores Universitatis Californiensis: Has Literas **Edunt;** Ut omnes qui easdem perlegerint, certiores fiant —— ——, probatum Candidatum primi Gradus Universitatis Californiensis, definitive Collegii Literarum Humaniorum, a Gubernatoribus Universitatis donatum esse Titulo Artium Liberalium Baccalaurei et hujusce Universitatis Alumnum esse creatum. Quod publicum Universitatis Sigillum cum chirographo et Praesidis Secretariique Gubernatorum Consilii et Praesidis Professorumque Universitatis testantur.

Datum ex Aedibus Academicis **die** —— ——, Anno Salutis millesimo octingentesimo —— ——, Annoque Hujus Universitatis —— ——.

—— ——, Praeses Gubernatorum.

—— ——, Secretarius Consilii.

—— ——, —— ——, —— ——, —— ——,
Praeses et Professores Universitatis.

ARTICLE 346.

The Regents of the University of California, by authority **of the** State of California, have conferred the degree of *Bachelor of (Science)*, with all the rights and privileges thereto pertaining, on —— ——, a student in the College of (Mechanics), who has been examined by the appropriate Faculty and presented to the Regents as worthy to be admitted to the honor of said degree.

In witness whereof, **the** Regents **of the** University of California have caused their official **seal** and the signatures of their officers to be hereto affixed.

Dated at Berkeley, the seat of the University, this —— day of ——, in the year A. D. eighteen hundred and ——.

—— ——, President of the University.

—— ——, Governor of California and President of the Board of Regents.

—— ——, Secretary **of the Board** of Regents.

—— ——, —— ——, —— ——,
Professors and Instructors of the University

ARTICLE 347.

The Regents of the University of California, by authority **of the** State of California, have conferred the degree of *Bachelor of Philosophy*, with all the rights **and** privileges thereto pertaining, on —— ——, a student of the College of ——, who has been examined by the appropriate Faculty and presented to the Regents as worthy to be admitted to the honor of said degree.

In witness whereof, the Regents of the University of California have caused their official seal and the signatures of their officers to be hereto affixed.

Dated at Berkeley, the seat of the University, this —— day of ——, in the year A. D. eighteen hundred and ——.

—— ——, President of the University.

—— ——, Governor of California and President of the Board of Regents.

—— ——, Secretary of the Board of Regents.

—— ——, —— ——, —— ——,
Professors and Instructors of the University.

CHAPTER V.

Article 348.

Monthly Salary Roll of the University of California.

Names.	Monthly.
W. T. Reid, President	$375 00
John LeConte, Professor of Physics	275 00
Joseph LeConte, Professor of Geology and Natural History	275 00
Irving Stringham, Professor of Mathematics	250 00
Martin Kellogg, Professor of Latin Language and Literature	250 00
Frank Soulé, Professor of Civil Engineering and Astronomy	250 00
W. B. Rising, Professor of Chemistry	250 00
E. W Hilgard, Professor of Agriculture, etc.	250 00
A. S. Cook, Professor of English Language and Literature	250 00
G. W. Bunnell, Professor of Greek Language and Literature	250 00
Bernard Moses, Professor of History and Political Economy	250 00
F. G. Hesse, Professor of Industrial Mechanics	250 00
Geo. H. Howison, Mills Professor of Intellectual and Moral Philosophy, etc.	333 33
A. Putzker, Professor of German Language and Literature	200 00
Ross E. Browne, Instructor in Mechanical Drawing, etc.	200 00
F. Slate, Jr., Superintendent of Physical Laboratory and Instructor in Physics and Mechanics	150 00

George C. Edwards, Instructor in Mathematics_____$150 00
H. B. Jones, Instructor in French and Spanish_____ 150 00
A. W. Jackson, Jr., Instructor in Mineralogy, etc.____ 150 00
J. C. Rowell, Librarian_____ 150 00
William Carey Jones, Instructor in United States
    History and Constitutional Law_____ 150 00
C. B. Bradley, Instructor in English Language and
    Literature_____ 150 00
S. B. Christy, Instructor in Mining and Metallurgy__ 150 00
J. B. Clarke, Instructor in Mathematics_____ 150 00
J. J. Rivers, Curator of Museum_____ 100 00
E. C. O'Neil, Instructor in Chemistry_____ 125 00
W. W. Deamer, Recorder to Faculty and Instructor
    in Latin_____ 100 00
—— ——, Instructor in Civil Engineering_____ 75 00
Adolph Sommers, Assistant in Chemistry_____ 50 00
J. P. H. Dunn, Assistant in Chemistry_____ 50 00
—— ——, Assistant in English_____ 50 00
J. H. C. Bonte, Secretary and Superintendent of
    Grounds_____ 250 00
J. Ham. Harris, Assistant Secretary and Land Agent_ 220 00
John B. Mhoon, Attorney for Board of Regents_____ 100 00
John Hart, Janitor of Mechanical Arts College Build-
    ing_____ 60 00
George Gleason, Janitor of North Hall_____ 60 00
William Ellis, Janitor of South Hall_____ 60 00
Abel Whitton, Superintendent of Printing Office____ 60 00
W. J. Variel, Armorer_____ 12 00
E. A. Sawyer, Janitor of Gymnasium_____ 60 00
G. T. Clark, Janitor of Library Building_____ 30 00
Robert T. Bush, Janitor of Library Building_____ 30 00
—— ——, Policeman_____ 62 00
C. H. Dwinelle, Lecturer on Practical Agriculture___ 150 00
Joseph A. Sladky, Foreman of Mechanical Shop_____ 125 00
F. W Morse, Assistant in Agricultural Laboratory__ 75 00
W. G. Klee, Gardener to the College of Agriculture__ 75 00
M. E. Jaffa, Assistant in Viticultural Department___ 75 00

CHAPTER VI.

Inventory of real and personal property.

ARTICLE 349.

University site_____ 193$\frac{345}{1000}$ acres
The Tompkins farm_____47 acres
The Toland lots_____2 lots in San Francisco
The Cogswell property_____1 lot in San Francisco
    (The Lick Observatory not yet transferred to the Regents.)

ARTICLE 350.

From the Inventory, June 30, 1884.

COST OF BUILDINGS.

North Hall	$99,527 64	
South Hall	197,223 06	
Equipment for N. and S. Halls, etc.	29,293 84	
Mechanic Arts and Mining College	48,622 45	
Bacon Library and Art Gallery	54,145 47	
Furniture of	11,443 62	
Harmon Gymnasium	10,000 00	
Students' Cottages	27,226 06	
Barn	1,305 00	
Propagating houses, etc.	2,178 83	
		$480,965 97

PROPERTY IN DEPARTMENTS.

Physics	$8,239 09	
Civil Engineering	3,836 50	
Military	863 13	
University printing office	3,036 99	
Geology	1,635 00	
Museum of Natural History	17,468 56	
Museum of Mineralogy	28,131 94	
Mining	12,133 10	
Physical Laboratory	934 19	
Art Gallery	54,750 00	
Library	54,015 00	
Chemical Laboratory	8,394 01	
Agriculture	9,492 94	
Mechanical	9,414 02	
		$212,344 47
Total		$693,310 44

CHAPTER VII.

Funds and Endowments.

ARTICLE 351.

SEMINARY LAND FUND.

Derived from a Congressional grant of seventy-two sections of land (46,080 acres). This land was sold by the State Land Office at Sacramento at $1 25 per acre. (Transferred to Seminary Land Investment Fund.

ARTICLE 352.

PUBLIC BUILDING FUND.

Derived from a Congressional grant of ten sections of land (6,400 acres). The land was sold by the State Land Office at Sacramento at $1 25 per acre.

ARTICLE 353.

UNITED STATES ENDOWMENT FUND.

Derived from a Congressional grant of one hundred and fifty thousand acres. This land has been sold by the Regents of the University at $5 per acre. A permanent endowment, interest only to be used. (See Chapter II, Title I. Now invested in bonds, $518,000.)

ARTICLE 354.

BRAYTON PROPERTY FUND.

Derived from the sale of blocks Nos. 172, 173, 192, and 193, and buildings thereon, located in the City of Oakland. This fund took its title from the fact, that on one of the blocks the Rev. Mr. Brayton had his school buildings. The money for the purchase of the four blocks came from funds belonging to the University of California. The four blocks were sold for $169,760. From this amount the Regents paid off a mortgage of $50,000, and returned to the General Fund $32,255; reserving the balance of $87,505 for a permanent fund known as the Brayton Property Fund.

ARTICLE 355.

STATE ENDOWMENT FUND.

By Act of April 2, 1870, the State Controller was required to invest in bonds from the proceeds of the sale of tide lands an amount sufficient to yield an annual income of $50,000 for the benefit of the State University. This required an investment in bonds of the par value of $811,500. The Controller only purchased bonds of the par value of $750,-000, but added to this amount bonds held by the University prior to the passage of said Act, of the value of $61,500, claiming in his biennial report of 1873-5 that the law had been fully complied with. The Legislature by a subsequent Act, restored to the University the $61,500 with accrued interest thereon.

ARTICLE 356.

DIVERTED FUND INTEREST.

By Act of March 4, 1881, the annual interest of $4,785 is to be paid to the University until the State elects to and does return to the Perpetual Endowment Fund of said University, the sum of $79,750. This sum was to restore the $61,500 of bonds held by the University prior to Act of April 2, 1870 and the accrued interest thereon of $18,250. (See Articles 134 and 135, page 67.)

ARTICLE 357

LAND ADMINISTRATION FUND.

Derived from accrued interest on special funds deposited with savings banks. In bonds, $22,000.

ARTICLE 358.

SEMINARY LAND INVESTMENT FUND.

Derived from investment by the Regents in bonds of the par value of $19,000. These bonds were purchased with money belonging to the General Fund, to restore to the Seminary Land Fund the amounts that had been used from time to time in payment of current expenses; the Regents not having been informed by the State Controller of the sources from which said sums were derived.

ARTICLE 359.

MICHAEL REESE LIBRARY FUND.

Donation by Mr. Michael Reese of $50,000, the interest only to be used for the purchase of books. (See Chapter XVII, Title III, page 143.)

ARTICLE 360.

D. O. MILLS FUND.

Donation of $75,000, to which is to be added the accrued interest to June 1, 1884, of $11,638 35, making a total of $86,-638 35, to be invested as a permanent fund, the interest of which shall be used to provide for a Chair of Intellectual and Moral Philosophy and Civil Polity. (See Chapter XXXIV, Title III, page 156.)

ARTICLE 361.

MEDAL FUND.

Donations by subscription amounting to $2,383 68, the interest on which only to be used for the purchase of a gold medal to be awarded to the most distinguished graduate of the year. (See Chapter X, Title III, page 119.)

ARTICLE 362.

ENDOWMENT BY HON. EDWARD TOMPKINS

Of the "Agassiz Professorship of Oriental Languages and Literature," by donation of forty-seven acres of land in Oakland, the same to be held by the Regents of the University until it can be sold for $50,000, which sum is then to be invested as a permanent endowment, the interest only to be used. The land has been rented and rents deposited with the Union Savings Bank of Oakland, which, with accruing interest, amounts to some $2,250. (See Chapter XI, Title III, page 119.)

CHAPTER VIII.

Deed purporting to transfer interest in lands and reserving water rights—The Regents to Mary E. Brayton.

ARTICLE 363.

This indenture, made the twenty-eighth day of November, A. D. one thousand eight hundred and seventy ——, between the Regents of the University of California, party of the first part, and Mary E. Brayton, of Oakland, Alameda County, California, party of the second part, witnesseth: That the said party of the first part, for and in consideration of the sum of thirty thousand dollars, lawful money of the United States of America, to it in hand paid by the said party of the second part, at or before the ensealing and delivery of these presents, the receipt whereof is hereby acknowledged, has granted, bargained and sold, conveyed and confirmed, and by these presents does grant, bargain and sell, convey and confirm unto the said party of the second part, and to her heirs and assigns forever, all those certain pieces or parcels of land, situate, lying, and being in the County of Alameda, State of California, bounded and described as follows, to wit:

First—Commencing at the southeast corner of plat number eighty-two (82), as known upon the map hereinafter referred to, and running thence north 50° 30' west fifteen (15) chains; thence south 80° 30' west twelve (12) chains and sixty-eight (68) links, thence south 9° 30' east fifteen (15) chains; and thence north 80° 30' east eleven (11) chains sixty-three (63) links to the point of beginning, containing eighteen $\frac{21}{100}$ (18$\frac{21}{100}$) acres of land, and being a portion of plat number eighty-two (82), as designated and numbered on a certain map of the ranchos of Vicente and Domingo Peralta, surveyed by one Julius Kellersberger, and on file in the County Recorder's office in and for the said County of Alameda.

Second—Commencing at the northeast corner of plat number eighty (80), as designated and numbered on the said map of the said Kellersberger, and running thence south 5° 30' east forty-three (43) chains and fifty (50) links; thence south 85° 30' west six (6) chains and seventy (70) links; thence north 13° 30' east two (2) chains; thence north 33° east seven (7) chains and sixty (60) links; thence north 13° 30' west two (2) chains; thence north 82° west seven (7) chains and eighty-nine (89) links; thence south 50° 45' west three (3) chains and forty-four (44) links; thence south 79° 30' west two (2) chains and eighty-six links (86 l.); thence north 8° 45' west two (2) chains and eighty (80) links; thence south 81° 15' west six (6) chains and ten (10) links; thence north 8° 45' west eight (8) chains and eighteen (18) links; thence north 29° 40' west one (1) chain and seventy-nine (79) links; thence north 32° west five (5) chains and ninety-one (91) links; thence north 44° 15' west four (4) chains and thirty-two (32) links; thence north 46° 15' west two (2) chains and seventy (70) links; thence north 72° west one (1) chain and thirty-nine (39) links; thence north 19° 30' west one (1) chain and seventy-five (75) links; thence north 60° 15' west one (1) chain and sixty-five (65) links; thence south 58° 15' west two (2) chains and twenty-one (21) links; thence north 84° 30' west seventy-five (75) links; thence north 40° 30' west eighty-four (84) links; thence south 72° west three (3) chains and seventy-four (74) links; thence north 6° east one (1) chain and seventy-five (75) links; thence north 79° 30' east two (2) chains and twelve (12) links; thence north 89° 45' east two (2) chains and seventy-six (76) links; thence north 46° 45' east one (1) chain and ninety-eight (98) links; thence south 64° 45' east two (2) chains and eighty-one (81) links; thence south 28° east one (1) chain and forty-eight (48) links; thence south 52° 45' east three (3) chains; thence south 75° 30' east one (1) chain and fifty-eight (58) links; thence south 44° 45' east one (1) chain and twelve (12) links; thence south 59° 15' east two (2) chains and fifty-eight (58) links; thence south 64° 30' east one (1) chain and seventy-seven (77) links; thence south 86° 30' east four (4) chains and fifty (50) links; thence north 89° 30' east three (3) chains and three (3) links; thence north 36° 30' east three (3) chains and three (3) links; thence north 86° 15' east one (1) chain and eighty-three (83) links; thence north 9° 30' west twelve (12) chains and fifty-six (56) links; and thence north 80° 30′ east eleven (11) chains and sixty-three (63) links, to the point of beginning, containing sixty-three $\frac{49}{100}$ ($63\frac{49}{100}$) acres of land, and being a portion of said plot number eighty (80).

Third—All those certain lots numbered one (1), two (2), three (3), four (4), five (5), six (6), seven (7), eight (8), nine (9), ten (10), and eleven (11), in Block B; lot number forty-nine (49), in Block F; and lots numbered twenty (20), twenty-one (21), twenty-three (23), twenty-four (24), twenty-six (26), twenty-seven (27), twenty-eight (28), twenty-nine (29), thirty-one (31), and thirty-two (32), in Block D, as designated and numbered on a certain map of a portion of the Berkeley property, situated between the University of California and the State Deaf, Dumb, and Blind Asylum, Oakland, Alameda County, as laid out by Frederic Law Olmstead, and surveyed by W. F. Boardman, Surveyor for the said County of Alameda, and filed for record in the County Recorder's office, in and for the said County of Alameda; the said lots being twenty-two (22) in all, and a portion of said plot numbered eighty (80) as designated on said map of Kellersberger.

Fourth—All the right, title, and interest of the party of the first part of, in, and to all the undivided mountain land, situate easterly of the said plots numbered eighty (80) and eighty-two (82), as known and designated on the said map of the said Julius Kellersberger, the same being the undivided interest in lands not embraced in any of the numbered plots upon the said map of Kellersberger, said undivided interest supposed to be two hundred and thirty (230) acres of land, more or less, and more particularly described in a certain deed, bearing date November 6th, A. D. 1858, made and executed by one John A. Bonneron to one Orrin Simmons, and recorded in the County Recorder's office in and for the County of Alameda on March 21st, A. D. 1859, in Liber "H" of Deeds, page 717, and also in a certain other deed bearing date August 10th, A. D. 1864, made and executed by the said Orrin Simmons and Hannah, his wife, to the President and Board of Trustees of the College of California, and recorded in the County Recorder's office aforesaid, on August 19th, A. D. 1864, in Liber "P" of Deeds, page 687, to both of which said deeds for greater certainty reference is hereby made, together with all the right, title, and interest, possession, claim, and demand, conveyed to the President and Board of Trustees of the College of California (and since by them to the party of the first part) by the said last above mentioned deed from the said Orrin Simmons, and Hannah, his wife, of, in, and to all that certain portion of the undivided mountain lands, hereinabove referred to, which had been included and inclosed within a fence by the said Simmons, and was in the possession of and occupied by the said Simmons at the date of the execution and delivery by himself and wife, of the said deed last above mentioned, and since then continuously has been and now is in the actual, notorious, and exclusive possession of and occupied by the party of the first part.

Together with all and singular the tenements, hereditaments, and appurtenances thereunto belonging or in any wise appertaining, and the reversion and reversions, remainder and remainders, rents, issues, and profits thereof. And also all the estate, right, title, interest, property, possession, claim, and demand whatsoever, as well in law as in equity, of the said party of the first part of, in, or to the above described premises, and every part and parcel thereof, with the appurtenances.

To have and to hold, all and singular the above mentioned and described premises, together with the appurtenances, unto the said party of the second part, her heirs and assigns forever. Excepting and reserving out of and from this conveyance and out of the premises, firstly, secondly, and fourthly above described, the right to the water arising upon or flowing across the same, so far as it shall be needed for the use of the University of California, and the right to enter upon said land for the purpose of constructing and laying the necessary pipes to make the same available, the same to be exercised in such manner as not to interfere with the use and occupation of the land for cultivation and to do no damage to the crops thereon.

[Recorded in Liber 61, p. 198, Records of Alameda County.]

CHAPTER IX.

1. Map of grounds.

BOUNDARIES.

No.	Course.	Distance.	No.	Course.	Distance.
1	N. 80° 34′ E.	593.30	19	S. 81° 10′ W.	79.40
2	N. 9° 30′ W.	41.92	20	N. 46° 5′ W.	49.70
3	N. 80° 30′ E.	4,546.74	21	N. 85° 15′ W.	49.50
4	S. 9° 30′ E.	1,799.00	22	S. 69° 30′ W.	71.30
5	S. 86° 15′ W.	120.78	23	S. 4° 37′ E.	115.20
6	S. 36° 30′ W.	200.00	24	S. 62° 00′ W.	1,231.90
7	S. 89° 30′ W.	200.00	25	S. 68° 45′ W.	206.58
8	N. 86° 30′ W.	297.00	26	N. 4° 46′ W.	17.93
9	N. 64° 30′ W.	116.82	27	S. 70° 10′ W.	405.25
10	N. 59° 15′ W.	170.28	28	West.	176.22
11	N. 44° 45′ W.	73.92	29	N. 77° 00′ W.	140.58
12	N. 75° 30′ W.	104.28	30	N. 70° 30′ W.	97.02
13	N. 52° 45′ W.	198.00	31	N. 85° 00′ W.	209.29
14	N. 28° 00′ W.	97.68	32	S. 89° 30′ W.	1,004.52
15	N. 64° 45′ W.	185.46	33	N. 4° 56′ W.	652.30
16	S. 46° 45′ W.	158.19	34	N. 80° 30′ E.	8.58
17	S. 77° 33′ W.	56.30	35	N. 5° 14′ W.	948.05
18	N. 61° 00′ W.	57.80			

TITLE FIVE.

ORDERS OF THE BOARD.

TITLE FIVE—ORDERS OF THE BOARD.

DIVISION ONE—RELATING TO THE BOARD.

CHAPTER I.

BY-LAWS.

Officers and Meetings.

ARTICLE 364.

The regular officers of the Board shall consist of a President, who shall be the Governor, as provided by law; a Secretary, and Treasurer.

ARTICLE 365.

The regular meetings of the Board shall be on the first Tuesday of September, December, March, and the last Tuesday of May.

ARTICLE 366.

Special meetings may be called at any time by the President of the Board, or by any seven members through the Secretary, who shall notify each member of the time, place, and object of such meetings by notices addressed to the members at their respective places of residence and deposited in the Post Office at least six days before the meeting.

ARTICLE 367.

The Treasurer of the University and the Deans of the affiliated colleges shall be notified of the time of meetings of the Board.

ARTICLE 368.

As provided by law, seven Regents constitute a quorum for the transaction of business; and any meeting may be adjourned, and its business continued, by the vote of a majority of the Regents present.

13

ARTICLE 369.

The absence of any appointed Regent for four successive regular meetings of the Board shall—unless the Board for good cause, such as sickness, temporary absence from the State, by a vote of record expressly excuse such absence— make it the duty of the Secretary to address such Regent, in writing, inquiring whether he intends by such absence to express his desire to resign his office; and in the absence of any reply thereto, or reasonable excuse for such absence, he shall be requested to resign.

ARTICLE 370.

It shall be the duty of the President of the Board to preside at its meetings, and to direct the calling of special meetings when they shall seem to him expedient. In case of his absence, or of his inability to act, his place may be supplied, *pro tempore*, for that meeting, by any member of the Board who may be chosen for that purpose by a majority vote.

ARTICLE 371.

A Secretary and a Treasurer shall be elected by the Board by ballot, who shall give bonds for such amounts and in such form as the Board shall prescribe, immediately after their election.

ARTICLE 372.

It shall be the duty of the Secretary to call all meetings of the Board when so directed; to keep and duly record the minutes of its proceedings in a book provided for that purpose; to discharge the duties required of him by law; and to assist the President, the committees of the Board, and the Treasurer, in the discharge of their duties, whenever required by them. In case of the absence of the Secretary, or of his inability to act, his place may be supplied, *pro tempore*.

ARTICLE 373.

It shall be the duty of the Treasurer to collect, receive, and take charge of all moneys of the corporation or subject to the use of the Board; to disburse them on the warrants of the President and Secretary of the Board drawn upon the Treasurer in pursuance of the orders of the Board, and to make a full report of his receipts and disbursements at the regular meetings of the Board and at such other times as the Board may specially direct.

All moneys received by or paid to the Regents or its officers shall be deposited, without delay, in a bank to be selected by the Treasurer, to the credit of "The Regents of the Uni-

'versity of California." All checks drawn against such bank account and deposits shall bear the signature :

"The Regents of the University of California,
" By ----------------------
"Treasurer."

Committees.

ARTICLE 374.

There shall be five standing committees, as follows:
On Endowment, Finance, and Audit.
On Buildings, Grounds, and other property.
On Law.
On Congressional Land Grant.
On the Library and Museum.

ARTICLE 375.

These committees shall consist of three members each, and the Secretary of the Board shall notify the members and attend their meetings (except in the case of the Land Committee) and keep a minute of their proceedings in a suitable record book. The Board, at its regular meeting in May, may nominate the members of the several standing committees, and recommend them to the President for his confirmation.

ARTICLE 376.

The standing committees are specially charged with the immediate care and supervision of the subject-matters indicated respectively by their titles. All questions relating to their particular departments, requiring reference, shall be severally referred to them, and they shall report progress, or finally, at the meeting next following the date when the matter was referred to them. In case any matter is referred to two or more of said committees, or of a special committee appointed to act with any standing committee, then the proper committees shall unite and form a joint committee, and a majority report of said joint committee shall be regarded as a majority report of each of said committees so joined. The joint committee shall elect its own Chairman.

ARTICLE 377.

Special committees may be raised at any meeting of the Board to execute such business, not properly belonging to the department of a standing committee, as may be intrusted to them. They may be appointed by the President or by resolution of the Board, and must report at the meeting of the Board next after their appointment, or as the resolution may direct.

ARTICLE 378.

A majority of any committee may act and agree upon a report at any meeting thereof, when all the members are present, or at any meeting of which all the members have had due notice. No action of a committee shall be valid unless had at a meeting of such committee convened as herein authorized.

ARTICLE 379.

In case vacancies occur at any time in the committees, they may be filled by the Board.

ARTICLE 380.

The Finance Committee shall present the annual budget at the quarterly meeting in September. (See Art. 429.)

Reports.

ARTICLE 381.

The annual report of the Secretary and Land Agent shall be made up to the first day of July of each year.

ARTICLE 382.

No documents, other than reports of committees, shall be spread upon the minutes unless so ordered.

ARTICLE 383.

All reports, letters, and other documents presented to the Board must be immediately placed in the hands of the Secretary, who shall place them on file in the archives of his office.

ARTICLE 384.

All reports shall be presented in writing.

ARTICLE 385.

All resolutions shall be presented in writing, when requested by the Chairman.

Article 386.

The Secretary shall report to the Board all communications received by him, and intended for the Board, at the next meeting after their reception.

Article 387.

The Secretary shall indorse upon all documents presented to or considered by the Regents the date of the filing, and the number of the same, in the order of filing, and shall preserve the same and keep an index thereof by subjects.

Article 388.

All recommendations and testimonials of candidates for professorships must be printed or filed, and copies must be furnished to each member of the Board if desired.

Regents.

Article 389.

Regents shall submit their commissions upon their first introduction to the Board, and the Secretary shall enter upon the minutes the fact, with an abstract of the commissions.

Article 390.

No Regent shall be elected or appointed by the Board to any position with a salary.

Article 391.

No Regent shall be interested, directly nor indirectly, in any contract with the Regents, nor in goods furnished for the University, nor make any purchases, nor secure the transportation of any goods with those purchased or transported for the University.

Article 392.

The corporate seal of the Regents shall be of the size of a Mexican dollar, and the legend around the rim shall be: "University of California—Organized 1868." And the motto shall be: "Let there be light."

Article 393.

No amendment to any article of this chapter shall be made at the meeting when such amendment is first proposed.

CHAPTER II.

RULES OF ORDER.

ARTICLE 394.

The following rules of order are adopted:

RULE 1. The President shall state every question coming before the Board, and before putting it to vote, shall ask "Is the Board ready for the question?" Should silence indicate their readiness, he shall rise to take the question, and after he has risen no Regent shall be allowed to speak upon it. He shall pronounce the decision of the Board on all subjects; he may speak to all questions from the chair, having preference of other Regents in speaking on points of order; he shall decide questions of order without debate (unless entertaining doubts on the point, he invite it). When his decision has been appealed from, the question shall be put thus: "Will the Board sustain the Chair in its decision?"

RULE 2. Every Regent, when he speaks, shall rise and respectfully address the Chair, and shall not proceed until recognized by the President. While speaking, he shall confine himself to the question under debate.

RULE 3. Should two or more Regents rise to speak at the same time, the Chair shall decide which shall be entitled to the floor.

RULE 4. No Regent shall disturb another in his speech, unless to call him to order or for the purpose of explanation, nor pass between the speaker and the Chair, nor indulge in audible conversation during the meetings of the Board.

RULE 5. If a Regent, while speaking, shall be called to order by the Chair, he shall cease speaking, and take his seat until the question of order is determined and permission given him to proceed.

RULE 6. No Regent shall speak more than once on the same question, until all the Regents wishing to speak shall have had an opportunity to do so; nor more than twice, without permission of the Chair; nor more than five minutes at one time. On questions of order no Regent shall speak more than once.

RULE 7. When any communication, petition, or memorial is presented, before it is read, a brief statement of its contents shall be made by the introducer to the Chair; and after it has been read, a brief notice of its purport shall be entered on the journal.

RULE 8. No motion shall be stated until it has been seconded, nor open for debate or consideration until stated by the President, and, at the desire of any Regent, shall be reduced to writing.

RULE 9. No more than two amendments shall be in order to any proposition at the same time; except that a substitute for all the pending propositions may be offered at any time, and in that case the adoption of the substitute shall be the first question. If the substitute is adopted it shall become the only proposition before the Board, and may then be amended or passed upon without amendment. A proposition to strike out all after the word "Resolved," in a resolution, or to strike out the body of a resolution, shall be deemed to be a substitute.

RULE 10. When a blank is to be filled, the question shall be first taken on the highest sum or number, and the longest or latest time proposed.

RULE 11. Any Regent may call for a division of a question, when the sense will admit of it.

RULE 12. When any two of the Regents rise in favor of taking a question by "yeas and nays," it shall be so taken and recorded.

RULE 13. When a question is before the Board, no motion shall be received, unless: First, to adjourn; second, to lay on the table; third, the previous question; fourth, to postpone indefinitely; fifth, to postpone to a particular time; sixth, to divide; seventh, to refer; eighth, to amend—which motions shall severally have precedence in the order herein named, and the first three shall be decided without debate.

RULE 14. When a question is postponed indefinitely, it shall not be acted on again for three months.

RULE 15. After any question, except one of indefinite postponement, has been decided, any Regent who voted in the majority may, at the same or next succeeding stated meeting, move for a reconsideration thereof.

RULE 16. On the call of two Regents, if seconded by a majority, the "previous question" shall be put in this form : "Shall the main question be now put?" If carried, all amendments not already adopted shall be acted upon in their order, but the questions must be taken without further debate.

RULE 17. While the President is putting the question or addressing the Board, no Regent shall walk about, leave the room, or entertain private discourse.

Order of Business.

ARTICLE 395.

The following shall be the order of business at each meeting:
1. Roll call.
2. Reading, correction, and approval of the minutes of the last meeting.
3. The special business for which the meeting is called, if the meeting be special.
4. Reports of standing committees.
5. Report of the President of the University.
6. Reports of special committees.
7. Report of the Secretary, Treasurer, and Land Agent.
8. Unfinished business.
9. New business.

ARTICLE 396.

This order of business may be suspended at any meeting by a vote of two thirds of the Regents present.

ARTICLE 397.

Cushing's Manual of Parliamentary Law is adopted, in so far as not inconsistent with the orders of this Board and statutes governing the same.

DIVISION TWO—RELATING TO INSTRUCTION.

CHAPTER I.

The Academic Senate.

ARTICLE 398.

The Academic Senate shall organize and perform such duties as are required by law, and exercise such other powers as the Board of Regents may confer upon it, and hold at least two sessions each year, at Berkeley.

ARTICLE 399.

All persons authorized to engage in instruction in any of the departments of the University, by authority of this Board, are entitled to participate in the discussions of the Academic Senate, but the power of voting is confined to the President and professors, resident and non-resident.

ARTICLE 400.

The Secretary of the Board of Regents shall be also Secretary of the Academic Senate.

CHAPTER II.

Colleges of Letters and Science, at Berkeley.

ARTICLE 401.

The following colleges are established:
1. College of Letters (classical course).
2. College of Agriculture.
3. College of Mechanics.
4. College of Mining.
5. College of Engineering.
6. College of Chemistry
7. Literary Course.
8. Course of Letters and Political Science.

ARTICLE 402.

The full course in each of these colleges extends through four years.

ARTICLE 403.

Commencement Day of each year is the last Wednesday in May.

ARTICLE 404.

For the purpose of facilitating the work of the agricultural experimental stations the Professor of Agriculture is authorized to use the grounds and laboratories attached to his department, provided that the total expenditures to be made in connection with the agricultural experimental station shall not exceed the special legislative appropriation.

Article 405.

All that portion of the University grounds west of the main road—being west and northwest of the northerly branch of Strawberry Creek—is set apart for the purpose of the culture of economic plants and botanical garden, under the direction of the Professor of Agriculture.

Article 406.

Two hours a week for military tactics in the University shall be required for four years.

Article 407.

Applications for promotion in rank, or for an increase of the salary of any officer, professor, instructor, or other employé of the University, can only be made in writing, and must be submitted to the Board at the regular meeting next preceding the annual meeting, and can only be considered at such annual meeting, or at the next regular meeting thereafter.

CHAPTER III.

Affiliated Colleges.

Article 408.

The affiliated colleges are as follows.
1. The Hastings College of the Law
2. The Toland College of Medicine.
3. The College of Dentistry.
4. The College of Pharmacy.

Article 409.

All other colleges of the University now existing, or which may be added to, or affiliated with, the University, shall be subject to the control of the Board of Regents to the same extent as the Colleges of Science and Letters, except in so far as the authority of the Board may be limited by law, or by agreement of affiliation with such other colleges.

CHAPTER IV.

The President of the University.

ARTICLE 410.

The President is required to report to the Board of Regents at its regular meetings the condition, wants, and prospects of the University, in writing.

ARTICLE 411.

The President is required to obtain monthly from each professor and instructor a report of the number of hours of each day actually employed by him in his class duties, and the number of students in actual attendance in each class, and make report quarterly thereof to the Board.

ARTICLE 412.

The President is authorized to make such visits as he may deem expedient and practicable to the schools and teachers' institutes of this State, in order that a more intimate relation may be established between the University and the schools of the State.

ARTICLE 413.

The President is authorized to assign the lecture and recitation rooms, and to permit the use of halls for lectures and other purposes.

ARTICLE 414.

The printing press at Berkeley is placed in charge of the President.

DIVISION THREE—RELATING TO STUDENTS.

CHAPTER I.

ARTICLE 415.

Every applicant must be at least sixteen years of age, and must present a certificate of good moral character.

Article 416.

Women shall be admitted into the University on equal terms with men.

Article 417.

No tuition fee is required from any student in any of the academic colleges, at Berkeley.

Article 418.

The willful damaging or defacement of the buildings, appurtenances of the University, or the conversion or theft of any of the property of the same, by any student, aside from the usual remedy at law, shall be deemed sufficient ground for expulsion.

Article 419.

The following regulation, adopted by the Board of Regents, March 4, 1884, is in effect:

"Upon the request of the Principal of any public school in California, whose course of study embraces, in kind and extent, the subjects required for admission to any college of the University at Berkeley, a committee of the Academic Senate will visit such schools, and report upon the quality of the instruction there given. If the report of such committee be favorable, a graduate of the school, upon the personal recommendation of the Principal, accompanied by his certificate that the graduate has satisfactorily completed the studies of the course preparatory to the college he wishes to enter, may, at the discretion of the Faculty of such college, be admitted without examination."

DIVISION FOUR—RELATING TO ADMINISTRATION AND FINANCE.

CHAPTER I.

Article 420.

The President of this Board is ordered to draw from the State Treasury, upon an order drawn upon the State Controller for a warrant on the State Treasurer, in favor of the Treasurer of the University of California, at any time during each fiscal year ending June thirtieth, any or all moneys realized from the "Consolidated Perpetual Endowment **Fund of** the University of California," as interest, profits, income, or revenue arising therefrom, which is subject to disbursement, to meet the current annual expenses of the University; also, the annual interest of forty-seven hundred and eighty-five dollars, provided for by Act **of** March 4, 1881, "providing **for the** restoration **of** certain diverted **funds.**"

ARTICLE 421.

The **President of this** Board is **ordered** to draw **from the** State Treasury, upon **an** order drawn upon the State **Con**troller for a warrant on **the** State Treasurer in favor **of the** Treasurer of the University of California, at any time during each fiscal year (ending June thirtieth), any and all moneys appropriated by the Legislature for the use or benefit of the University during such current fiscal year.

ARTICLE 422.

The State Treasurer is directed to pay over all amounts paid into the State Treasury for the redemption of bonds belonging to the University to the Treasurer of the University of California, in accordance with **the** terms of an Act entitled an Act to provide for the better control and management of the several funds of the University of California, and for the investment and security of the same, approved March 9, 1883.

ARTICLE 423.

The Treasurer of the University is authorized and instructed to advance from the General Fund of the University to the Treasurer of the State of California, an amount sufficient to pay the interest coupons that may be due on all bonds belonging to the "Consolidated Perpetual Endowment Fund of the University **of** California," **three** days be**fore** their maturity.

ARTICLE 424.

The Treasurer of the University is authorized and instructed to advance, from the General Fund of the University to **the** Treasurer of the State of California, at such times as may **be** required, an amount sufficient to redeem all bonds belonging to the "Consolidated Perpetual Endowment Fund of the University of California," which may be required to be sur**rendered** for cancellation.

ARTICLE 425.

In remitting bonds belonging to the University, to be placed in the "Consolidated Perpetual Endowment Fund of the University" to the State Treasurer, by the Treasurer of the University, the latter is required to advise the State Controller accordingly, at the time of such remittance.

ARTICLE 426.

All bank certificates of deposit issued on account of the University shall be made payable to the order of the Regents of the University, and the Treasurer of the University is authorized to indorse the same.

ARTICLE 427.

The President of the Board and the Secretary are hereby authorized to draw upon the Treasurer of the University, and the Treasurer is hereby authorized to pay such checks as may be drawn upon him by them, for the payment of the current expenses of the University, to wit: The salaries of the Faculty, Instructors, Janitors, Land Agent, Secretary, and other permanent employés whose salaries have been or may be fixed by this Board, and such other demands as have been or may be hereafter properly audited and approved by the Board.

ARTICLE 428.

The Finance Committee are authorized to invest the money in the treasury of the University belonging to the separate permanent funds, in such securities as they may deem best.

ARTICLE 429.

At the regular September meeting of the Board of Regents, a budget shall be made up by the Finance Committee and submitted to the Board for its approval, apportioning specific sums to the several departments of the University for that year.

ARTICLE 430.

The President of the University and the Secretary shall closely supervise all current expenditures of the University, excepting such as the Board may definitely incur, and bills therefor shall not be approved by the Finance Committee without the indorsement of one or both of said officers. This shall not apply to investments in securities.

ARTICLE 431.

All bills must be approved by the various committees by whom they are incurred, before being audited by the Finance· Committee.

Article 432.

No demands or bills shall be ordered paid by the Board until approved by the proper committee and audited by the Finance Committee, except **upon a** two-thirds vote by yeas and nays of all the members present **at** a meeting of the Board.

Article 433.

The Secretary of the Board shall keep a book, to **be called** "The Abstract Book," wherein shall be opened an account with each fund, crediting the fund with its appropriation, and debiting it as warrants are drawn upon said fund, from time to time, bringing down quarterly balances, and reporting the same to each regular meeting of the Board of Regents, and that no change or transfers shall be made of said funds without the consent of the Board of Regents.

Article 434.

In all cases relating to the collection of compound interest due the University, the Finance Committee of the Board is hereby directed to instruct the Secretary and Land Agent of the Board as to the adjustment and collection of the same.

Article 435.

All expenditures for salaries, material, and labor, on account of any special appropriations made by the Legislature, shall **cease** with the exhaustion of said funds, respectively.

Article 436.

No liability shall be incurred on behalf of the Board of Regents by any officer or officers of any affiliated college.

Article 437.

No professor, or employé, in any affiliated college of the University, shall receive any salary or wages as such from the funds of the University under the control of this Board.

Article 438.

Whenever leave of absence is granted to any professor or instructor his salary shall cease during such absence.

ARTICLE 439.

No salary or compensation shall be paid to professors, instructors, or employés unless actively employed in some department of the University.

ARTICLE 440.

Before any purchases not authorized previously by the Board, can be made, a requisition addressed to the Secretary must be made out giving in detail the articles to be purchased, with the prices thereof, and approved by the Finance Committee.

ARTICLE 441.

No purchase shall be made without a written order from the Secretary.

ARTICLE 442.

All students using the several laboratories must make a deposit with the Secretary for each term in advance.

ARTICLE 443.

The amount of such deposit shall be designated by the President of the University, and shall be estimated to cover the cost of the materials to be used.

ARTICLE 444.

Upon the recommendation of the President of the University, and the approval of the Finance Committee, the amount of such deposit may be remitted to students unable to pay.

ARTICLE 445.

When such deposits are made the Secretary shall give deposit receipts.

ARTICLE 446.

The Secretary shall require all students who may have made deposits on account of chemicals or other purposes, to make settlement before Commencement Day of each year. In case of their failure to make such settlement, all their deposits shall be forfeited to the University and paid over to the Treasurer.

ARTICLE 447.

Such deposits, or the balance thereof, after settlement, shall be returned to the student only upon the surrender of the deposit receipt therefor.

Article 448.

All delinquencies must be collected by the Secretary, and students in arrears refusing or failing to pay such delinquencies shall be suspended, and the Academic Senate or the proper Faculty are instructed to enforce this provision.

Article 449.

A fee of ten dollars shall be collected by the Secretary for every diploma issued to graduates of the colleges at Berkeley, and two dollars for every diploma furnished in blank to the affiliated colleges of the University.

Article 450.

All orders and requisitions upon the State Printer shall be made by the President of the University and the Secretary or by the Board.

CHAPTER II.

Land Administration.

Article 451.

In case an applicant for lands procures a certificate of deposit to the order of the Regents of the University, as security that he will take and pay for the lands, if title can be procured, and subsequently the application of the University to locate said lands is rejected by the United States land officers, the amount of the certificate shall be returned to the applicant by the Treasurer.

Article 452.

It is hereby declared the duty of the Land Agent to act as Secretary of the Land Committee, and as such to keep papers, minutes, and records of all their official proceedings, and to attend meetings of the Board during the discussion of land matters.

Article 453.

The Land Agent of the University is authorized and empowered to commence and prosecute, in the name of the Regents of the University of California, all suits necessary to enforce the collection of arrears of interest due, or that may become due hereafter, on account of sale of land by the University, when the purchasers fail to comply with the terms of their contracts with the University.

14

Article 454.

All applications for unsurveyed lands on which the twenty per cent payment required to be paid in advance has not been made, are hereby ordered canceled.

Article 455.

All bondsmen must be residents of the State.

Article 456.

Upon the accumulation of five thousand dollars to the credit of the Land Fund, the same shall, in accordance with the laws of Congress and of this State, be invested by the proper officers of the Board.

Article 457.

The Land Agent is authorized to abandon to the United States all surveyed applications made in behalf of the University on which no preliminary deposit has been made.

Article 458.

The Land Agent of the University is instructed to demand the balance of principal and excess of one dollar and twenty-five cents per acre due on all certificates of purchase now due, or that may become due, by reason of the expiration of the five years credit, and all interest due. Said interest, if not paid as it becomes due, to be added to the principal, and to become a part thereof, and to bear interest at the same rate per annum, and if default be made in the payment of the interest, as herein provided, then the principal and the whole thereof shall immediately become due, at the option of the Regents of the University. Both principal and interest shall be paid in the gold coin of the United States.

Article 459.

The Land Agent of the University is required and instructed to collect the following fees for issuance of patents under the Agricultural College Grant of one hundred and fifty thousand acres: For each and every application, a fee of five dollars. For each one hundred and sixty acres, or fractional part thereof, one dollar, to be paid to the Secretary of State for affixing the seal of the State to said patents.

ARTICLE 460.

The list of **fees** and rules of the Land Office of the University shall be printed and posted in the office of the Land Agent.

The following is a copy of said rules and fees as now posted in the Land Office:

Rules and Regulations of the Land Department of the University of California.

To the Land Agent of the University of California

SIR: Whenever it is brought to your notice that applicants for lands under the Agricultural College Grant have interfered, or are attempting to interfere, with the rights of settlers or persons in possession, you will report the facts to the Committee on College Lands for their action. You will not approve any location until after the expiration of thirty (30) days from date of the United States Register's acceptance of the same.

It will be your duty to communicate with the United States Land Offices, and ask that they take action upon all college applications that have been filed in their offices over ninety (90) days. If the Registers and Receivers of the United States Land Offices cannot decide in that time, you will get from them a statement of their reasons, and submit the same to the Committee on Lands.

In all applications for timber land applicants will be required to furnish bonds for the payment of deferred payments, with two sureties, to be approved by the Finance Committee of the Board.

FEES.

Applicants shall pay to the Treasurer the following fees:

For filing and making out papers for the United States Land Office, for every location of 320 acres or less, $5.

For certificate of purchase, $3.

For patent for each and every application, $5.

For each 160 acres or fractional part thereof, $1.

For locations embracing more than 320 acres, the same fees shall be paid for each 320 acres or fraction over in the location.

The fee for certificate of purchase shall be paid at the time the first payment of principal is made. The fee for patent, when the same is issued. The fee for filing must accompany the application.

ARTICLE 461.

The Land Agent of the University of California is directed and required to collect a fee of two ($2) dollars for each certified copy of papers on file in his office, and deposit the same with the Treasurer to the credit of the Fee Fund of the University.

ARTICLE 462.

The Land Agent of the University shall not receive any money for the University, and all money due from the sales of land, or in connection therewith, shall be paid direct to the Treasurer by the persons owing the same, upon the certificate of said Land Agent showing the correctness of the amount due. And said Agent shall notify all persons owing or who may hereafter owe the University as aforesaid.

ARTICLE 463.

The Land Agent is hereby authorized to receive applications for unsurveyed lands; *provided*, that the Regents reserve the power to revoke said applications, whenever it may appear that through misapprehension or misrepresentation, injustice may have been done to actual settlers.

ARTICLE 464.

The Land Committee is authorized to extend for one year all payments of interest where the parties have offered the same upon certificates of purchase upon which the five years' time has expired.

ARTICLE 465.

On sales of land, under the grant of one hundred and fifty thousand acres, interest shall be charged at the rate of seven per cent per annum. On new contracts to be made hereafter, when the five years' time has expired under the former contract, in the discretion of the Land Committee, interest may be charged at a rate not less than seven per cent per annum; *provided*, that all interest due under said former contract, up to the time of the making and execution of the new contract, shall have been fully paid, *and provided further*, that the certificates of purchase originally issued shall have been surrendered and canceled.

ARTICLE 466.

In addition to the power now conferred on the Land Committee to take measures to collect delinquent interest on land sales, said committee is also authorized to take measures to foreclose the interest of delinquent purchasers when failure has been made in payment of principal or interest, so as to recover the land to the University and place said land again on the books for sale.

ARTICLE 467.

Interest on payments made in the purchase of lands from the Board of Regents shall in no case be refunded or paid to the purchaser or his successors in estate.

NOTE.—The articles following in Chapter II contain the blanks used by the Land Agent in the Land Office of the University in the disposal of the grant of 150,000 acres for Agricultural College purposes.

ARTICLE 468.

Application for **location** under the State. **Location** No. ——, —— Land District, ——, 188-.

To —— ——, *Land Agent of the University*

I, —— ——, of —— County, State of California, do hereby apply, under the provisions of an Act to create and organize the University of California, approved March 23, 1868, and of an Act entitled "An Act to provide for the management and sale of the lands belonging to the State," approved March 28, 1868, and of an Act amendatory thereto, passed April 4, 1870, and of an Act entitled "An Act concerning the selection and sale of University lands," approved March 13, 1874, to purchase and locate the following described land in —— County: —— containing —— acres, according to the returns of the United States Surveyor-General, and which I agree to accept in lieu of the full amount of —— acres, for which I agree to pay to the University of California —— dollars per acre, if minimum, and —— dollars per acre, if double minimum land, payable in gold coin of the United States in the following manner, viz.: twenty per cent of the purchase money, together with yearly interest on the balance at the rate of seven per cent per annum, in advance, from the date of approval of the location by the Land Agent of the University, and at any time after the expiration of five years from date I agree to make payment in full when demanded by said agent. It is agreed and understood that this agreement shall become void, unless said land shall be listed and patented to the State, and that no demand will be made for the return of interest that may have been paid by me on said location.

Affidavit for Location.

State of California, County of ——, *ss.*

I, —— ——, of —— County, State of California, being duly sworn, depose and say: That I am —— a citizen of the United States, and a resident of the State of California, of lawful age; that I desire to purchase said lands, viz.: ——, and that there are no improvements of any kind on said land other than those of myself, who am the applicant therefor ——. That the above described lands are not timbered lands, and that each legal subdivision in the above described tracts is more valuable as agricultural than as mineral land.

Subscribed and sworn to before me, this —— day of ——, 18—. Witness my hand:

I, —— ——, Land Agent of the University of California, do hereby accept the above offer, under the following conditions: That if such location be accepted and approved by the United States, it shall be for the use and benefit of the applicant, on his complying with all the conditions and provisions of his agreement or contract.

—— ——, Land Agent of the University.

Land Agent's Office, ——, 18—.

Indorsed: 150,000 acres for Agricultural College purposes, —— Land District; Location No. ——; —— Meridian; Township No. ——; Range No. ——; Section ——; Containing —— acres; In satisfaction of —— acres; Located for ——; Received and filed ——, 18—; Approved ——, 18—.

—— ——, Land Agent of the University.

Land Agent's Approval of Location.

ARTICLE 469.

STATE OF CALIFORNIA, ⎱
OFFICE OF LAND AGENT OF THE UNIVERSITY, ⎰
SAN FRANCISCO, ——, 188-. ⎰

Location No. ——.

I hereby certify, that under the directions of the Board of Regents of the University of the State of California, I have located as a portion of the University Lands, —— acres of public lands in the County of ——, at the request and for the use of —— upon his application therefor. Said land is described as follows: —— acres taken for —— acres, ——. This location has been made by ——, in the name and for the benefit of the University of California, at the United States Land Office for the —— District, in the City of ——, and in accordance with List No. —— of the United States —— Land District, dated the —— day of ——, A. D. 188-, and the said application is entered and numbered upon my Register of Locations. The said location is hereby approved, and the Treasurer of the University shall receive in payment therefor, from —— dollars, within fifty days from the date of the Land Agent's approval, being twenty per cent of the purchase money, and interest on the balance, at the rate of seven per cent per annum from the —— day of —— 188-, to January 1, 188-, and the further sum of —— dollars, being the excess of one dollar and twenty-five cents per acre due on double minimum lands.

Whole amount (including excess), $——.

Twenty per cent at five dollars per **acre**_____ $——
Interest to January 1, 188-_____ $—— $——
Excess of $1 25 per **acre** on —— acres_____ $——
   First payment_____ $——
Balance due, $——.
Annual interest, $——.
Please return this document **for** signature **of Treasurer,**
with the amount due by you on **first** payment, **viz.:**

            Amount **of first** payment **and fee**__ $——.
            Credit by amount paid ___ _____ $——.
                Balance due_____ $——.
        —— ——, Land Agent of the University.

Treasurer's Receipt.

ARTICLE 470.

OFFICE OF THE TREASURER OF THE UNIVERSITY
OF THE STATE OF CALIFORNIA,
SAN FRANCISCO, —— 188—.

Received of —— the sum of —— dollars and —— cents,
being **twenty** per cent of the purchase money and first fractional year's interest upon **the balance, to January 1, 188—,**
and the further sum of —— dollars, being the excess of one
dollar and **twenty-five** cents per acre due on double minimum lands.

$——
        —— ——, **Treasurer of** University.

Received, also, —— dollars for the certificate of purchase,
and —— dollars for filing application.

$——
        —— ——, Treasurer of University.

Land Agent's Application to the United States Land Office.

ARTICLE 471.

OFFICE OF THE LAND AGENT OF THE UNIVERSITY
OF THE STATE OF CALIFORNIA,
No. ——.   SAN FRANCISCO, ——, 188-.

Under the provisions of an Act of the California Legislature,
approved March 28, 1868, "To provide for the management
and sale of the lands belonging to the State," and an Act
amendatory thereto, approved April 4, 1870, I hereby apply,
in behalf of the State of California, for the following described
tract— of land, to wit: ——.

The above described lands are selected for said State under the Act of Congress entitled "An Act donating public lands to the several States and Territories which may provide colleges for the benefit of agriculture and the mechanic arts," approved July 2, 1862, and the Acts amendatory thereto, including the one which provides for the selection of Agricultural College Lands granted to the State of California, approved June 8, 1868, and the one approved March 3, 1871.

The above described tract— contain —— acres, which I agree, as Land Agent of the University of the State of California, to accept in satisfaction of the full amount of —— acres of the grant of Congress above mentioned.

—— ——

—————————————————————————————————
Land Agent of the University of the State of California.

Indorsed: One hundred and fifty thousand acres for Agricultural Colleges, —— Land District; Location No. ——; —— Meridian; T. ——; R. ——; S. ——; Subdivision ——; —— acres, taken in satisfaction of —— acres; Rec'd and filed —— 188–: Approved —— 188–; —— Register U. S. Land Office.

—————

Certificate of Acceptance by the United States Register.

ARTICLE 472.

—— LAND DISTRICT OF THE STATE OF CALIFORNIA. No. ——.

U. S. LAND OFFICE, ——, 188—.

It is hereby certified that —— ——, Land Agent of the University of the State of California, has this day presented at this office an application to select the following described tracts of land: ——. Which application I have filed and placed on record, to be forwarded to the General Land Office for approval.

The above described tracts of land contain —— acres, and are selected under the provisions of an Act of the California Legislature, approved March 28, 1868, and of an Act amendatory thereto, approved April 4, 1870, in part satisfaction of the grant made by the Act of Congress, approved July 2, 1862, entitled "An Act donating public lands to the several States and Territories which may provide colleges for the benefit of agriculture and the mechanic arts," and the Acts amendatory thereto, including one which provides for the selecting of Agricultural College Lands granted to the State of California, approved June 8, 1868, and the one approved March 3, 1871, and are taken in satisfaction of —— acres of the grant of Congress above mentioned

And it is further certified that there is no valid preëmption or homestead right to the lands within described, nor any other valid rights thereto of record, except the claim of the State of California made herein.

—— ——, Register.

Certificate of Purchase upon the Payment of Twenty Per Cent.

ARTICLE 473.

LAND OFFICE OF THE UNIVERSITY OF THE
STATE OF CALIFORNIA,
No. ——. SAN FRANCISCO, —— day of —— 188—.

It appearing from the certificate of the Treasurer of the University of California, bearing date the ——, A. D. 188—, has paid into the Treasury of the University the sum of —— $\frac{}{100}$ dollars, being twenty per cent of the purchase money and fractional first year's interest to January 1, 18——, on the balance in advance for —— acres of University land, described as follows: In Location No. ——, —— Land District, —— in Township No. ——, Range No. —— Meridian. Date of location in United States Land Office, the —— day of ——, 188—.

Now, therefore, be it known, that the said —— having made payment of said twenty per cent and the first year's interest for the above described tract of land, under the provisions of an Act entitled "An Act to provide for the management and sale of the lands belonging to the State," approved March 28, 1868, and the Act amendatory thereto, approved April 4, 1870; and of "An Act to create and organize the University of California," approved March 23, 1868, and the Codes of the State, is the purchaser of the same; and after having, in all other respects, complied with the provisions of said Acts, and the terms of his agreement, and full payment has been made, and on the presentation of this certificate to the Board of Regents of the University, and after the said land has been confirmed to the State, the said —— shall be entitled to receive a patent for the same.

—— acres taken for —— acres.

Balance of purchase money due, —— $\frac{}{100}$ dollars.

Annual interest on balance, —— $\frac{}{100}$ dollars.

In witness whereof, the Land Agent of the University has hereto set his hand and affixed his seal of office the day and date above mentioned.

—— ——, Land Agent of the University of California.

University lands. Acts of March 23 and 28, 1868, and Acts amendatory thereto, and the Codes of the State. Interest—Seven per cent per annum in advance.

Price per acre, —— dollars.

——, 188—.

I certify that —— has paid to the Treasurer of the University the sum of —— dollars, being the excess of one dollar and twenty-five cents ($1 25) per acre on —— acres, due on double minimum lands.

—— ——, Land Agent of the University of California.

(Receipts for payment.)

Full Paid Certificate of Purchase.

ARTICLE 474.

LAND OFFICE OF THE UNIVERSITY OF THE)
STATE OF CALIFORNIA,
No. ——.   SAN FRANCISCO, —— day of ——, 188—.)

It appearing from the certificate of the Treasurer of the University of California, bearing date the —— A. D. 188—, that —— has paid into the Treasury of the University the sum of ——$_{\tau\sigma\sigma}$ dollars, being payment in full for —— acres of University land, described as follows in Location No. —— Land District; —— in Township No. ——, Range No. —— Meridian.

Now, therefore, be it known, that the said —— having made payment in full for the above described tract of land, under the provisions of an Act entitled "An Act to provide for the management and sale of the lands belonging to the State," approved March 28, 1868, and "An Act to create and organize the University of California," approved March 23, 1868, is the purchaser of the same, and after having, in all other respects, complied with the provisions of said Acts, and on surrendering this certificate to the Regents of the University, and after the said lands have been confirmed to the State, the said ——, or his assigns, shall be entitled to receive a patent for the same.

—— acres taken for —— acres.

In witness whereof, the Land Agent of the Land Office of the University has hereunto set his hand and affixed his seal of office, the day and date above mentioned.

—— ——, Land Agent of the University.

Payments in full—Acts of March 23 and 28, 1868.
Grant of 150,000 acres—University lands.
Price per acre, —— dollars.

Land Agent's Certificate to the Governor for Patent.

ARTICLE 475.

LAND OFFICE OF THE BOARD OF REGENTS,
UNIVERSITY OF CALIFORNIA,
SAN FRANCISCO, ——, 187—.

Certificate No. ——.

To his Excellency Governor —— :

I hereby certify that —— did, on the —— day of ——, 187—, receive a certificate of purchase for the following described land, to wit : ——, containing —— acres, and that payment in full has been made for the same, that said certificate of purchase has been surrendered and is in my possession, and do further certify that the above described land has been listed to the State of California by the United States, as a portion of the 150,000 acres granted to the State under the provisions of an Act of Congress entitled "An Act donating public lands to the several States and Territories which may provide colleges for the benefit of agriculture and the mechanic arts," approved July 2, 1862, and that the said —— is entitled to receive a patent for the land.

—— ——, Land Agent of the University.

Form of Patent.

ARTICLE 476.

UNITED STATES OF AMERICA, STATE OF CALIFORNIA.

To all to whom these presents shall come, greeting:

Whereas, Under the provisions of an Act of the Congress of the United States entitled "An Act donating public lands to the several States and Territories which may provide colleges for the benefit of agriculture and the mechanic arts," approved July second, eighteen hundred and sixty-two, one hundred and fifty thousand acres of the public lands were granted to the State of California; and whereas, the Legislature of the State of California has provided for the sale and conveyance of said lands by statutes enacted from time to time; and whereas, it appears by the Certificate of the Land Agent of the University, No. ——, issued in accordance with the provisions of law, bearing date the —— day of ——, A. D. 18—, that the tracts of Agricultural College land hereinafter described have been duly and properly located in accordance with law, and that —— entitled to receive a patent therefor;

Now, therefore, the State of California hereby grants to the said ——, and to —— heirs and assigns, forever, said tracts of land, located as aforesaid, and which are known and described as follows, to wit: ——, containing —— acres, taken in lieu of —— acres, together with all the privileges and appurtenances thereunto appertaining and belonging. To have and to hold the aforegranted premises to the said ——, and to —— heirs and assigns, to —— and their use and behoof forever.

In testimony whereof, I, ——, Governor of the State of California, have caused these letters to be made patent, and the seal of the State of California to be hereunto affixed.

Given under my hand, at the City of Sacramento, this the —— day of ——, in the year of our Lord one thousand eight hundred and ——

—— ——, Governor of State.

Attest: ——, Secretary of State.
Countersigned: ——, Land Agent of the University.

Indorsed
Letters Patent from the State of California. Issued ——, 18—, to ——, for —— acres of Agricultural College land, lying in —— county.

CHAPTER III.

Management of the Library.

ARTICLE 477.

The Library to be formed by virtue of the bequest of the late Michael Reese shall be general in its character, and shall include judiciously selected works pertaining to Literature, Science, and the Arts. The principal shall remain as an invested fund, and the interest only shall be used for the purchase of books.

ARTICLE 478.

The professors and instructors shall, at least once a year, present to the Library Committee lists of books relating to their respective departments of knowledge, which they recommend for purchase for the University Library at Berkeley.

ARTICLE 479.

The Librarian shall examine said list and see that no unnecessary duplicates are ordered.

Article 480.

The professors and instructors shall hand their lists to the Librarian between the fifteenth of November and the first of December of each year, and the Librarian shall present the same to the Library Committee with the least possible delay.

Article 481.

The Library Committee and Librarian shall thereupon revise and adopt the list of books to be purchased: the Librarian shall ascertain and report the prices, publishers, etc., of such books to the committee, who may adopt the same; and the said list of books and prices shall be filed with the Secretary, who shall issue the necessary orders and receive the books, provided, the total expenditure shall not exceed the amount previously authorized by the Board to be so expended.

Article 482.

Any person who may fail to return any book of the library by reason of the loss thereof, shall, upon the demand of the Librarian or Library Committee, pay to the Librarian the price necessary to be paid for replacing such book. Such failure to return or pay for any book shall deprive such person from further privileges of the library. The Librarian shall report all such cases, and pay all money received therefrom to the Secretary.

Article 483.

The Secretary of this Board is directed to make public the readiness of the Regents to receive donations of books, maps, and engravings for the Library of the University, and in particular that they will accept volumes of the Congressional Globe, History of Congress, Mexican Boundary Commission, State Geological Surveys, Smithsonian Reports, Coast Surveys, and the like. Such volumes shall be placed on the shelves of the Library by the Library Committee, and shall contain a presentation plate inscribed with the name of the donor, and donations shall be acknowledged by the Secretary by circulars in the usual form, and also statedly in the public prints in a compendious form.

DIVISION FIVE—RELATING TO PROPERTY.

CHAPTER I.

ARTICLE 484.

The boundaries of the University site, as set forth in the survey made by M. G. King, C.E., maps and field notes of which were presented to the Board and filed on April 11, 1883, are declared to be the boundaries of the University site.

ARTICLE 485.

The present site of the University of Berkeley is adopted as its permanent location.

ARTICLE 486.

The privilege of using any of the roads in or to the University grounds is a mere license, revocable at the pleasure of the Board of Regents.

ARTICLE 487.

Picnics upon any of the grounds, except as set apart for that privilege, are prohibited.

ARTICLE 488.

The agricultural and botanical work on the grounds of the University, except as to the location thereof, is left with a committee consisting of the President of the University, the Professor of Agriculture, and the Superintendent (Secretary) of the Grounds, with power to employ such labor as may be necessary, not exceeding $250 per month, and materials as needed, not exceeding $1,200 per annum, the same to be audited by the Finance Committee and paid out of the Special Agricultural Fund. Said limits of expenditure, however, may be changed by special order of the Board. (See Articles 404, 405.)

ARTICLE 489.

The Secretary is charged with the control of the grounds at Berkeley and the care of all University property, except as herein otherwise provided.

Article 490.

The President of the University is authorized to direct the use of all property set apart for purposes of instruction.

Article 491.

All rents from property of the University must be paid in advance to the Secretary.

Article 492.

The care and management of all the University cottages devolve upon the Secretary, who shall make quarterly reports to the Board.

Article 493.

It is the duty of the Secretary to keep in his office duplicates of all the keys of the several rooms and buildings at Berkeley.

Article 494.

The Secretary is authorized to employ, dismiss, and regulate the duties of the Watchman and day laborers.

Article 495.

The President and Secretary are authorized to employ, dismiss, and regulate the duties of Janitors, and they must promptly report their action to the Board.

Article 496.

All orders, rules, and resolutions not contained in Title Five are rescinded.

INDEX.

15

D

	Article.	Page.

	Article.	Page.

www.ingramcontent.com/pod-product-compliance
Lightning Source LLC
Chambersburg PA
CBHW020850270326
41928CB00006B/635